What, no baby? takes us on a journey into the lives of contemporary women who plan to have it all — marriage, motherhood and work — yet have been derailed by reluctant men, insatiably demanding jobs and ever-climbing expectations of what it takes to be a 'good' mother.

The Australian Bureau of Statistics predicts that 25% of Australian women who are currently in their reproductive years will never have children. Yet respected researcher and ethicist Leslie Cannold argues that women want to mother as much as they ever did. What has changed is their willingness to sacrifice everything they've built — everything they are — to do so. Drawing on demographic data, social research and insights gained from interviews with women in their 20s, 30s and 40s, Cannold shows that the easier society makes it for women to combine parenthood and paid work, the closer women get to having the number of children they want.

At the end of the 21st century it is women's freedom to mother that is most at risk. Guaranteed to reshape the current debate around declining fertility, *What, no baby?* is a must-read for everyone concerned about Australia's fertility decline and for women who want to better understand — and to solve — the social problems keeping them from fulfilling lives in which children play a part.

WHAT, NO BABY?

Why women are losing the freedom to mother, and how they can get it back

LESLIE CANNOLD

Curtin
University Books

FREMANTLE ARTS CENTRE PRESS
in partnership with Curtin University of Technology

First published in 2005 by Curtin University Books
A Fremantle Arts Centre Press imprint
25 Quarry Street, Fremantle
(PO Box 158, North Fremantle 6159)
Western Australia
www.facp.iinet.net.au

Editor Sarah Shrubb
Cover illustration and design Caitlin Moffatt
Printed by Griffin Press, Australia

National Library of Australia
Cataloguing-in-publication data

Cannold, Leslie.
        What, no baby? : why women are losing the freedom to
        mother, and how they can get it back.

        Bibliography.
        ISBN 1 920731 88 1.

        1. Childlessness. 2. Parenting - Social aspects. 3.
        Motherhood. 4. Women - Social conditions - 21st century.
        I. Title.

        306.87

For my grandmother, who has never let me down and who, through her dedication and love for us all, taught me the value of children
and
for SP, with love

About the author

Dr Leslie Cannold was born in New York but has lived in Australia since 1989. She has degrees in psychology, medical ethics and education, and works as a researcher at the Centre for Applied Philosophy and Public Ethics at the University of Melbourne. She is heard regularly on radio and TV, and her opinions appear in the *Sydney Morning Herald*, the *Australian*, the *Age*, the *Herald Sun* and the Brisbane *Courier Mail*. Her previous book, *The Abortion Myth: Feminism, Morality and the Hard Choices Women Make*, was rated outstanding by the prestigious *ALA 2002 University Press Books*. Leslie lives in Melbourne.

Women make their own reproductive choices, but they do not make them just as they please; they do not make them under conditions they create but under conditions and constraints they, as mere individuals, are powerless to change. That individuals do not determine the social framework in which they act does not nullify their choices, nor their moral capacity to make them. It only suggests that we have to focus less on 'choice' and more on how to transform the social conditions of choosing, working and reproducing.

Rosalind Pollack Petchesky[1]

Acknowledgements

First and foremost, I want to sincerely thank my agent, Fiona Inglis, and my publisher, Margaret Whiskin. They believed in this book and fought for its existence against a phalanx of doubting Thomases. Here's to proving the doubters wrong.

I am also extremely grateful to my partner, my father and stepmother (Michael and Mimi Cannold) and my mother and stepfather (Libby and Arnie Margoluis). They have been more than generous with their emotional and financial support during the writing of, and necessary breaks in writing, this manuscript. Special thanks go to Helen Barnett for help with research, and to Sarah Shrubb for her incisive editing.

Contents

Note to readers

This book is the first of its kind. It's about women who don't have children not because they are childless by choice or infertile, but because circumstances have limited their freedom to choose motherhood. Women who are childless by choice are those whose desire to be childless is longstanding, and who pick and discard life partners on the basis of their willingness to go along with these women's strong, unwavering desire to avoid motherhood. There is an adequate and ever-expanding literature about these women. Similarly, many books exist that speak eloquently about the experiences of women struck by infertility.

I know voluntarily childless and infertile women exist. I respect their choices and support their struggle to have their stories heard and acknowledged. But this book is not about them. Instead, it is devoted to putting a hidden group of childless women — those childless by circumstance — on the map and offering some solutions to the problems they face.

I dedicate it to them.

Preface: Why this book?

You probably think I'm mad. Most people believe that it is the freedom women have to choose childlessness — not motherhood — that has long been and remains under threat. But I promise you, I am perfectly sane. After some five years of researching the issue of childlessness, I fear my predictions about the threats contemporary women currently face to their reproductive freedom are frighteningly accurate. In fact, if most women knew what I do about the obstacles many will face getting to motherhood, they'd choose the challenge of an unplanned pregnancy over the ethical and practical dilemmas of unplanned childlessness any day of the week. These days it is mothers, not the childless, who are an endangered species.

The extent of the problem is mind-boggling. At the peak of the baby boom, just over 40 years ago, Australian women were averaging close to three children each. Now they each have fewer than two (1.75 to be exact), and the numbers are still falling. By 2008, experts predict that Australian women will have 1.3 children, or just slightly more than one child, apiece. The US situation is much the same, though high birth-rates among subgroups such as Hispanics and teenagers have reduced the fertility free-fall somewhat, and kept fertility at around two children per woman. However, this is significantly down from the 1957 figure of 3.8 children per woman, and if we adjust this for these subgroups, the United States' rate is just 1.8 and — like the Australian one — falling.

This decline in what experts call the fertility rate includes two sorts of women: those who are having fewer kids, and those who are having no kids at all, though it is the spiralling number of women in this latter category that has left so many observers open-mouthed. In fact, so staggering has the rise in childlessness been that the Australian Bureau of Statistics predicts that one in four Australian women currently in their reproductive years will never become mothers. In the United States, the figure is one in five. This downward trend is sweeping the developed world, with fertility falling in from 1.9 in 1990 to 1.6 in 2000. Indeed, Italy's current fertility rate — 1.1 — is so low that unless things turn around quickly, demographers predict that there simply won't be any Italians in 100 years' time. The Greeks and the Spaniards are in a similarly bad way.

But why should things change? Don't low birth-rates simply reflect the choices Western women are making about children, choices that not all that long ago — in the bad old pro-childbearing days of the 1950s — women were denied the freedom to make? And even if it is true, as many experts say, that these trends have worrying implications for society as a whole, what can be done about them? Expel women from the workforce and lock them back behind suburban picket fences? Confiscate all forms of contraception and return abortion to the backyard? In any case, surely the decisions women make about if and when to mother are private ones for them alone to make. Personal choices that should rightly remain beyond public scrutiny and political interference.

Well yes ... and no. The first thing to understand is that plunging fertility rates in Western countries don't reflect what women want when it comes to motherhood; they just reflect what women are getting. Ask young women in their late teens or early twenties what they *want* their lives to look like by the time they turn 35 and the vast majority (92%, according to one large Australian study) say the same thing. They want to be partnered for life with a man, working in a good job, and the mother of at least one or two kids.[2] In the United States, a recent survey of childless career women found that a mere 14% of them said they had not wanted to have children; another survey found that 60% of childless women wished they'd had children.[3] And it wasn't only childless women who were dissatisfied with their reproductive results: one in four mothers said they would have preferred to have more children than they actually did.

In fact, you may be surprised to learn that the more educated and ambitious a woman is, the greater the number of children she wants to have. In one study, university-educated women were found to want, on average, just over two kids (2.6), while those without a degree hoped for slightly fewer (2.4). But while education and ambition don't dampen a woman's desire for motherhood, they severely restrict her chances of achieving it. By the time they reach their early thirties, women with degrees have sharply revised their childbearing ambitions downward, to just 1.8 children: a number that they don't even come close to reaching. This story contrasts with that of less educated women who each give birth to, on average, slightly less than two children and in so doing come far closer than the more educated to achieving their motherhood dreams.[4]

What sort of procreative difficulties do upwardly mobile women face? No prizes for guessing that the time it takes to get a degree and establish a career is a major one. Most graduates are somewhere north of 30 (particularly if they're looking to have 'Dr' before their names) before they skid into the workplace and start searching in earnest for someone to share and build a life with. As one researcher put it, this doesn't leave them much time to identify Mr Right, get him up the aisle and convince him he wants kids before the decline in fertility — which begins in earnest when a woman hits 35 — really starts to complicate matters.[5]

Not surprisingly, many women find it hard to get their lives to conform to such rigid social and biological timetables. The longer a woman waits to have her first child, the more likely she is to fall short of her childbearing goals. This is not rocket science, just common sense. There are only so many cycles in a month, and so many pregnancies a woman can carry in a year. If a woman has her first pregnancy at 38, she'll have to keep her finger on the fast-forward button if she's to have any hope of fitting in the other two she planned before her body 'just says no'. And if she's 40 by the time she starts trying to fall pregnant, she'll be lucky to hold even one squalling newborn in her arms before the final physiological curtain falls.

Is this choice? Most people understand a choice as a decision a person makes when she has a full range of possible options from which to select, and is equally free to choose any one of them. Yet while increasing numbers of Australian and American women are finding themselves without children (or with fewer children than they want), only a handful would say this outcome was a result of free choice. Those in the know, such as Professor Peter McDonald, who heads up the demography and sociology program at the Australian National University, estimates that of the 25% of Australian women predicted to remain childless, only about 7% will actually choose not to mother. Another 7% will be waylaid by medical infertility, and the rest, about 11%, want and fully intend to mother but miss out because of circumstance. What this means is that while the percentage of women choosing childlessness or suffering infertility has remained relatively steady over the last few decades, the number of women who are circumstantially childless is rising at an astronomical rate. It is the phenomenal rise in circumstantial childlessness, not the childlessness that women choose, that explains a good chunk of the downward spiral of fertility rates across the developed world.

There is no question that women should be in charge of decisions about their bodies and their lives. Choices about motherhood — the whether and the when — are unquestionably theirs, and theirs alone, to make. But in order to be free, really free, to make a choice, people need a range of external supports. Such support can take various forms. It can manifest as supportive social attitudes or practices, or the absence of laws or other restrictions on what we say and do. Resources of various kinds are nearly always necessary. For women to have the freedom to choose abortion, for example, laws criminalising the procedure had to be repealed and clinics that women could easily access, and that offered the procedure at affordable rates, had to be set up. In fact without safe, accessible and affordable abortion services, the legal freedom to choose becomes an 'empty', or meaningless, right.

It is no different with motherhood. While conservative governments like to pretend that there is nothing they can do to influence women's reproductive decisions, it's doubtful that even they believe such nonsense. Respected political commentator Paul Kelly recently called the Australian government's insistence that it could not influence women's fertility 'irresponsible, self-defeating … inconsistent … [and] dangerous'.[6] Neither Kelly nor any of the other political commentators looking for a change in the attitudes of decision-makers on this issue is calling for governments to reassert control over women's bodies. Far from it. What they are asking for is what feminists like to call *enabling* social policies: policies that provide women of reproductive age with the attitudinal and practical support they need to have the children they want.

The childless by circumstance: why no-one wants to talk about them

But while calls continue to be made for changes to the way the Western world treats actual parents, and those who want to be parents someday, the circumstantially childless themselves remain eerily silent. The reasons for this are complicated, and include the embarrassment some women feel about admitting that they wanted kids, but at close to 40 (or beyond it), they still don't have them. This is particularly the case when there is no man in the picture. For some, standing up to be counted as a woman who despite all efforts has been unable to achieve the life she wanted for herself is tantamount to a public admission of failure as a human being. I will say much more about this later, but for the moment I note only that such feelings are understandable for women who live in countries like Australia, where we are all raised to believe that we are fully in control of our own destiny and that everything bad that happens to us is therefore all our fault. The truth is, however, both more complicated and less finger-pointing. Many of the decisions women make about having children are in reply to circumstances beyond their control; consequently, their outcomes should attract neither shame nor blame.

Unfortunately, there are a number of groups who would be quite happy if the childless by circumstance remained a political force that dared not speak its name. The motives of these groups range from the venally self-interested to the thoroughly well intentioned. Those concerned with their own interests are the leaders of the business world, and their political lackeys. Because the sad fact is that all women, but particularly mothers, suffer dreadful inequality at work. Harassment and discrimination still exist in many workplaces and, most critically as far as reproduction is concerned, women still make around 84 cents, in Australia, and 77 cents, in the United States, to every man's dollar. When they become mothers, the pay and conditions gap increases, mostly as a consequence of reduced working hours, and women find themselves unceremoniously booted out of the competitive scrum seeking advancement.[7] The unapologetic and unrelenting family-unfriendliness of the modern workplace is one of the most critical circumstances forcing tomorrow's mothers to delay — and in some cases put off altogether — their procreation plans.

The massing of a political movement of the childless by circumstance would send alarm bells ringing in CEO suites across the nation because its very existence would call attention to all that is wrong with modern-day workplace attitudes and practices, and to the laissez-faire approach of governments that allow them to continue. If business leaders and politicians can continue to push the plight of the childless by circumstance below the public awareness radar, then no-one need know about the countless frustrations and lost opportunities that young women on the bumpy road to motherhood encounter at work. Much, much more on this problem, and how it also affects men, later.

Less self-serving motives are behind the urge of childless by choice and feminist activists to deny the existence of the childless by circumstance. What they fear is that unless all women without children are deemed to be childless by choice, those who did really choose childlessness will be catapulted back to the bad old days: as deviants, or pitied as unwomanly. Back then, social conservatives got away with claiming that all 'normal' women instinctively craved children and knew, in ways that men could not, how to raise them.

There is no doubt that feminist activists should feel proud of their success in removing the stigma attached to women without children: after all, only 40-odd years ago such women tended to be treated in social situations like a bad smell. But it is time for feminist successes on this front — huge, substantial, significant successes — to be acknowledged, and for the debate to become more nuanced and complex. Things have changed a lot since the 1960s, and this includes attitudes to the childless. While just over a decade ago only 2% of Australians believed having none or one child was ideal, by 1997, 30% saw a childless life as complete. In 2000, this figure had ballooned to 48%, and it's likely that such rapid opinion shifts will continue apace. Even political activists in the childless by choice or 'childfree' movement admit that society's views are changing quickly, with a number reporting that an increasingly common response of friends who are parents to the activist's own decision not to have children is envy. When high-profile feminist historian Anne Summers conducted a series of round-table interviews with women of reproductive age years ago, she was amazed at the high levels of tolerance women had for each other's choices about children. Gone, she said, were the 'shrill accusations' of selfishness aimed at those not having children that were a feature of Australian life just a few decades earlier. They had been replaced, she said, with a 'compassionate realism' and acceptance that 'life is about making choices and decisions and then living with those decisions'.[8] Indeed, this high and growing level of acceptance backs up the assertions of many social scientists that it is the motherhood decision, rather than the experience of motherhood, that constitutes the contemporary woman's rite of passage to adulthood.

It is unseemly for feminist activists, some of whom are researchers, to insist with a straight face that in today's world women who choose not to have children are 'commonly reproached for selfishness' or 'pitied for their immaturity', when this claim is based on data that is biased, poorly analysed, or simply out of date. It is also sloppy for feminist activist researchers to use women's ultimate acceptance of, or even happiness about, being childless as proof of choice. The reality is that women may ultimately live a fulfilling and happy life despite being childless by circumstance, but this doesn't justify rewriting history to say they *chose* not to have children. It would be better for activists and researchers to take well-deserved credit for having led the charge on achieving much-needed changes in attitudes to the childless by choice, to welcome those changes, and then to switch their focus to those in need of their attention and passionate advocacy: the childless by circumstance.

The need to speak out

I feel extraordinarily grateful to the women who invited me into their lounge rooms, gave me a cup of tea, and then honestly answered all my questions about intimate aspects of their lives. What a privilege! Along with it, however, came a whole host of responsibilities, one of which was to make the sacrifice of their time and privacy *amount* to something. It simply wouldn't do to let fear of how my findings might be misused, or anxiety that they might impede some women from getting over their disappointment about missing out on motherhood, stop me from making them public. As I see it, the women whose lives form the basis of this book trusted me enough to share the joys as well as the disappointments of their reproductive lives. If telling their stories to the world, and naming the source of their disappointment, might change their circumstances or those of the generation to follow, then I am obligated to do it.

However, I did seriously consider shirking this responsibility. Not by rewriting women's personal histories, or altering my analysis in order to conform to existing theoretical frameworks, but simply by keeping my findings locked up in some dusty PhD dissertation that practically no-one would read, and moving on to something else. The reason for this vacillation was that a few years back I wrote another book, about abortion, that told a number of researchers and activists things they didn't want to hear about women's attitudes to abortion. Many of these people were colleagues, a few were friends, and I found it painful to be on the wrong side of their anger. At a conference organised a few years after the book was published, I was surprised to find it still the centre of attention. While I had my defenders, much of what was said about the goal of the book — which was to describe and defend women's abortion freedoms in moral terms — and consequently about me, was, shall we say, far from flattering.

I knew that this book would set me up for attack, too. At the heart of my argument are contentions about the nature of choice that don't toe well-trod and simplistic lines. I insist that we see a woman's childlessness, whether chosen or circumstantial, as the outcome of a decision that is worthy of respect. Women without children are neither victims nor candles in the wind of fate. Alongside this claim, however, is my assertion that some women may have made a different decision about motherhood had they had more reproductive options and a greater ability to choose among them. I affirm the capacity of circumstantially childless women to survive the disappointment of missing out on motherhood and build happy, meaningful lives, but at the same time castigate the wealthy societies in which these women came of age for not providing them with the same freedom to embrace motherhood as they had to avoid it. The difficulties contemporary women have getting to motherhood are not personal but political, and it's going to take political action to ameliorate the devastating impact they are having on women's freedom to have the number of children they want, or any children at all. The rarity of such arguments in the public domain makes them ripe for misunderstanding and abuse.

Before I began writing this book, I rang up one of my closest friends and told her I didn't think I could go through with it. I wasn't as young or as bulletproof as I used to be, and didn't feel up to being on anyone's ideological hit list. Again. My friend is stunningly beautiful, extraordinarily talented but, at 39, somewhat insecurely partnered and trying — as yet unsuccessfully — to get pregnant using sperm from an anonymous donor. She is, in other words, one of the women this book is about.

'But you must write it!' she shouted down the line, genuinely appalled. 'What you're saying is so important and no-one else is saying it! It's so *zeitgeist*! You must speak up! If you don't, there'll be another lost generation like ours. More women who'll be misunderstood, and who'll miss out on a chance to have children!'

So I considered it and, after asking her to explain what *zeitgeist* meant (the outlook characteristic of a generation), decided to push ahead.

Why worry about circumstantial childlessness?

There would surely have been others, had I sought their counsel, who would have advised me against writing this book. Foremost among them are the population drones. These are the people who are convinced that low birth-rates, no matter where in the world they happen, or how they are achieved, are always a good thing. They are easily recognised, because they use the same old 'arguments', both in and out of their usual habitats — Sceptics Society bashes and other venues for the loud and earnest, but desperately ill-informed. Their arguments go something like this: 'Doesn't the world already have too many mouths to feed?' and 'Why would you bring a child into such a screwed-up world?'

Such arguments are mistaken, and are tragically beside the point. It is just silly to think that overpopulation in one country in any way cancels the tragic consequences of rapidly declining population in another. It doesn't. And for Western countries, the costs of decreasing populations are very serious indeed. They include — but are not limited to — shortages of young innovative workers, shrinking tax bases at precisely the time when populations are ageing, a less competitive economy and, as a result, plunging standards of living. And even if large-scale immigration were politically saleable at the moment, which sadly it is not, it is no substitute for the 'natural' increases that come through people having babies. Basically, this is because babies don't migrate on their own; they come with parents, and sometimes grandparents too. This means that absolutely enormous numbers of migrants are needed to make even the tiniest change in the ratio between the young and the old and a dent in the social difficulties that low fertility brings.

In fact, once a population shrinks beyond a certain level, the downward momentum takes on a life of its own, and among those crushed by the landslide are those who already have children (and may have been thinking of having some more). With declining population go schools, hospitals, maternal health care and child-care centres ... and all the other services that ease the burden on parents. This adds degrees of difficulty to parenthood that in turn discourage all but the most hearty and determined of prospective parents from taking the plunge, and so the population shrinks more, eroding services even further, and on and on it goes. Philosophers describe this as an 'infinite regress', but demographers and parents call it a bloody disaster, particularly because the point at which the population spiral goes critical is somewhere around 1.3 babies per woman — the level Australian society is predicted to reach as early as 2008. Unless, that is, unless something is done — and fast — to stop it.

But I want to make clear from the beginning that the main concern I have about population decline is not to do with absolute numbers or the social disruption caused by rapid change, though these things do matter. The main reason I worry about population decline is because, upon closer inspection, it reveals the lack of choice many women are experiencing when it comes to motherhood. Circumstantial childlessness is a problem, in other words, because it is the consequence of the lack of real options experienced by contemporary women who want to have children. This lack of options begins with the way our society defines 'good' mothers and implicitly questions the rationality of those who procreate. It then moves on to the lack of men who are willing and able to play the husband and father part in the procreative drama, and is sadly rounded off by the Byzantine constraints the contemporary workplace imposes on employees who dare to dream of a life beyond the office.

The limits that the combination of these forces places on women's freedom to choose motherhood are no trifling matter. Real reproductive freedom is not a middle-class luxury, but a moral good and political right essential to women's identity, as well as to their capacity to build a meaningful life. Nothing corrodes the essential dignity of a person — male or female — more than being told what they must do, or must not do, with their bodies and lives. This is as true of motherhood as it is of abortion.

What this book *won't* be

It won't be a harangue against women. There'll be no blaming of women for their failure to reproduce, or to reproduce enough, or to reproduce on time. There will be no telling younger women to partner early and to forget about their careers or risk missing out on children altogether. No attempts to stampede older childless women into grabbing a partner to procreate with (any partner — QUICK!) before it's too late. I will not be criticising women for not realising what they are up against, nor will I imply that with just a bit of foresight and careful planning, any girl with a Palm Pilot can beat the odds.

There are, unfortunately, a number of people involved in the debate about childlessness who do this. And not only is it truly annoying, it's also damaging to both women's self-esteem and their chances of achieving the social change needed to have the children they want. One such commentator is wealthy businessman cum leader of the failed Australian Republican Movement cum Liberal Member of Parliament Malcolm Turnbull. In a recent newspaper piece, Turnbull urged women to close their eyes, think of England — oops! I mean the birth-rate — and get down to marrying at a younger age so they could produce more babies for 'the nation'. What was most ridiculous about Turnbull's intervention was not his fretting about the birth-rate, but his presumption that women's failure to breed was caused by their bad attitude, rather than competing demands. Then there's columnist Cathy Sherry, a young partnered mother and part-time legal academic who never tires of advising single and childless women to take a leaf out of her book when it comes to marriage, work and motherhood. In one article she chastised women who did not act as quickly as she did on the knowledge that fertility declines with age.

I also have no intention of blaming 'feminism' for the difficulties facing the circumstantially childless, despite the unprecedented popularity of this strategy as of late. Take-a-leaf-out-of-my-book Sherry, for instance, argues strongly that the cause of Australia's declining birth-rate is that feminists never told her while she was at school that she should 'aspire to have a part-time job and raise children'. Virginia Haussegger agrees. In a 2003 opinion piece in the *Age* that got nearly as much attention as President Bush's declaration of war on Iraq, the childless Australian

TV news presenter blamed what she describes as purple-clad you-can-have-it-all feminism for her unwanted childlessness.

It isn't feminism, but the unrelentingly sexist world that the women's movement tried, but in some cases failed, to change that is the source of the obstacles women are encountering on their way to motherhood. Biological clocks were never the professed nor acknowledged expertise of feminism, though over the years there have been a number of feminists who've intimated, or said outright, that career was more important than motherhood. Others in the sisterhood, however, have disputed this, and it's fair to say that robust debate on this matter has been taking place ever since the late 1960s and 1970s. Whose fault is it that Haussegger was — quite obviously — totally unaware of this debate? More importantly, who — or what — is really to blame for the fact that Haussegger didn't wind up with a career as well as a child? Feminists? Or the world that feminism failed to change? There are only around 5% of Fortune 500 companies run by women, and only one in every four of Australia's elected representatives is a woman. Am I the only person who has noticed that women, feminist or otherwise, are not running the world?

What this book *will* be

An unflinchingly honest but compassionate look at the lives of childless women: some of them chosen, more of them not. The stories of women's lives related here have been taken from extensive interviews I undertook with both Australian and American childless women. I have tried to tell them in a way that will encourage childless women, as well as those who did finally manage to have a child, to recognise their own life paths, and to sympathise with the journeys of others. I also hope to bring comfort to those for whom the quest to have a child — or more children — is still not over. Most of all, I seek to demonstrate, beyond a shadow of a doubt, that the circumstances many contemporary women face severely restrict their freedom to choose when, and whether, to mother.

I have also tried to give a detailed account of the people, organisations and institutions that are currently standing in the way of the lives that most childless women are trying to build for themselves: lives that include stable partnerships, challenging work, and at least one or two kids. Only after we have a clear picture of the obstacles women are confronting on their journey to motherhood can we possibly — as I do in the last chapters — have a stab at proposing some ways in which we might overcome them. While the book has been written for, and is dedicated to, the circumstantially childless, I suspect many mothers will enjoy it too. I document the tough and complex aspects of maternal life that scare many women away from diving into motherhood too soon, or at all. In the final chapters, I speak about the need for parents — actual and prospective — to work together politically for change. Only when people stand together is there any hope of changing the conditions that make contemporary parenthood so hard.

We must solve the problem of circumstantial childlessness. Not just because of the high cost of low fertility, but because justice and equal opportunity are at stake. It isn't as if women who want children are standing in line for handouts, author Sylvia Hewlett said recently. All they want are the same opportunities that men have always had, opportunities which they rightly see themselves entitled to. Opportunities that allow them to reach out and grab the very stuff of life: a partner and a chance to contribute to the community they live in, both through work and through the raising of children, without sacrificing all they've earned and achieved in the past.

Surely, this isn't too much to ask.

Chapter 1

THE CIRCUMSTANTIALLY MANY

Only she who says she did not choose, is the loser in the end.

Adrienne Rich

What bothers fertile women without children most? Is it the false accusation that 'selfishness', or 'hedonism', is behind their childlessness? Or the totally inappropriate use of the word 'choice' to describe the reason why they end up without kids? Even though a handful of women do choose to be childless, the majority don't. They just end up that way.

It is hard to over-emphasise how indignant circumstantially childless women feel about being called selfish, and having their childlessness lumped together with that of women who actually made a choice. Andrea Cook's letter to the editor of the *Age*, aptly titled 'Childless Neither Selfish Nor a Choice', gives a good feel for how frustrating and distressing circumstantially childless women find the insult, and the all too commonly made conceptual mistake:

> Another simplistic editorial about why women aren't having children these days ... I'm your 'subject' — a 34-year-old, university-educated, childless woman. Not by choice. It just happened that way. That's the way my life has unfolded. I never once sat down and tallied up the pros and cons with children on one side of the balance sheet and work/finances on the other. Your editorial is not unique in giving the impression that women like me are consciously and selfishly deciding to abandon family and children in favour of getting ahead. The truth is more complicated, far less self-absorbed and much less rational. My list of 'reasons' goes on and on. Not on the list, however, is a sense of duty to my career or a fear of not getting enough tax breaks. Thanks, though, for joining in the black-and-white, us-and-them argument

sustained in our society that winds up with me feeling selfish and greedy because I haven't sorted out my reproduction to other people's satisfaction.[9]

Sylvie, 33, a high-profile museum curator, is constantly upset by the way friends, colleagues and clients interpret her relationship break-ups and her childlessness as evidence that she's coldly indifferent to marriage, and has 'chosen' her career over motherhood. In fact, says Sylvie, while her work is terribly important to her, her childlessness was no choice:

> I remember when I broke up with the last man I [had] a long-term relationship with, people saying, 'Oh, you've let a good one go', as though I actually had options. I hadn't wanted the relationship to end, I was very distressed about it ending … They assumed that I had left him because I am this kind of single career gal, when actually it hadn't worked out for other reasons, nothing to do with that … [People I work with think], 'If you have a career you can't be a mother', and so they feel [that because I am childless] I have chosen to be a 'hardbitten career woman' … My working life is just the air I breathe … [but having said that,] I could also imagine giving it up and trying other things [for a while] because … Having a deep loving relationship [and] having children is kind of an exciting challenge for me.

The naked truth about selfishness

The standard insult hurled at all women these days is that they are 'selfish'. Women who work rather than stay at home with their kids full-time? Selfish. Women who don't go out to work and deprive their daughters of 'role models'? Selfish. Women who have children? Selfish. Those who have pain relief rather than natural births? Feed their baby by the bottle instead of the breast? Abort rather than raise an unwanted child? Choose highlights rather than perms? Well, you know what I mean. Sometimes, it seems that no matter what women do, we are accused — by some self-appointed someone somewhere — of getting it totally wrong. We're also highly sensitive to the criticism. We want to do the right thing by ourselves, our families and our communities, but our roles have transformed so radically in the last 40 years that it is a rare female who feels she is doing and living right.

However, all this may simply be the inevitable outcome of gaining the historically unprecedented freedom to live according to our own rules. The downside of there being no strait-jacketing role to which all women must conform is that no woman's life choices are eligible for society's shiny stamp of approval either. Consequently all women feel 'out of step' with what everyone else is doing, most of the time. According to researcher Grace Baruch and her colleagues:

> Never-married women can feel out of step because they are not married; divorced women can feel that way because they aren't married any longer. Childless women often feel different because they don't have children, and employed women who do have children often feel anxious because they have departed from the 'proper' role they were socialized to play. And the one group of women that did follow the expected route of marrying, staying home, and raising children now find that rules have changed — suddenly, society is questioning the value of what they are doing.[10]

The 'selfish' insult has a long history in Australia and in the United States. It probably dates back to the very first woman who ever gave birth, and the very first lazy-ass man who — having noted the extent of her workload — began worrying what might happen if she decided one day to stand up for herself. Australian women without children, or with fewer children than the patriarchy of the day deems enough, have come under particular pressure to sacrifice and breed. Indeed, as far back as the turn of the 20the century, men in high places were commissioning reports to explain declining birth-rates and, as the following ditty suggests, pinning the blame on women who refuse their breeding 'responsibilities' in favour of their own 'selfish' desires:

A woman's duty is to wed,
And mind affairs domestic.
And every man should work, but *entre nous*,
If every place and trade'll
Be occupied by women, who
Henceforth will rock the cradle?
Then won't the coming census show
A shocking alteration,
With no posterity, and oh!
No rising generation![11]

Though mercifully sparing us the doggerel, today's opinion makers pass similar value judgements about the moral character of women who remain childless or insufficiently fecund. The only difference is that in place of the word 'selfish', they employ the more fashionable euphemism, 'hedonistic'. Journalist Tim Colbatch, in his front page report on why Australian women are refusing to breed, says the reasons are simple: first, women's 'hedonist[ic] unwillingness to invest their time or money in raising children', and second, women's 'lack of emotional feelings for children'. The more things change, huh? Yet the truth remains the same: calling women selfish is a way of keeping them in line and working hard; it is a slur that gets trotted out whenever the female of the species threatens — individually or collectively — to stop bearing the 'motherload' of parenting. Whenever women start factoring themselves into the equation, we are accused of selfishness by those who hope we'll meekly return to the bowing and scraping that has throughout the ages enabled men to have so much yet do so little.

The race to motherhood

How do I know that Andrea and Sylvie's stories are the rule rather than the exception? What makes me so certain that the vast majority of the childlessness of fertile women, and the cause of most of the decline in birth-rates over the last 30 years, is the result of women's circumstances, not their choices? I know because I've had a look at a whole range of fertility data: from the birth trends in all Western nations (Australia and the United States included) to the whys and wherefores of the decisions individual women and childless couples make. The facts are simply beyond question.

But before we swan-dive into the numbers, we need to get some basic facts about the reproductive capacities of the female body straight. The first is that biologically speaking, women do it tougher than men on nearly every count. Not only do they have to carry pregnancies, give birth and breastfeed, but their window of opportunity to pursue these pleasures is far smaller than that available to men. We're talking a letterbox versus a post office. Men can and regularly do father children in their forties, fifties, sixties and even beyond. Who can forget the hoo-ha when David Letterman's much younger partner gave birth when he was 56? This is not to say that male fertility does not deteriorate with age. In fact, both quantity and quality of sperm decline on a yearly basis from age 24 onwards, and there is increasing evidence that a whole range of birth defects and problems, including miscarriage, can be sheeted home to the humble old sperm. What it also means, though, is that the infuriating image of a grey-haired, pot-bellied bloke meandering casually along the path to fatherhood — a spring in his step and a relaxed smile on his face — is highly accurate. They have all the time in the world to contemplate and complete Mission Parenthood. It's totally infuriating. I wish that tubby, whistling bloke would bend over and pick up a flower. I'd kick him up the bum.

Female fertility, as many women have been distressed to discover, is nowhere near as laissez-faire. Medical opinion differs about when precisely the easiest or 'best' age is for a woman to fall pregnant. Some say the teens, some say the early to mid-twenties and some say the early thirties, but for the purposes of this conversation, the debate is irrelevant. This is because all fertility experts agree that female fertility falls off at age 35, and then declines steeply at 37. By age 40, half of those who struggle to achieve pregnancies will fail and one-third of those who succeed are likely to have their pregnancy end in miscarriage. By age 45, natural family-planning guru Evelyn Billings says, only 1% of women will still be fertile.

What this depressing statistical litany means is that unlike men, women don't have three-quarters of a lifetime to muse on the question of motherhood. They have no alternative but to wake up, smell the parental coffee and — if brewing up a bub is what's intended — get on with it. The 'biological press', as one expert has dubbed it, simply doesn't allow women to shilly-shally around.

What the statistics *don't* imply is that someone, or more precisely a particular coterie of someones, is responsible for these highly irritating limits of female biology and their often unintended consequences: namely, circumstantial childlessness. Despite this, desperate attempts are occasionally made to find someone human, rather than divine, to blame. In Australia, the shrill accusatory finger is pointed either at particular women or at 'feminists' in general, and it is often pointed by highly educated and accomplished women who insist that had the women's movement told them 'the truth', they wouldn't be ending their reproductive years childless.

The most accomplished of such accusers is Haussegger, who lists her varied accomplishments as ABC TV news presenter, former host of the *7:30 Report*, and reporter for *Witness* and *A Current Affair*. In an opinion piece accompanied by a winning cartoon of a woman chained to her briefcase tearfully bidding goodbye to a child, Haussegger accused feminist mums and teachers of preaching the lie that you can have it all. They induced girls like her to become successful editors, doctors and engineers, but intentionally withheld the truth about women's time-limited fertility. 'I am childless and I am angry,' seethes Haussegger. 'Angry that I was so foolish to take the word of my feminist mothers as gospel. Angry that I was daft enough to believe female fulfilment came with a leather briefcase.'

Haussegger's rave got on more than a few people's nerves — the letters page was buzzing for weeks — and mine were definitely among them. I hate that 'oh no-one told me' rubbish that has increasingly characterised the plaints of young anti-feminists such as those in the 'Women Hurt by Abortion' movement. First of all, I'm only a few years younger than Haussegger and I certainly have no recollection of feminists telling me anything at all about my biological clock — true, false or otherwise. And given how enthusiastically the media has embraced the 'it's all the fault of the feminists' line, I find it hard to believe that if a hapless women's libber from the past *had* proffered fertility advice of any kind, a journalist wouldn't have uncovered it by now and broadcast it across the globe. The deafening silence suggests that nothing of the sort was ever said. Further, I actually did know by the time I was in my twenties that fertility declined with age, as did a number of my contemporaries. Some of these are now mothers; others are not. We may be a rarefied group, of course, but this does imply that the truth Haussegger so desperately needed was in circulation. As a colleague of mine — a high-profile media personality herself — grumbled after the article appeared: 'What's wrong with her? Doesn't she read?'

It is true that feminists urged all women to shed their domestic shackles and seek fulfilment and financial independence outside the home. But what is Haussegger? A brainless puppet? A mindless drone? There were plenty of women around at the time, a whole movement of them in fact, who rejected the feminist message and urged women to cling fast to 1950s values and social roles. She could have taken their advice … and don't we all wish she had, so that we weren't now forced to tolerate her unseemly assault on the very women who made her career success possible.

Social forces, including ideas about social change, may *constrain* women's thought horizons and by so doing *limit* their awareness of their options and their confidence to choose freely among them. However, even if the existence of such restrictions can be demonstrated, they don't render women mindless robots whose decisions aren't worthy of respect. Indeed, the object for anyone really trying to make a difference in women's lives is to challenge such limits in a way that doesn't invalidate or disrespect the authenticity or worthiness of their own or other women's reproductive decisions. This means getting the balance right between recognising the responsibility we have and must take for our lives and the real limits on our freedom to choose: something that Haussegger's unseemly whinge utterly fails to do.

Let's now turn to the evidence that shows, incontrovertibly to my mind, that there is a new, unrecognised social phenomenon in our midst: the woman who is childless by circumstance.

Most childlessness is circumstantial

The big studies show this effortlessly. In developed countries, the more family-friendly a society is, the closer women get to having the number of children they want — and, consequently, the higher the birth-rate is. In family-unfriendly societies, the reverse is true. That is, where the 1950s model of family and economic modelling prevail, women and their desired family size are like ships passing in the night: they never even get close. Indeed, so tight is the relationship between family-friendliness and high fertility rates in Western nations that virulently family-unfriendly societies such as Spain, Greece and Italy now face the prospect of national disintegration. Even though this has been thoroughly ignored by policy makers, experts now predict, some with a slight tremor in their voice, that unless things start changing — and fast — in 100 years' time, there simply won't be any Italians left!

So what kind of family-friendliness are we talking about here? We are talking about tax, industrial relations and family policies, and about work practices. To be family-friendly, all of these must be based on the assumption that both parents do, should do, and have a right to paid work. This means that childcare is a responsibility that must be shared by both partners (if there are two), and by the family and society at large. This is in stark contrast to the assumption that underpins most tax, industrial relations and work policies and practices in most Western societies, including Australia: that everyone lives, wants to live and should live in a male-breadwinner household. You know, the sort of home where the wife raises the kids, feeds the dog, picks up the dry-cleaning and generally does all the unpaid domestic work, while Dad works long hours, takes few holidays and doesn't look after or even speak to Junior for more than seven minutes a day.

You may already have guessed that Italy, Spain and Greece (with rates of 1.2, 1.2 and 1.3 babies per woman, respectively) are on the bottom of the ladder when European countries are ranked according to family-friendliness. As a consequence, Italian, Spanish and Greek women have downed fertility tools in an unprecedented — and in many instances, one suspects, an unrelished — birth-strike: one that will only be broken when Italian, Spanish and Greek men and societies change their ways and start pulling their weight at home. Speaking specifically about Italy, demographer Jean-Claude Chesnais explains:

> Educated along the same lines and performing similarly or better than their male partners in the labour force, women have altered their self-image as well as their outlook on marriage and family. They seek a social status based on jobs they themselves hold and on the related financial rewards such jobs provide. Education has made them conscious of their own capability ... and they wish to be considered as autonomous individuals ... Italian men, even the young, are ill-adapted to this new equality of genders. Even those who shared school classes with girls from early childhood are not prepared for family life in which women are on equal footing with men. But young women no longer accept the family arrangements their mothers or grandmothers considered natural; ... they do not tolerate subordination. The link between these attitudes and fertility behaviour is direct. A woman who engages in repeated childbearing runs the risk of being

relegated to roles from which young Italian women struggle to escape.[12]

Men are instrumental in how today's fertile women judge their prospects of a family-friendly future. In other words, one in which motherhood does not equal career death. Indeed, the evidence indicates that while some women might be game enough to battle through the family-unfriendliness they face at work, and in society more generally, the family-unfriendly attitude of the bloke sleeping beside them is the real reason they delay first-time or repeat motherhood. (Who says that when it comes to having kids, women don't live and learn!) This is why the birth-rates of Italian-Australian and Greek-Australian women are as low as those of their compatriots in the home countries, and significantly lower than that of Anglo-Australians, despite Australia's attitudes and work policies and practices being somewhat better than those found in either country. It seems that while young women of Italian and Greek origin are taking full advantage of the educational and job opportunities available in Australia, their husbands retain the same chauvinist approach to women as their brothers in the home country. McDonald puts it this way:

> Australians of Greek and Italian origin continue to adhere to conservative attitudes to the family and to the superiority of the adult male in the family context. As large groups in a multicultural society, Italian-Australians and Greek-Australians have been able to maintain significant features of their culture ... and patriarchy prevails.[13]

What is happening in these ethnic subcultures is a microcosm of mainstream trends. Having looked around at the available educational and work requirements and opportunities, and the reluctance (or inability) of their bloke to accept the labour and employment compromise required to bring up a child, women pursue education and paid work, and put motherhood on hold. The problem, however, is that babies delayed can become — courtesy of age-related infertility — babies forgone. Sex Discrimination Commissioner Pru Goward describes the Faustian 'choice' faced by contemporary Australian women as one between the 'job and the dirty nappy', and expresses little surprise that having been backed into the proverbial corner and forced to choose between them, many young women 'prefer the job'.[14]

This is not, I hasten to add, because most women don't want children. Indeed, there is ample evidence to show that they do. Many even want lots and lots; well over the 2.1 required to stabilise fertility rates. They want kids, that is, before they see the harsh reality of what a bitch it is to raise them without much in the way of help from their man or their society; at this point they quickly revise their fertility ambitions downwards. Studies suggest that on average, women, both in Australia and overseas, want about 2.5 children each. The Australian Longitudinal Study on Women's Health, for example, surveyed 39,000 women aged 18 to 22 and discovered that 91% of them said that by the time they were 35, they wanted to be in a stable relationship, employed, and a mother.

When women hit their thirties, however, a massive re-evaluation of their realities and priorities takes place. From the over 2.5ish they first intended, women begin to feel that a little less than two (1.8, to be exact) would be far more manageable. This is a starkly reduced figure that they won't, in the event, manage to achieve. Those in for the biggest disappointment when the final biological bell sounds are women with the most education. Not only are these gals the least likely of all women to have any kids; they are also the most likely — if they are mothers

— to have just one child. This is despite the little-known fact that it was this more educationally ambitious group who, back in their early twenties, desired a larger brood. In contrast, it is women who wind up with less education who end up having more children overall — and, more importantly, close to the number of children they said they wanted to have.

While there is no necessary linkage between highly educated women and childlessness or reduced fertility (indeed, it is precisely this nexus that family-friendly policies and practices break), the connection tends to be strong in family-antagonistic societies. It shouldn't require an Einstein to figure out why. Kids cost a fortune these days, so only those with a fortune (or perhaps those who are so low on the economic totem pole that they have given up hope of ever having a fortune) are willing to have more than one or two. A recent AMP/NATSEM report put the average cost of raising two children to age 20 as $448,000, or $310 a week. Such costs, notes Ross Gittins, the no-nonsense economist who writes regularly for the *Age*, are not only on the rise, but are prohibitive for those living below the poverty line, as they well and truly exceed social security benefit payments. That parenthood is increasingly becoming an option only for the rich is backed up by a 2004 report by the Australian Council of Social Services, which found that families with only one parent in the workforce spend $138 more a week than they get in government assistance to raise a child. And that's the good news. The shortfall for families where one parent works part-time is $212. Part of this gap is down to the reduced tax benefits the Howard Government gives to two-earner families in comparison with its preferred family form: the single-earner household.

But for the average Aussie family (which these days is one where one parent works full-time, and the other part-time), it is the cost of childcare that sends them to the wall. It is simply beyond the budgetary means of those on lesser incomes, even if they could secure a place (currently, more than 164,000 Australian women cite a lack of childcare, or its cost, as the reason they are out-of-work). Feminist Anne Summers describes childcare as an 'impossible luxury'. Even women on government assistance, she reports in her recent book *The End of Equality*, must pay '$200 plus per child per week'.[15]

The great irony of policies designed to make life more stressful and expensive for working parents, so that they will return to living as so-called traditional family units — the approach of the Howard Government — is that while it may drive some middle-class women *who are already mothers* back behind the picket fence, it has a chilling effect on the birth-rate: an unexpected downside that has social conservatives squirming in their seats. Not only have social conservatives traditionally supported larger families, but declines in the number of women willing to mother make the behaviour of women of the future far less vulnerable to manipulation by social policies designed to force them to choose between being a good mother and a high-achieving worker.

But it's the injustice of the situation that irks me. On the one hand it's good to know that prospective parents take their fiscal responsibilities to future progeny so seriously that they won't parent without being confident that they're in a financial position to manage the costs. But policies that either put the pleasures of parenthood out of reach of the average punter, or insist that affordability come at the price of playing house like Carol and Mike Brady, are patently unfair. 'Little wonder [low-income] couples are in no rush to add to their family,' former TV news anchor and columnist for the *Herald Sun* Jill Singer exclaimed recently. 'How could they possibly afford to do so?'[16]

Singer is on to something important here, something McDonald and other demographers are at pains to stress: the family-unfriendliness of social attitudes, tax systems and the workplace are causing birth-rates to decline in two ways. First, they push women and couples towards childlessness; second, they cause women and couples to have fewer children than they otherwise might have had. Research shows that the less relaxed and comfortable young people — particularly women — feel about their prospects in an increasingly globalised, competitive and highly insecure workforce, the harder they'll work to be fit for the treadmill, and the faster they'll run once they're on it. In economic terms, tough and mean economic times lead young people to 'invest in their own human capital' by spending 'longer years in education and in the full-time labour force before they can contemplate having a child'.[17] So the tougher and meaner the economic environment, the more young people will want to invest in themselves, and the longer they'll delay parenthood, or put off growing their existing family. During the economic downturn in Sweden a few years ago, the number of women pursuing further education nearly tripled, as women sought desperately to increase their competitiveness in a tight market by upping their skill level.

This not only demonstrates young women's high level of commitment to the paid workforce (a commitment that experts across the Western world now acknowledge is on a par with young men's) it also explains why 'no can do' is the response of most young women to occasional suggestions batted around in the public arena that they begin breeding in their early twenties, when fertility is at its peak. Instead, women are delaying their first child, in Australia, until on average, age 29, and age 25 in the United States. Many are then forced to delay further because of the difficulty they face gaining a toehold in the workforce and, once there, seeing a way to balance their career ambitions and their desire for kids. The unwillingness or inability of their partners to chip in is part of this equation, but the sum couldn't be completed without paltry or absent workplace provisions regarding paid maternity leave (available to only 38% of Australian women), quality part-time work, flexible hours and telecommuting (still a pipe-dream for most, and when available, offered mostly to executive men).

Indeed, as the Swedish success story of fighting declining fertility rates shows, it is precisely the availability of these sorts of policies in countries where women have equal access to education and training that make the difference between stable birth-rates and irredeemably rapid downward declines. Demographers like to call the correlation between equity between the genders and high birth-rates (one that contradicts the longstanding correlation in the developing world between improved circumstances for women and *lower* birth-rates) the 'feminist paradox'.

Sweden is a great example of how a country can turn things around through a commitment to gender equity at all levels of society, from home to office and beyond. Like the rest of Europe, Sweden suffered a precipitous decline in birth-rates at the end of the baby-boom. Never ones to close the gate after the horse bolted, the Swedes swung into action. Today, Swedish women not only enjoy equal pay, but are represented more or less equally at all levels of society, including in the Swedish Parliament. Women's participation in the Swedish workforce is twice that in Italy, with quality part-time work widely available, and parental allowances — including leave after a baby is born — that are not just generous, but must be shared by the mother and the father (a requirement that mercifully stops parental responsibility being, and being seen as, an all-female affair). Daycare centres and schools are well funded and receive strong support from the community. This is so much the case, in fact, that Swedish early childhood professionals express dismay and incomprehension at the repetitiveness and virulence of debates about the evils of daycare that are regular tabloid fodder in Australia and the United States. In sum, says demographer Jean-Claude Chesnais, the work and cost of raising children 'is more equally shared between fathers and mothers, and between the family and the community' than is the case in many other Western societies.[18] The pay-offs they receive for this approach are many, but among them are stable — and, in the European context, relatively high — fertility rates.

Fertility expert David De Vaus says that the high birth-rate in countries where women are emancipated and empowered can only be explained by:

> a change in preferences among women (and couples) concerning the desired trade-off between work and family ... [It] makes sense only in a world where most women wish to work and where the trade-off issues they must consider involve the possibility, practicability and timing of combining work and family ... The consequence is a reversal of much of the standard logic by which we comprehend the choices confronting couples in contemporary societies. The standard assumption is that more work means less fertility ... [But] the truth is that the greater the availability of women's work ... the easier it is for women to get that work ... and the weaker the voices (including those of policy makers) telling women that work and family are incompatible, the more likely it is that the birth-rate will be relatively high.[19]

The take-home message of such large-scale research is clear, and is eloquently revealed by differences in fertility trends across the Western world. Most women and couples do want to parent, and to have more children than they do currently. It is the family unfriendliness of the workplace, and the impact this has on the division of labour within families, that is standing in their way.

Turning to the smaller qualitative studies, I ask the same question: what do they tell us about the degree of freedom women (and couples) feel they have in their decisions about children? While the sample sizes used in such research make it impossible to generalise their findings, such studies are crucial in explaining — by adding names, faces and personal stories — the trends revealed in large-sample demographic data. Small-scale studies (which usually collect data through qualitative methods such as interviews, rather than in standardised formats such as questionnaires) reveal how childless people tend to think about their childlessness, how they became childless in the first place and how they feel about their decision to be childless.

One thing to note about this qualitative research is that it is nearly always conducted by researchers who are themselves childless. Another is that nearly all those who participate in such studies answered advertisements calling for women or men who were 'childless by choice'. The fact that such a recruitment strategy would actually bias the sample towards those who really did choose to be childless is something important to keep in mind when considering what many of the participants had to say about the voluntariness — or otherwise — of their decisions to remain childless.

The first thing such research reveals is that for a healthy handful of participants, childlessness was neither a consciously chosen, nor a freely made 'first choice' about parenthood. Rather, for some women, fertility troubles, the strong desire of a childless by choice partner to avoid parenthood, or the conflict they knew existed between work and family was enough to keep them on the mothering sidelines.

The influence of childless by choice men on the decisions of their more ambivalent and undecided partners cannot be underestimated. As one resolutely childless man bluntly put it:

> [If she became pregnant] my wife could have three choices. One, she could have an abortion. I hope she would do that, but I guess I couldn't make her do it. If not, two, she could have the baby and place it for adoption. Or three, she could have a divorce.[20]

In the same study, a supposedly childless by choice wife demonstrates her 'commitment' to her childless life this way: 'If he had really wanted to have a family, I'd go along with it wholeheartedly. Of the two of us, I'm the wishy-washy one … He was the one who made the decision …'[21]

For other 'voluntarily' childless women, the stark incompatibility of their chosen career with children (given most assumed that the entire domestic burden of parenthood was rightly theirs) was enough to cause them to delay having kids. For some, such delays led (courtesy of age-related infertility and fear of being — or being seen as — too old to parent) to a childlessness that was clearly not fully chosen. Helen McDonald, a married woman who loves her job, put the problem this way:

> One of the reasons I have some doubts about having a family is that I find it difficult to tie a family into the idea of a career. You know, I presume that if I had a family there would be a gap of a certain number of years … seven years … [My career is] very important [to me] … The longer you live with two incomes coming in and freedom and so on the less likely you

are to … want to bring this to an end, particularly when [staying at home with a child] would mean … tying me … to a street like this, which I hate.[22]

Helen McDonald demonstrates the sort of 'either/or' thinking many qualitative researchers claim is typical of childless women. It goes something like this: having accepted (or resigned themselves to) the fact that they will be the ones to bear the extra work and the cost to their personal and work lives that children bring, they delay rather than try to fashion some sort of compromise that might help them resolve these conflicts (such as having fewer children, employing paid help or — heaven forfend! — pressuring their male partner to do his fair share), these women put the dilemma in their own mind as 'either I mother or I have a career'. In her, at times inaptly named, book *Childless by Choice*, Jean Veevers describes the extreme type of thinking that childless couples and women use when deciding about parenthood:

> For most persons, having children is something which is done in *addition* to doing other things. Childrearing can be defined in ways commensurate with the resources available for their care. Men presumably find fatherhood to be less disruptive than women find motherhood, but most persons of either sex can usually manage to have and to raise children without making permanent or drastic alterations of their other priorities. In contrast, childless couples tend to define having children as something which can only be done *instead* of other things. For women, the choice is often defined not so much as 'Do you or do you not want to be a mother?' but 'Do you or do you not want to be *only* a mother?'[23]

Not surprisingly, this sort of either/or thinking leads a fair number of well-educated, middle-class women to give children the thumbs down.

This all makes sense. The problem comes when researchers such as Veevers characterise this kind of decision, which is based on reactionary assumptions about the proper role of women, extreme thinking patterns, and knowledge of a social world that makes motherhood a bitch in ways that fatherhood isn't, as a *choice*. Real childless by choice women are those who are what Veevers herself calls 'independents': women who decide to be childless early on and do not waver from this verdict; who would ditch a child-yearning partner; and who would choose childlessness no matter how easily society allowed them to balance their career ambitions with motherhood. As Veevers herself admits, only a handful of the 'voluntarily' childless women she interviewed for her research came close to fitting this description.

But ambivalent women with virulently childless by choice husbands and career women with socially conservative values are not the only ones researchers mistakenly toss in the childless by choice basket. Infertile women are in there too, as well as women who decide to make the most of the advantages a childless marriage and lifestyle have to offer.

Here is the way an 86-year-old widow describes her decision to remain childless: a decision that the researcher interviewing her unblinkingly described as a 'choice':

> When I married my husband, we tried very hard to have children. Of course, we didn't know anything about birth control in those days, so I never did anything to protect myself. We just never had any children. I don't remember feeling especially bad about

it though ... we were able to travel a lot. I worked for a business publisher. We had lovely friends. We were very popular ... I never had what you might call a 'career' but my boss liked me a lot. I was given more and more responsibility ... But children? Oh, yes, we wanted them. We just never had any.[24]

It gets even better. This recollection also comes from a married woman who is part of a couple the researcher also claims 'chose' to be childless:

We were going to have children ... and nothing happened and I got fed up with all this indecision ... I didn't know whether I was coming or going, going to be pregnant or not, so I went back on the pill ... Then we decided we'd try again [but we didn't conceive] and I was put on the pill. [Then] we decided we were quite happy the way we were ... We don't talk about it now. I still look in prams and say, 'Oh isn't she lovely!' I think I'll always do that, but it doesn't make me definitely want to have children ... I think who wants kids at 32 and Graham's 37. I keep thinking you're nearly 40 and it's far too old.[25]

Obviously, women who are infertile are not childless by choice. How can you choose to reject something that was never an option in the first place? Neither can 'choice' be deduced from the fact that a woman is coping well — or is even extremely happy about — being childless. A good example of this is photographer Judith, quoted by Mardy Ireland in *Reconceiving Women*. When Ireland interviews her, Judith is at the end of a long journey to overcome her sense of social isolation and come to terms with her childlessness:

I think I used to be sort of defensive and avoid situations [where people ask, 'Do you have children?'] And now the thing that comes forth sometimes is envy from other people. That's one aspect ... Another aspect ... is that I'm reasonably *in* what I am, so it isn't so much of a question of what I'm *not* now ... The word 'childless' is focusing on what you are not. So this has been another part of my own healing journey — the shift from what is not, to what is.[26]

'Hooray' for Judith, but 'boo' to Ireland, for confusing Judith's hard-won acceptance of her childlessness with her choice to be that way. Acceptance or even happiness about childlessness (or anything else, for that matter) is not the same as choosing it. The two may go together, or they may not. This is not to say, I hasten to add, that research findings that show women are coping well or even happy about being childless aren't good news, and well worth reporting. But women cope well with all sorts of events they don't choose. To trumpet this fact, and for a woman herself to feel proud of it, in no way implies that she chose those events or wouldn't — if she'd been given the chance — have tried to prevent them.

How happy lives became chosen ones (or when the best of intentions get in the way of good research)

Are most qualitative researchers really confused about choice and happiness? Do they really believe that if a woman winds up satisfied with her childless lifestyle, or looks back and says she is glad she didn't have kids, that she *chose* to be childless?

Few, I think, really do. The exception seems to be those who are so caught up in the endless circularity of Freudian thinking about the unconscious that they really believe that everything that happens to us proves that on some level, we wanted it to be the case. Missed out on ever getting to Europe because your elderly mum needed you at home? Had a child you didn't want because a legal abortion was impossible to get? Got caught in a traffic snarl and were late to your best friend's wedding? The true Freudian acolyte will claim that little is by chance, and that whatever you did to respond to these difficulties reflects what you really wanted to do anyway. Marian Faux is a great example of this sort of researcher. Her faith in the unconscious is so absolute that not only is there no room in her theory for circumstantially childless women, but she comes close to suggesting that infertility is a reflection of an individual woman' s covert 'hostility' to motherhood:

> The women prior to the 1970s who chose childlessness ... were hardly vocal about their decisions. But many women who were not technically sterile probably were only aware of their reluctance to mother on a subconscious level. That their childlessness might be rooted in some form of deep-seated maternal ambivalence was generally unapparent even to the women themselves ... Because people were a good deal less psychologically aware then than they are today, the notions of not having children because one did not really want them largely went unrecognized. Yet therapists have long been aware that a woman's ability to conceive depends in part on her psychological willingness to do so.[27]

Blind and (conveniently) unprovable faith in the power of the unconscious, however, is not the main reason why researchers 'confuse' women's happiness about childlessness with their choice to be that way. The main reason is that qualitative researchers are acutely aware of both the social stigma women will experience, and the high psychological cost they'll pay, if they continue to think about their childlessness as unchosen.

To understand why this is so, a brief detour into the fundamental values and beliefs of nations like Australia and the United States is required. For those who haven't yet noticed, the capacity to choose is at the heart of Western values. From cars to phone companies to the schools our children attend, we are daily exhorted to choose, and to believe that a lack of options from which to select, or of the freedom to decide from among them, deprives us of the individuality and freedom that is both our birthright and at the heart of what makes a life worth living. That choice is at the heart of what it is to be human is in essence what political philosopher John Stuart Mill was saying when he noted in his famous treatise *On Liberty* that:

> ... the only purpose for which power can be rightfully exercised over any member of a civilised community, against his will, is to prevent harm to others ... He cannot rightfully be compelled to do or forbear because it will be better for him to do so, because it will make him happier, because, in the opinion of others, to do so would be wise, or even right ... The only part of the conduct of anyone, for which he is amenable to society, is that which concerns others ... Over himself, over his own body and mind, the individual is sovereign.[28]

Mill's ideas frame the political ideologies and economic systems in Australia and the United States that place a premium on individuals, and the choices those individuals make. In such individualistic cultures the person is, to quote one scholar, 'conceived of as a product that is created by, and emblematic of, the self', while the life she's led is seen as the outcome of her 'volitional action'.[29] Translated, this means Australians and

Americans tend to see themselves as people whose identity and life course are direct outcomes of their (totally free and fair) choices. Lives, in this view, are 'coherent narratives': stories with beginnings, middles and ends. Australians and Americans, more than any other peoples on the Earth, believe that everyone sits at the steering wheel of their own destiny, and that each of us consequently deserves all the praise we get for the races we win, and all the blame when we fail to cross the finish line. This was vividly demonstrated by the results of a 2002 study that asked 38,000 people in 44 countries to agree or disagree with the statement 'Success in life is pretty much determined by forces outside of our control.' While Australians were not surveyed (humph!), they would probably not have been far behind the whopping 65% of Americans — the largest percentage of any national group — that disagreed that this was the case. This compared with about 46% of the English, a mere 30% of Germans, and a paltry 12% of Indians. Clearly, both the very existence of choice and control, and the degree to which we can exercise them in our life, are in the eye of the beholder.[30]

Many feminists, it is important to note in this potted intellectual history, have warmly embraced the idea of choice as central to the goals of the women's movement. Indeed, poster-feminist Naomi Wolf argues in *Fire with Fire* that the very meaning of feminism is 'choice and self-definition'. So, too, do individual women (whether they identify as feminists or not) believe that in order to be seen as emancipated and responsible women — or full citizens and moral agents — they must make choices and 'take control' of their lives. Indeed, perhaps in line with the most powerful and profound feminist demand — that women have a right to 'control their bodies' — it is in the area of reproduction that women tend to feel most strongly that they must exercise control. Whether it be in relation to contraception, abortion or the decisions that need to be made after 'negative' pre-natal diagnostic tests, study after study reveals that women feel inordinately responsible for what happens in their reproductive bodies and lives, even when they know they have little choice in or control over these matters. For example, in a study of women's experience of pregnancy in a technological age, researcher Robin Gregg found that women not only feel guilty about, 'choosing' to abort a wanted pregnancy after learning that the foetus is seriously damaged, but also blame themselves for miscarriages.[31]

All this sheds light on what qualitative researchers worry might happen if they openly admit what their data amply demonstrates: that some childless women don't choose to be childless, but end up that way through circumstance. First, they worry that in an age of oversimplification, the 'some' will quickly become 'all', and the hard-fought-for category of 'women childless by choice' will be lost. But they also worry that even if we can keep our conceptual categories clear (some women are childless by choice, others are childless by circumstance), circumstantially childless women will be compared unfavourably with their choosing sisters. That the circumstantially childless will be pitied as candles in the wind of fate: weak and passive victims, or what famous French feminist Simone de Beauvoir famously described in *The Second Sex* as 'immanent' — women who are incapable of acting as transformative agents in their own lives.

The risk of this would send chills up the spine of any feminist researcher who can remember the bad old days — which really only ended in the 1970s — when all childless women were either pitied as 'barren' or ridiculed as unlovable 'spinsters'. Such researchers worry that any depiction of women that doesn't show them as bold and fearless captains at the helm of their personal reproductive ship risks allowing the media, decision makers and the general public to fall back upon their old ideas about women being 'naturally' receptive or passive and unable to make and accept responsibility for important life choices: stereotypes that feminists have worked long and hard to undermine.

This fear is not without foundation. In the many interviews I have done with women on reproductive issues, most have seen themselves as choosers, and a great many have identified, at least in part, as feminists: as active, assertive women, confident of their place in the world. It is possible that such women could take umbrage at being called childless by circumstance, if they saw the description as implying that childlessness was the cost of their having failed to take the reins of their reproductive lives *when those reins were there for the taking.*

But this is the critical issue: how the experience and nature of circumstantial childlessness is described. The powerful — though unspoken — presumption that sits behind the glowing ideas we have about choosers is that everyone can be one, if only they have a good attitude and try hard; it's a sort of Nike 'just do it' stance on reproductive and other life decision making. Yet even the rawest facts about circumstantial childlessness reveal that women's options about children are extremely limited, and their capacity to decide between them is unfairly hedged. If this were not the case, there would be no connection between the family friendliness of developed nations and their fertility rates. If this were not the case, the number of children women say they want would closely match the number they have. If this were not the case, studies actively recruiting childless by choice women would not repeatedly report stories of women made childless because of fertility troubles, childless by choice husbands, and tortured zero-sum choices between motherhood and their careers. What the existence of such relationships and realities proves is not that Western women don't deserve real choice, and wouldn't benefit from it, but that as things stand now, real choice doesn't exist.

Demonstrating that women's freedom to choose motherhood is unfairly and unnecessarily constrained is the central challenge of this book, and one that I readily accept. But it is a challenge. On the one hand, I must show that women not only see themselves as 'choosers', but actively resist the limits they experience on their freedom, and utilise the freedoms they can access to shape their lives. On the other, I have to show that there are patterns in women's reproductive lives and decision making: patterns that reveal the negative impact social attitudes and institutions are having on their freedom to mother. Only when childless women acknowledge the shared and oppressive nature of many of the social forces in their lives can they work together to change them. The goal, in other words, is to credit:

> women (and others) for their survival skills in the face of real social constraints ... [while at the same time] mov[ing] beyond those constrained choices, to try to create situations where women's perceptions of themselves as choosers are mirrored more accurately by the opportunities for real choice within their larger social and political contexts.[32]

Circumstantial childlessness and the nanny state

For some, the most contentious aspect of my claims about circumstantial childlessness is that social attitudes, policies and practices can seriously affect women's decisions about children: that they can really deprive them of reproductive choice. Wouldn't solving such problems require greater government intervention in industry policy and practice, and people's lives? Wouldn't it invite the creation of what in Australia is disparagingly referred to as the 'nanny state'?

At the heart of this problem lies an important difference between negative and positive choice. A negative choice is the sort small-l liberal societies love to support. It is a decision that can be freely exercised with all the tools each person is assumed to have readily to hand — as long as the government keeps its grubby mitts off. Sexual freedom is negative freedom. We are all seen to be inherently free to control where and with whom we have sex, and what kind of sex we have. Our entitlement to such freedom has been used to oppose government attempts to control contraceptive use, or particular sexual practices — like sodomy — in the past (though most people accept that the state has some role in setting the age of consent and placing prohibitions on some sexual acts taking place in public). A positive choice, in contrast, needs more than just government standoffishness to be implemented, because decision makers don't — or can't be assumed to — have all the resources they need to make it. What this means is that it is not enough that governments resist passing laws which prohibit women from accessing pre-natal diagnostic testing such as amniocentesis, they must also ensure that there are medical practitioners trained to provide such screening, that Medicare rebates are available and that no social stigma attaches to women who use them. If they don't, the reality is that no women — or only those who are wealthy — are really free to choose them. And because social attitudes and institutions are known to impact on the capacity of individuals to make positive choices, governments are among the players with responsibility for ensuring that the necessary environment exists for positive choices to be made. Traditionally, reproductive choices such as abortion have been seen as negative ones: those available to women if governments would just keep their laws off women's bodies. However, the passage of time has made it clear that women are unable to exercise many of the reproductive options available to them without attitudes, policies and laws in place that are 'enabling': those that ensure that women don't have just in-principle freedom, but also the sort that can be realised on the ground.

In this day and age, childlessness is a negative choice. While once women's freedom to choose it would have been constrained by unforgiving social attitudes towards couples without children and poor availability of effective contraception and abortion, these limits on freedom have largely been removed. Given that there are no laws mandating that women breed, it is fair to say that the choice to remain childless is one women in Western countries today are at least relatively free to make.

The choice to mother, on the other hand, is a different kettle of fish. Not only does a woman who wants to mother need a male partner or at least male sperm to enact her choice; she also requires a host of other economic resources (a job, some sort of family endowment) and social supports (daycare centres, kindergartens, schools) for her dream to become reality.

Not surprisingly, positive choices tend to set small-l liberal governments, as well as the big-C (conservative) business sector, on edge. Not just because they take more 'taxpayer' funds, and dig deeper into commercial profits, but because the enabling role required of government and the private sector is seen by the overly paranoid as alarmingly akin to socialism: the invasion of government and society at large into the hallowed 'privacy' of the Family.

I admit that I find most of those who complain about Australia becoming a nanny state hypocrites, cheapskates, or both. You never hear social conservatives braying about government intervention into the privacy of families when they spy a chance to prohibit couples from freely choosing reproductive technologies to avoid the birth of a sick child, or to have yet another go at making abortion illegal. And while governments and businesses have finally come on board to support unpaid maternity leave, American and Australian women are still waiting for them to commit to a meaningful leave entitlement: the sort with a dollar sign attached to it.

Perhaps more important, though, is the fact that if the freedom to make choices in general, and reproductive choices in particular, is at the heart of what it means for us to be human, then whether making that choice possible is harder or easier resource-wise is neither here nor there. If as a society we believe that women (and men, for that matter) are entitled to full reproductive freedom, and that their dignity and moral agency depends on it, then there is no excuse for leaving the job half-done: we cannot enable women and couples to *avoid* parenthood, but not to *embrace* it. Fostering and defending the reproductive freedom of all citizens, not just some, wouldn't make Australia or the United States a nanny state: it would just make each a state that was a lot more fair.

Comedian Buddy Hackett used to joke that his mother's menu consisted of two choices: take it or leave it. The main thing that binds circumstantially childless women together, and differentiates them from women who are childless by choice, is that when it comes to motherhood, they want to 'take it'. This, however, is where the similarities end. Some circumstantially childless women are 'independently' committed to motherhood and among this group are women so desperate for children that when the man of their dreams — and even of their nightmares — fails to show up, or to stay around, they will trek interstate to have themselves inseminated with donor sperm. Others are ambivalent enough about their motherhood that a partner's opposition to parenting, or an early sign of fertility trouble, is enough to divert them to the happily childless path. For some circumstantially childless women their sense of self, and the future they imagined for themselves, are so bound up with motherhood that even thinking about missing out induces tears; others do a cost/benefit analysis of working motherhood and come down in favour of childlessness with barely a backward glance.

In fact, there are two distinct groups of circumstantially childless women: thwarted mothers and waiters and watchers. In the following chapters, we will meet them both.

Chapter 2

THWARTED MOTHERS

I know of one woman who had a child when she was 43. I collect these stories like trophies because they give me hope.

43-year-old childless woman

Most women in their thirties would know a thwarted mother: a friend, sister or cousin closing on the big four-zero with either no suitable man in sight, or none willing to have a child with her. In Australia, the award-winning TV drama *Simone de Beauvoir's Babies* dramatised the lives of a number of childless women, several of whom — notably a single doctor in her late thirties played by Sonia Todd — were thwarted mothers.

Thwarted mothers tend to be most noticeable, and to attract the greatest amount of public interest, near the end stages of their reproductive lives. It is then that, unable to have a child in what one woman I interviewed pithily described as 'the usual way', some reluctantly pair off with the last bloke left on the shelf or — just as half-heartedly — make their way to the sperm bank. It is at this stage that some thwarted mothers start to find being around babies or the sight of a pregnant woman painful, and begin collecting stories of older women's successful pregnancies. Crying jags, and a profound sense of being socially exposed as unloved — and unlovable — are common complaints.

Desperately seeking thwarted mothers

High-profile thwarted mothers aren't hard to find. Single infertile woman Leesa Meldrum, whose crusade to obtain infertility treatment made headlines in Australia is one. So is well-known New York playwright Wendy Wasserstein (of *The Heidi Chronicles* fame), who made her odyssey to older motherhood — courtesy of IVF — a matter of public record by discussing it at length in an article in the *New Yorker*. More recently, singer Kylie Minogue has also joined their ranks, when in a frank interview with British talk-show legend Michael Parkinson, she confessed her worry that at age 35 she was running out of time to mother.

Such women also abound in my social circle: the older sister of a friend, the aunt of a colleague. Yet when the time came for me to assemble a 'mixed bag' of childless women to interview, from those positive they had chosen childlessness through to those convinced they hadn't, it was the thwarted mothers who were scarcer than hen's teeth. The difficulty wasn't that people in my social network — friends, colleagues, family — didn't know one or two of these women: they all did. The problem was that nearly all my connections refused, point blank, to work their connections to get me some interviews. Nothing personal, they explained cheerily. It was simply that asking a childless woman to participate in my research would be to acknowledge their awareness that she was indeed childless, possibly also single, and not exactly thrilled about either — or both — of these aspects of her life. This, my connections felt, would both embarrass and distress the woman, something they were understandably reluctant to do.

Such fears, I was quickly coming to realise, were not unfounded. When a few of my colleagues bravely overcame their reluctance and asked their childless friends to speak with me, nearly all the women they asked said no. The reason for refusing was tellingly uniform: they'd be sure to 'cry hysterically' throughout the entire interview. I did manage to speak to one such woman — the trophy collector quoted at the top of this chapter — at considerable length on the phone, but at the end of the conversation she refused to be formally interviewed, both because to do so seemed to signify that she had given up hope of having children one day (which, she made clear to me, she had not), and because — you guessed it — she was positive she would cry hysterically through the whole thing. I tried desperately to convince her that speaking to me would not indicate an abandonment of hope, and that it was not a problem for me if she cried during all or parts of her story. I reassured her that she would be free to stop the interview at any time. But my pleas fell on deaf ears.

Good heavens, you might be thinking. What do thwarted mothers find so embarrassing and distressing about their predicament that they won't share it with a solitary interviewer who could promise them anonymity and — short of legal proceedings — complete confidentiality? And given that the subject is so sensitive, was it right for me to even try to get them to talk?

There are two reasons why circumstantially childless women in general, and thwarted mothers in particular, tend to feel so embarrassed and distressed about their situation. Comprehending both is not only essential for entering sympathetically into the mindset of these women, but critical to understanding why circumstantial childlessness is a real and important social phenomenon, despite languishing below the horizon of public awareness and concern.

Thwarted mothers feel embarrassed because often, though by no means always, their childlessness predicament is a by-product of being single — either chronically, or as a result of an ill-timed relationship split. Given the widespread social depiction of most men as hairy-chested creatures who'll settle more or less happily for any woman with a pulse and breasts (not necessarily in that order), singledom can make some women feel like Big (L-shaped finger on the forehead) Losers. Worse, some women feel guilty about feeling this way, instead of like Miranda and Carrie, the sassy and confident what-in-the-world-would-you-need-a-man-for single gals in *Sex and the City*. Not only are they Big

(L-shaped finger on the forehead) Losers, such women's logic seems to run, but they are failed feminists, too. It seems that despite the fact that up to 70% of Australian women swear they're not feminists, many measure their behaviour against feminist ideas of womanhood; perhaps giving credence to comic Kaz Cooke's assertion that women who don't call themselves feminists but decline to be treated like seagull poo on the windscreen of life have just got their terminology wrong. The upshot of all this is that thwarted mothers, particularly those coming to the end of their reproductive years, are not women whose confidence in themselves *as women* is at its peak.

Some thwarted mothers also get embarrassed, and not a little distressed, by the lack of control they feel they exercise over critical aspects of their reproductive lives, such as partnering and the decision to mother. The embarrassment comes from the expectation in liberal Western societies that individuals should and do control their lives. Those who confess to having lives that haven't gone to plan feel they are branded as 'victims' or 'failures'. Yet the reality is that, as 39-year-old single journalist Sushi Das puts it, women simply aren't in control of when they meet Mr Right, let alone when they can get him to settle down and play house:

> People do not have enough control over their lives to plan exactly when they have children. Sure, some people are lucky and meet their partners early. But not all childless women in their 30s have chosen to forgo having children so they can have a career. For many, childlessness is a result of not meeting the right person — of not finding 'a suitable boy', as my father would put it.[33]

Deakin University academic Colleen Murrell, who became a mother late in life, agrees with Das that many women feel they lack control of many aspects of their 'choice' about children:

I was an orphan when I entered the workforce some 17 years ago. I had a university degree, but thankfully no massive student debts. And I knew that I had to earn my living and build a career. It was not through avoiding the urge to merge that I didn't start trying to have children till my mid-30s, it was simply that a suitable boy hadn't materialised — and in the meantime I continued to work and gain promotion. When I then had several miscarriages — a problem more common in older women — I was lectured by many patronising male doctors about how I shouldn't have put off childbearing until my later years.[34]

How brave were Das and Murrell, given the stigma that is suffered by non-choosers, to invite the public into the complexity of their reproductive decisions, and their lived experience of circumstantial childlessness?

Which brings us to the question of whether it's even ethical to invite — or attempt to persuade — women to participate in research that probes and seeks to draw into the light personal issues of such sensitivity.

My answer is both yes, and no. Yes, because while many issues, including all things reproductive, are personal and sensitive, this doesn't mean we shouldn't do any research on them. Of course research is not the only way we can learn about things. Comments from therapists have, in the past, alluded to the existence and unhappiness of circumstantially childless women. But therapists are duty bound to keep secret what women tell them in the counselling suite. Research like mine makes the problem public and can provide a basis for change.

However, even the quest for knowledge has its limits, something I soon realised once I began interviewing thwarted mothers. Initially, I chose to interview women aged 38 to 42: ages at which I thought women would see the parenting option as still open, though coming to a close. I was wrong. Thirty-seven seemed to be the final crunch year for many women considering parenthood, and 38 the age at which they began the process of coming to terms with their childlessness. By age 42, the resolution process of those I spoke with was complete: women of this age and older could calmly and confidently recount to me a journey to childlessness clearly marked at various stages by conscious and deliberately made choices.

The problem was that even the most delicate of poking at many such narratives revealed the illusoriness of many of the women's choices. Requests for details brought out accounts of fertility difficulties, failed efforts to persuade independently childless partners, and frustration at relationship breakdowns that occurred just when children were being planned. It also brought matter-of-fact revelations of depression, anger or sadness about childlessness; emotions all now happily in the past. Renata was one such woman. She was intending to mother, but a split with her long-term partner Justin when she was 36, and a long string of short-term relationships since, put an end to her plans. But Renata doesn't want to dwell on the 'journey' she took coming to terms with how her life has turned out; she wants to talk about the fact that she has arrived at a place where she feels comfortable and happy:

> Having a special partner-type of relationship is quite important. I haven't had one that's gone longer than about five or six months for five years. You miss the intimacy of someone knowing something about you, or being able to read you, or just being that little bit more caring. That's of course if it's that kind of relationship. You can only hope that it is. But while I think they're

important and if it's a good working relationship, it's very fulfilling, I'm not going to slash my wrists because there isn't one happening currently. It's like anything; you make your life. You could sit home and close the doors and not go out, or you can get out there and be part of just what's happening and things that interest you.

What was I to do? If I pushed at Renata's story too hard, I might collapse her narrative of choice, the narrative mental health professionals say women like her need if they are to successfully resolve mixed feelings about childlessness, and move on. But if I didn't — and in the end I didn't — I would end up with a whole stack of poorly conducted and boring interviews, instead of just that one. More critically, I'd never find out if my hypothesis was right: that not all women without kids were childless by choice.

I fretted and gnashed my teeth about this problem for a while before finally hitting on a solution. Instead of interviewing older women, I decided to speak to younger ones: those aged 28 to 38. While the fertile years ahead meant such women might still wind up with children, it also meant that the parenting decision was still very much 'live', rather than one they'd gone past, and were being retold for my benefit. The hope was that I would get access to the decision making before the outcome of all those decisions made revisions to earlier motivations and plot lines too tempting to resist. I would catch women's decisions, and the motives and emotions behind them, as they happened.

Thwarted mothers: who are they?

Real childless by choice women are childless 'independents': their desire to avoid motherhood comes from within; and is barely affected by what others say or do. Thwarted mothers are 'independents' too, but their internally driven commitment — one that formed early and rarely wavers — is to motherhood, not childlessness. In the same way that childless by choice women can't see themselves with kids, thwarted mothers find it hard to imagine a future in which they don't mother. Hilary, aged 35, is a typical thwarted mother. Sure, she's had a few miscarriages, but she's determined to do whatever it takes — even IVF — to ensure she has children. She simply can't imagine her future any other way:

> [The way] I was raised, there was just no question that I would have children ... I feel there's someone that's meant to be ... By the time we're ready to move to the country and live down there, the child will be ready to go to school and there is an excellent school down there ... That fits in well ... I haven't actually entertained that thought of being pregnant at 40. I don't think I could survive if it was another five years away ... I haven't seriously entertained the thought that I'm not going to get pregnant soon ... If I'm a parent at 39 — no, I just can't see having my first child at 39. It has to be before that.

Barbara has wanted to have a child since she was young. Now, experiencing the first signs of menopause, she struggles to imagine a future in which she isn't a mother:

> I have wanted children since I was eight. I have been clucky my whole life. I've felt that urge to have children my whole life. When I was about eight, I had a scrapbook of pictures of babies, that I cut out of magazines ... Now I don't know any other kid who had done that ... And I know that I might

have missed the boat ... [because] I've got pre-menopausal symptoms ... [Throughout my life] it was ... like I'd made a decision not to have a child at that time, but I always thought I'd have a child. I always thought [that].

Thwarted mothers also approach partnering with their long-term goal of mothering firmly in mind. While childless by choice women pursue partners who are similarly averse to ever hearing the patter of tiny feet, thwarted mothers shop for a man they are confident they can last the distance with, and who they believe will make a good father. As a consequence, it is these women who find the male line about 'still being a child myself; so how could I possibly father a child?' particularly trying. It is also these women who, particularly as they age themselves, can spot such men at 100 paces.

Kylie, who was a fashion model in her late teens and early twenties, married her husband young, always knowing that she would one day want kids. But early in the marriage her husband insisted she abort a pregnancy and she left him soon after, having realised that he'd never agree to becoming a father:

I was married at 20 ... My husband, who was a hairdresser, steered me into modelling, which I did for five years ... he didn't want to have children at that stage ... I could have ... [but] he didn't want them. And friends would come over and try to convince him. You know, he was stuck on the economics of it or whatever. ... [My new husband] Paul says, 'Well, when are we going to have babies?' ... I like the fact that he's keen ... and it's not like, 'Oops, I'm pregnant.' [Instead] it's like, 'Honey, when are you getting your IUD out? Let's have a family.'

Thwarted mothers: the real maternal superwomen?

In some senses, thwarted mothers are maternal superwomen: dodging and vaulting obstacles to motherhood that would halt less determined women in their tracks. Recalcitrant men? Thwarted mothers either leave them or, as one woman I interviewed did, pack them off to therapy. Repeated miscarriages or delays in getting pregnant? Thwarted mothers pursue fertility treatment straight away. But there is one major obstacle to motherhood that even the most determined thwarted mother finds it difficult to tame. It is the one that most seriously impeded the journey of nearly all the thwarted mothers I spoke with, and the one they felt the most unable to address. The obstacle was men (or in the case of the few lesbians I spoke with, women): the men they dated or lived with or — perhaps more importantly — the men they lacked.

A woman's age determines how she approaches her particular troubles with men. When a thwarted mother is young, she treats a reluctant father in only one way: she leaves him, with nary a backward glance. Former model Kylie is one such woman; 28-year-old Tina is another. Tina divorced her much-loved husband Daniel when he bought her a dog instead of acceding to her desire to have kids:

> Everybody used to call us 'clutch and squeeze': wherever one was, the other one was, too. We were always together. Even after eight years we would sit on the couch and hold hands. We were just really compatible ... I always loved kids ... I was ready [to have children] after we'd been married for one [year]. I would have been roughly 25. I kept saying, 'Oh, we should start a family', but I didn't push the issue ... [because] Daniel just didn't have the patience for

children. He just so wasn't ready ... I kept saying to Daniel, 'Come on, let's have a child.' He said, 'No, I'll get you a dog.' ... When I eventually bring up children I want it to be with a person who really wants children as well, and who is prepared to help ... to play an active role in parenthood.

What thwarted mothers want is what one woman called 'The Whole Package': a sexy 'for life' type of bloke, a nice house and a couple of kids. When thwarted mothers are young, and the insistent ticking of their biology is more than a decade in the future, they will hold out for the man with whom they can have it all: a top-shelf relationship and a guarantee of children. Judi, aged 28, explains:

[My boyfriend] Lyndon called me in the middle of the night and he was having this major drunken epiphany of wanting to get married ... We had been together for three years. We were really compatible in a lot of different ways. We both wanted the same thing: eventually to be in a relationship with kids ... But the bottom line was I wasn't emotionally satisfied, I wasn't intellectually satisfied ... The bottom line was I knew I'd be sacrificing my own happiness. And that I had to make a choice. To choose to have this life that's probably pretty much OK, and secure, and you get to have kids ... and you're positive of it, it's a sure thing. But you'll probably always wonder if there's some other relationship that could have been more satisfying, or [in which] you could be happier ... And so I said, 'At 28, I'm ready to take the chance and assume I'll meet somebody. And I can have both: happiness with that individual and kids' ... I just wasn't ready ... to settle.

In fact, if women who were keen to mother were quick to leave unsatisfactory or dead-end relationships, many did successfully re-partner with Mr (wants to have children) Right, and had the number of kids they wanted. This is certainly what happened to Tina (whom I ran into recently — she is now remarried and has a young child), and it's likely to end up being Brenna's story, too. A 33-year-old personal trainer, Brenna dumped her bodybuilding husband Kirk, who didn't want kids, for a Mr Right who did:

> I'm not married to Kirk any more … I'm remarried to a wonderful guy and we want to have children … Sam is such a wonderful guy … And he'll be a great father. He's a great husband … Kirk is very selfish …
>
> *Me:* Was that what led you to end the marriage?
>
> Absolutely … I should have … tried to talk to him about it … Kirk and I could have worked it out … but I think we were at different points in our lives.
>
> *Me:* You could have worked it out, but you chose not to?
>
> … Yes. [Because of] Sam. He and I were friends since about 1991 …
>
> *Me:* So you could see clearly that there was someone else? Someone who could give you more of what you wanted?
>
> Right …

However, as we all know, breaking up can be hard to do. The problem for women keen to mother is that when they leave the leaving too late (I swear there's a Tammy Wynette lyric in there), they may find themselves single just when their physiology starts screaming 'Now or never!'

This is what happened to Darcy, an accountant who was forced to end her relationship with her Mr (doesn't want children) Right and begin her search for Mr (wants children) Right in her mid-thirties:

> The relationship that I have just come out of [was] the … first person that I would consider having as the father of my children … I said to him, 'OK, we need to have a look at this. I want to know are we committed to one another here because I want to start looking at a family. Are we going to do this or are we not? Because if we are not, we shouldn't be together' … He bottled up. And basically we ended up splitting …

In fact, some women find the prospect of pursuing a new man so near to their personal fertility D-day so unattractive that they will stay with Mr (doesn't want children) Right, or even Mr (doesn't want children) Approximate — if it comes to that — to avoid having to go there. This is Sharon:

> If [my boyfriend becomes] absolutely convinced he doesn't want to have kids, do I go and find someone else? … I don't really relish the idea of going out there trying to find a partner to have kids with. That's a bit of an ordinary scene.

Ageing thwarted mothers who leave anyway are women like Darcy; women whose standards for Mr (wants children) Right are uncompromising because when push comes to shove, they'll abandon their plans to mother before agreeing to have a child on their own:

> I don't have a problem with [being childless] at this point … What's important for me is the fact that I

actually wouldn't go ahead and [have kids] without having a partner. One of my closest friends, a wonderful woman, has actually the exact opposite viewpoint. We don't fight about it, but we are just aware that we have different viewpoints on it. Her viewpoint is that she is financially secure and she wants a child, and that she would actually have a child without the male participating.

Me: And why do you disagree with that?

Because I want the input from the father.

Me: So much so that [if you go close to the wire] and still haven't found the right guy you would forgo the chance to become a mother?

I would. I think I would forgo that.

Rhyll, aged 36, agrees with Darcy. While she's always wanted kids, and her relationship with Jock is travelling well, she would immediately abandon her plans to have kids if Jock ended up being Mr Wrong. For Rhyll, a decision to mother isn't made separately from the right relationship. Rather, it arises from it:

I have yet to get to the point of being sure that the relationship is going to go on and on and on, because I have absolutely no desire to be a single mother. I don't think there is any point of discussing having babies with him, unless that discussion is held within the context of, 'This is a relationship for life.' ... We can't deny that the biological clock exists ... It's a recognition that, 'Shit, if I'm going to do it, I'm 36 now, I really wouldn't want to do it after 38.' ... Knowing there is a deadline means ... you've got to start saying, 'Time is up. Sometime in the next four years, I've got to have a baby.' … But that doesn't mean I'm going to rush any decisions about anything. I wouldn't have a baby with Jock just because I wanted to have a baby. I would because it seemed like the right thing to do, as a partnership … If it was like, 'OK, this seems like the right thing to do,' as opposed to, 'Oh God, I'm 36, I've got a man around, so I'll get pregnant now because it's my last chance.'

Things are not so simple for women like Peta, for whom motherhood is not a take-it-or-leave-it prospect. Indeed, at age 33, Peta wants to have children so badly she has decided to abandon her desire to get back together with her Mr Right and settle for her Mr (wants kids) Approximate so that she can start trying to get pregnant straight away:

I was going out with Allen, but Mitchell and I … were lusting after one another. But the whole time I was saying, 'I'm never going to have sex with you, and I'm never going to break up with Allen.' And then … Mitchell and I ended up kissing. And it's the classic. Allen discovered us … Allen said, 'I don't want to do it any more. I still love you, but I can't live with you.' I was absolutely devastated … I mean Allen was quite a special person really; he wasn't like your average bloke … Now I'm with Mitchell. He's 26 and … doesn't want to have children yet: he'd like to wait until he's at least 30. So do the calculations: I'll be 37, and I just think, 'I don't know if that's too late.' So we're actually going to see a counsellor this week [to talk about it.] Mitchell has talked about the fact that he does want to have children … At this stage we are committed to one another, but I am still getting over Allen. I find that quite difficult. I struggle with that daily.

Karla's predicament makes Peta's look good. Aged 35 and feeling that time was running out, she abandoned her dream of the Whole Package and began pursuing a match that was far from made in heaven, with a Mr Very, Very Approximate:

> I've always wanted 'it' to happen. The package: the husband and the life and the kids and everything else that goes with it … [But] I haven't met anyone who I thought might be a possible father. Well, I have, but it didn't work out … He lived overseas and was coming to terms with his own sexuality. We would meet together every year or so and then he said, 'Look, let's do it. Let's get married and do the whole thing.' And then a few months later it was like, 'I'm sorry I can't, it's a lie.' That was awful. It was shocking. It was traumatic. [I told my father] that I was thinking of having a baby and he said, 'Well, can't you wait till you get married, dear?' and I said, 'At this point, Dad, not really. Whatever comes first, the kid or the marriage, I'm not fussed.'

Shaney, too, is a woman for whom motherhood is a non-negotiable affair. At age 37, when her last attempt at making it work with Mr (wants to have children) Right foundered, she determined to take matters into her own hands. She visited a dating agency and placed an ad for a Mr (wants to have children) Approximate:

> I decided to go to an agency … That was Plan A for having a child. I figured that 35 or 36 was the latest I'd be wanting to have a child because I didn't feel it

was fair to have anything older than a 15-year-old with a 50-year-old mother …

Me: You wanted to meet someone and partner quickly, or meet someone who would help you get pregnant?

… I had in mind to make an arrangement. The ideal at the time for me was to have met say a businessman that was a bit of a workaholic, would love to have kids, but didn't have time for it and didn't have time for a wife either. I thought that would be ideal for me. To have children, to be able to have a break every now and then by giving these children to their father, who wanted to spend a little bit of time with them, but not too much. That would work out perfectly, plus to be able to have the children at not too late an age …

Me: So you told the agency this?

Yes, and they suggested not hitting the men with it straight away, which is fair enough. But I had no intention of — I can't think of the word — being dishonest at all. I would have been quite honest about it …

It's hard to overestimate how important motherhood is to the identity of women like Karla and Shaney, and how non-negotiable is the place it occupies in their imagined futures. Explains Karla:

[I think about having children] pretty much every day, and 50% of the day. It's sort of a big feature … in the last three years or so. I went through a really clucky stage when I was 28 or so. That lasted a couple of years then it went off. I thought no, that's not going to happen. Don't even think about it. Reject it. But now

I'm feeling that biological clock [and] … it's becoming so important now … What disturbs me most is that I don't really want to go on if I don't have children. And yet I love my life and I love my friendships, but I just — it's awful, but I just feel I'm not worthy, I'm not enough to be on my own. I'm not enough for me. I really want to love a child and bring a child into a world, and give what I can to it. (She cries.)

All thwarted mothers have a strong desire to have children, and to have them in the traditional way: in stable relationships with men. For women like Darcy, men remain a non-negotiable part of the plan, while women like Karla and Shaney abandon their desire for the Whole Package only when time is really running out and they feel forced to choose between having a child in a less-than-ideal way, and not having a child at all. Recently, said Karla, she had begun thinking about sperm donation:

I'm tossing up … the sperm donor thing. I think I'd like to see the person, and meet them and know what their life was like and how they live. I know they have all those details: colourings and interests and careers and medical history and all that. But to me there is something too clinical about it. And yet it's not totally out of the question, it's a last resort.

Shaney's plans were considerably more advanced, and by the time we met, she had been inseminated at a clinic several times. Yet the Whole Package remained an ideal she was reluctant to relinquish. Indeed, as Shaney's story shows, its power exerted considerable drag on the momentum of the plans of even those thwarted mothers who were determined to become mothers any way they could:

I … went to a clinic to try and get pregnant … Mum said to me, 'Whatever you do, I'll support you … I just feel I should let you know that I've been praying a lot about this, and I feel that God might have other things in store for you.' … She's entitled to her opinion but it put me off going, and it made me feel like I was ruining my life … It was actually quite subtle, [and] it wasn't until months later I thought, why did I stop, dammit? Why didn't I just say to Mum, 'What do you know? You've never been in my situation?' … She is the one that has the fairytale that there is somebody out there for me … And I've started saying, 'It's a fairytale. It's not going to happen. Don't hold your breath here. I'm 37 now, and nothing has happened yet.'

Me: So you don't actually feel that it is going to happen?

No, not really. I still hope it does. And that's where Mum's influence comes into it. Every time she says that, it sparks that hope again. And then after a couple of months I've got depressed about it all again and nothing happens and I don't meet anybody and rah rah rah. I squash it down again and start realising that it's not necessarily going to happen … When I was going to [the clinic] … I felt, 'what a shame I'm having to do it this way.' But it's the only avenue I have to have a child at this point in time … But the fact that I was going to get pregnant and have a child helped me there. That was a glimmer of hope for a future for me … I was doing something about my life and making my life what I wanted it to be, and hopefully bringing a lovely child into this world. I feel that that has been knocked on the head. It was because I still had that underlying hope that there'd be a male around there somewhere.

And I felt that I had to trade one off against the other. If I went down this avenue, then I was going to have to give up this one. And I immediately changed tack …

Karla's hope that she might be rescued at the last minute by the arrival of a Mr (wants children) Right on the scene has also led her to delay 'getting on with it':

> I would probably have [my parents'] support. They love me enough to probably give me that uncon- ditionally. It would be a hassle at first, the tenth degree, the Spanish Inquisition, but it would be OK in the end … I know women have babies in their early forties, but I still want to be reasonably young. I mean, even if I got pregnant today, I'd still be 36 by the time I had it. And I just want it to start happening now, at this age. Just to get on with it … I keep extending the time and I guess that's pretty common … But it's like, is [the Whole Package] going to happen or not? How long am I going to just hang on?
>
> *Me:* How long do you feel you can [wait]?
>
> I don't know (Crying). Not much longer, I don't think …

As Shaney and Karla's stories make clear, ageing thwarted mothers face a painful Catch-22. Biologically, the sooner they find a donor and start getting inseminated, the better: for the simple reason that younger women have a greater chance of falling pregnant and taking home a healthy baby than older ones do. But the sooner a woman enrols at a fertility clinic or becomes pregnant using donor sperm, the less time she gives herself to pursue Mr (wants to have children) Right and the Whole Package. Indeed,

Shaney now worries that her delay in returning to the clinic may ultimately cost her the successful pregnancy she so desires:

> That's why I'm probably still angry with Mum ... I went [to the clinic] in March of last year ... I'm just considering [going back now], but I'm getting a bit old. Back then I was 36. They said 'A lot of people come to us at 38 and 39, and it's really too late.' ... They said, 'It's good you came to us now.'

Not surprisingly, ageing thwarted mothers resent the hard equations — and the constant recalculations — forced on them by their ever-ticking clocks: especially given the large number of unknowns. This was not, explains Karla, how they expected their motherhood journey to be:

> Some people meet someone and it all happens really quickly. And I can probably imagine that happening with me, because things like that do happen with me. But then it just may not happen at all ... It pisses me off that ... for some people it just happens ... They don't think about it ... But for others like me it's like, 'Oh God.' You sit around waiting and wondering, and it takes away from it.

Some worries about sperm

Thwarted mothers are the women who, when infertility strikes or when time is disappearing and not even an Approximate bloke is to hand, consider the use of donor sperm to have a child. Waiting and watching types, those we'll discuss in depth in the following chapter, don't want children badly enough to go to such lengths.

But even for women who are clear as water that they want to mother and will end their days disappointed if they don't have children, the donor sperm option remains daunting. Now, as the stories of thwarted mothers that I've presented should make clear, some thwarted mothers will go through quite a song and dance to have a man, even a sub-standard one, in tow when they have children. But sometimes — as women like Karla and Shaney discovered — donor sperm is the only way. Both Karla and Shaney speak eloquently, in my view, about the frustration and despair they feel about having to even think about becoming a mother this way, let alone going through with it. But once they have faced up squarely to the prospect of the cloudy-white syringe, they discover that there are further unknowns and worries associated with becoming a mother in this way.

There are two options when it comes to sperm donations: known or anonymous. The advantage of a known donor, particularly if he's willing to meet the child, is that he can ensure that the child knows her medical history and has a clear sense of who she is and where she came from once she is old enough to start asking questions. Some known donors may even agree to act, in some limited ways, as a parent or a male role model to the child.

But the legal waters are murkier around known donors, and some women don't want to risk the biological father changing his mind and demanding greater parental rights than were originally agreed to: especially when there's some chance the courts might back him up. And that's not the only complication with a known donor. One woman I know ultimately rejected an offer from an old male friend of hers because she feared it would complicate her relationship with the man's wife, despite the wife swearing it wouldn't. Other single mothers are happy with an anonymous donor because they simply don't accept the oft-made claim that biological fathers provide the only suitable male role models for children. Single mother Lyndal

Dornan, a radio producer, has a pack of male relatives (granddad, father, brother), all of whom she describes as 'great men', and all of whom spend time with her 3-year-old son Edward.[35]

The most critical issue for women considering known donors is one of respect: not the 'will he still love me in the morning?' sort, but whether or not she respects the man as a person. It doesn't matter if the child is going to see the bloke once a year, once a week or only when she asks, 'Where is my daddy?'; a woman knows that once she's accepted a man's sperm to make a child, she is going to be stuck in some sort of relationship with this bloke for life — and so will the child. Sadly, it is in this area that many donors come up short. Here Rhyll tells how she had an abortion in her early thirties in large part because she simply could not imagine having an ongoing relationship with the biological father or allowing him to parent her child:

> When I was 32 ... I STUPIDLY got pregnant to this bloke who I really didn't even like very much ... [When] I realised I was pregnant, I cut it off straight away. Because I didn't want this man in my life, at all ... I have never wanted to be a single parent ... The decision was quick. Just because of who the father was ... There are not many men around I really like or respect. Lots of men I fancy, but respect is ... a tricky one.
>
> *Me:* Was the problem that you didn't like him and his genes were in this child or ...?
>
> No, no, no. Not his genes ... I couldn't bring a child into the world and know who its father was and where its father was, and deny it the right to know that father ... It would be immoral for me to deny [the father] the right to develop a relationship with the child: it would be immoral for me to deny the child a

relationship with him. So who the father is matters a lot, because single parenthood or not, I would still be tying up my life with this man ... I would be sharing a child with him. And I didn't want to because I didn't like him and I didn't respect him.

On the other hand, anonymous donors force women to confront their basic beliefs about the input of nature and nurture into what a child is, and will become. One single girlfriend of mine who, after much agonising, decided to use an anonymous donor found herself becoming increasingly antsy about the unknown nature of the genetic contribution the donor would be bringing to the reproductive table. Having relied on the scant donor descriptions provided by the clinic, she had finally decided on one who listed 'swimming' as a hobby. But from that point until her ultimate abandonment of the quest for pregnancy a number of months later, she spent a fair bit of time wondering what having swimming as a hobby actually meant. Was the donor's penchant for the pool an inherited or a learned quality? The swimmer also had a university education, but again she wondered, was this achievement the result of innate intelligence or economic privilege? This same woman also confessed to finding the pursuit — with a stranger — of the intimate project of creating a child together unbearably strange at times; she was desperate to know more about her donor than could be gleaned from the dry, one-page report she'd read and reread. She spent copious amounts of time swimming laps at the local pool, eying off each of the men pacing up and down beside her, and wondering if any of them was the one.

Such anxiety about the composition and 'quality' of the genes of sperm donors is not unusual. It is similar for eggs. The Ron's Angels website saw infertile couples bid extraordinary amounts of money for the eggs of models who did well at school (it has since been claimed that the site is a hoax). There was widespread panic recently in Denmark when the news broke that one sperm donor to an infertility clinic was a two-time child killer serving a life sentence in a psychiatric ward. Interestingly, the disagreement that broke out between Danish authorities and the clinic about how to settle the panic only underscored the potency of the disagreement among experts and the public at large about whether it is nature or nurture that determines the person a child becomes. While the clinic has vowed that all future donors will need to provide police certification that they are not criminals, the government defended the absence of laws requiring donors to have a criminal check on the ground that 'there is no evidence that a tendency towards criminal behaviour can be inherited'.[36]

Of course, sometimes women or couples seek donors with particular genetic characteristics (blue eyes, blond hair) — not so much because they see such qualities as 'superior', but because they increase the likelihood that the child will look, and therefore can be passed off as, biologically 'theirs'. Unfortunately, given the extremely tiny pool of available sperm donors worldwide, women from racial or ethnic minorities have almost no chance at the moment of securing a donation from a man from a similar background.

(An emphatic) Conclusion: the truth about thwarted mothers

In recent years, the mass media has spent a fair bit of time spinning a tale about hordes of hairy-chested (and legged, it's implied) single women who, having laughed off the idea of forming relationships and raising children with men, are now marching lock-stepped to the corner sperm bank to the triumphant beat of 'Sisters Are Doing It for Themselves'. A cover article in the Melbourne magazine

SundayLife! is typical. Amid a pink phalanx of cute little swimming sperm is the bold black headline: 'Wanted: one sperm (no strings attached)'. Below runs the tag line, 'Thirtysomething, single and solvent: the women who go it alone'. The implication is that increasing numbers of women are *choosing* to have children without men. Turn the page, however, and the truth emerges, in the stories of 'Sue', Lyndal and midwife Jane MacGregor. These are women who have come to the end of their biological rope with no man in sight, and have consequently been forced to snatch at single motherhood in preference to the only alternative left: single childlessness. The only ones talking about 'choice' are the subeditors. Says MacGregor:

> Finding a partner [was] impossible. Everyone [I met was] either married, divorced [and] with truckloads of emotional baggage or gay … I would have preferred to have done things in the conventional way, but it just wasn't happening — and at 36, time was running out.

'Sue's' journey to single-motherhood was depressingly similar: a yearning to become a mother at age 33; a long-term relationship with a man who lived overseas but who wasn't interested in making it a forever thing; and what I would consider an extremely wise reluctance to take her strong desire for a child into a new relationship.

The point here is simple, though it's one I feel I can't make too strongly. Women go to extraordinary lengths to conceive and raise children with all sorts (and in some instances, any sort) of men rather than going it alone. It is only when push comes to shove — a minute left on the biological clock and all attempts at wooing even the most Approximate of men having failed — that a handful of determined women take matters into their own hands and turn their considerable intellect and energy towards the pursuit of single motherhood. And even then, the heartfelt desire of most for the Whole Package leads many to continue to procrastinate, to recalculate odds, and to cast about for some other means of escaping their predicament: despite knowing that such delays could cost them dearly in the end. And indeed, many do agonise and postpone for so long — or have bad enough reproductive luck once they finally get into gear — that they do end up missing out on their dream of a child.

This isn't choice. Moreover, such tragic tales provide no support for the tiresome contention that is hashed and rehashed in the media: women are 'uninterested in' or 'indifferent to' men and the prospect of having and raising kids with them. Quite the contrary.

In later chapters, I'll return to the question of men: the role they play in the so-called motherhood strike, and what can be done to help men ante-up more effectively in the parenthood stakes. I'll be speaking about the institutional obstacles men face when they try to be active and effective fathers — and about the legitimate reluctance some of them therefore feel about making babies in the first place.

But before we get there, we must first look more closely at another group of women who are finding their freedom to have children uncomfortably constrained. Unlike the thwarted mothers, these circumstantially childless women don't see motherhood as a must, but as a mildly preferred life option to be pursued only if the conditions are right. These are women who are ambivalent and undecided about motherhood. I call them waiters and watchers, and it is their footsteps on the rocky road to motherhood that we will trace next.

Chapter 3

WAITERS AND WATCHERS

No-one knows what the right thing is. First we come to believe that developing ourselves is the right thing. Then we hear that motherhood is the right thing after all. But how are we supposed to integrate the two? The only role model presented to us that attempted the mix has been the 'having-it-all' woman who has a slick career and perfect children, and collapses from exhaustion each night after the last dinner plate is cleared.

Judith Schwartz, author of The Mother Puzzle:
A New Generation Reckons with Motherhood

Many women have made the choice to have children early and *try to establish careers, and we've all watched those exhausted but determined women being punished for not staying back late in the office, or for needing to take time out to care for a sick child. Indeed, many of we childless women have inched past them in the career race, feeling guilty but powerless to help. And if they dare to take time out from the paid workforce in those wonderful early years of a child's life, we've watched many of them get left far behind in the race.*

Sian Prior, columnist and radio personality

All things being equal, waiters and watchers want kids. But in a world that gives an awful lot of lip service to the wonders of motherhood yet never stops contriving to make the having of children — never mind the raising of them — difficult in the extreme, all things are far from equal. First of all, most waiters and watchers need the right man on board, and securely strapped in, before having children is even seriously considered. But while having a Mr (wants to have children) Right to hand is a *necessary* condition for a waiting and watching woman, it is definitely not *sufficient*. This is because waiting and watching women don't just carefully observe the woes of women attempting to combine work and motherhood; they adjust their plans for motherhood accordingly. This willingness to let what they see alter what they do when it comes to having kids is the key difference between waiting and watching women and their opposites, the thwarted mothers (for whom motherhood is a far less negotiable goal). Not long ago, Australia's Sex Discrimination Commissioner, Pru Goward, made a passionate plea for increased family-friendliness in the workplace, arguing that when women are forced to choose between 'a job and a dirty nappy/diaper', many today choose the job. But as we've already seen, it isn't thwarted mother types who, when push comes to shove, choose work over motherhood. The women Goward was speaking about are the waiters and watchers.

I had no trouble getting waiting and watching women to speak with me — another clear difference between them and the thwarted mothers. In fact, most ambivalent and undecided women were busting to talk about their worries and hesitations when it came to parenthood. When the interview was over, many thanked me for giving them the chance to run through their pros and cons of motherhood list, and thus mull the decision over a bit further, in range of a sympathetic ear.

Initially, I found the considered nature of these women's deliberations, not to mention their sheer volume, surprising. I am a fan of academic and commentator Susan Maushart, and believed one of the central contentions of her bestselling book *The Mask of Motherhood*: that mothers do everything they can to shroud the challenges of motherhood in 'silence, disinformation and outright lies'.[37] Consequently, I had assumed that the childless women I'd be speaking with would be totally clueless about — and therefore make decisions about parenthood untroubled by — the travails of contemporary Australian and American motherhood.

This had certainly been Maushart's story. She had confronted her sister several weeks after the birth of her sister's first child and breathlessly insisted on the truth about motherhood.

'I'm going to tell you this now, and I want you to remember it,' her sleep-deprived sister replied sharply. 'Everyone lies. Do you hear me? Everyone lies about what it's like to have a baby. Don't listen to them. Just watch me, and remember.'

Maushart nodded her head sagely, but not long after became pregnant with the first of her three children.

There is a moral to this tale, but not the one drawn by Maushart. The truth is that mothers do tell childless women about the difficulties they face, but many childless women simply don't listen. Maushart is a perfect example of this: she is a woman who was already so committed to having kids herself that really listening to the less-than-happy experiences of her mothering relatives and friends would pose too great a threat to her longstanding maternal imagined future and identity. So she didn't.

Waiting and watching women, on the other hand, are horses of an entirely different colour.

Waiters and watchers: who are they?

Waiters and watchers are women with a profoundly undecided and ambivalent attitude towards motherhood. Women who, when asked around the campfire to share a bit about themselves, would include neither 'mother' nor 'childless woman' in their self-description. Waiters and watchers are women who have a philosophical approach towards motherhood. They neither pursue it nor actively avoid it; they simply wait to see how their feelings and their circumstances develop. When told about the trials and tribulations of motherhood, not only do women of this persuasion not ignore it, they practically have to restrain themselves from taking notes. They are also the sort of women who, with only minimal provocation, can recite chapter and verse of every problem that any mother anywhere has ever encountered. Lack of sleep? They know about it. Nonexistent sex life? They are more than aware. Guilt over using childcare? Mastitis? Incontinence? The Mummy-track? Check, check, check, check.

In the 1950s, when motherhood was as *de rigueur* for women as a regular pap smear is today, most waiters and watchers probably ended up having kids. Social structures pushed women strongly towards motherhood, as did social pity and scorn for single and childless women. However, in today's world, which is both more child-hostile and, thankfully, more accepting of broader roles for women, ambivalent and undecided women are being pushed just the other way.

The key to waiters and watchers is that they don't *need* to mother: their sense of self is independent of whether or not they have children. This means two things. First, they are the connoisseurs of current mothering conditions: it is these women who pay the greatest amount of attention to parenting realities on the ground and make and change their personal decisions about motherhood accordingly. Second, waiters and watchers are strongly influenced both by what others say about motherhood in general, and by their own assessment of the costs and benefits of parenting in their particular case. Unlike thwarted mothers, who will leave a parenting-averse man if they possibly can, waiting and watching women tend to sit tight; they may even eventually adopt their partner's aversion to kids. Equally, partnering with a man keen to father may be enough to tip a waiting and watching woman over the mothering edge. Waiting and watching women are 'dependents' when it comes to mothering: mirror opposites of the 'independent' thwarted mothers. It is the people and circumstances of their lives that dictate their decision about motherhood, not a drive from within.

Dumpy mums (or the high cost of motherhood in a sexist society)

How does parenthood come to have such a vague place in the imagined future and identity of waiting and watching women? The answer can be found in their childhoods. Unlike thwarted mothers, raised to see motherhood as an essential ingredient for a good and happy life, waiters and watchers are women who saw when they were young — often in their own mothers — that children threatened all they were being taught to value in life: financial independence, romantic relationships, high-powered careers.

Martine is 36, and a museum director. When she was young, her mother explicitly warned her not to get married. However, Martine always knew that it wasn't her mother's early marriage, but her unexpected first pregnancy, that spoiled all the plans her mother had had for her own life:

Mum said she would've left [Dad] if she could have. But she had nowhere to go because she was an immigrant. So her family were in South Africa [and] had no money; [she had] no family to go to in New Zealand, so that was that. She stayed. And she reached some point or other where she said it was too late for her to leave ... And I don't, to be honest, I can't remember that she ever said to me, 'Don't have children.' She did use to say to me, 'Don't marry.' My parents always wanted me to do the things that they didn't do ... They wanted to travel the world and they didn't do it because Mum fell pregnant with me. If they had any aspirations for me, one [was] that I would go to university, probably because Dad hasn't had that much schooling. And the other was that I would do interesting things and that I would travel the world and explore and not get tied down in suburbia.

The eldest sister in a working-class Catholic family, Kaitlin spent her own childhood helping her mother raise her brothers and sisters. While Kaitlin has not ruled out having kids one day, she is reluctant to make the personal sacrifices she knows contemporary motherhood entails:

At work I see a lot of women really struggle to be a mother and work at the same time; women just being incredibly stressed. They've got to work part-time but they've got to work in a job that's unsatisfying. They're torn because they want to be with their babies. And then they can't do their fitness, because that's taking time away from their babies, let alone their partners. So where is their personal time for themselves? It isn't there. So many roles and still thinking about what's going to get cooked for dinner … I feel like I've already had a family … [and] I just love only being responsible for myself … I feel so free, so light … I just don't want the burden of a child. I feel like my life would have to go on hold, and I still haven't done all the things that I want to do. Maybe in a few years' time when … I've achieved a few things in my new career that I really want to achieve, then maybe I'll think, 'Yep, I can step back a bit, and go into mothering.'

Jacinta, a 33-year-old administrative assistant, has also been strongly influenced by the high price her own mother paid for having children, and what she perceives motherhood has done to her mothering neighbours. Her greatest fear is of becoming what she calls a 'dumpy mum':

My mother is one of nine kids. She's the second … [and] raised a lot of the younger kids … My dad drank most of my childhood away. He was a pretty absent father. When we were young kids Mum had no support from him … When I think about having a baby … I worry about … losing touch with the big wide world out there. I worry about becoming concerned with things like how much the nappies are going to cost me when [important political debates] are going on. I worry about losing perspective … and becoming a dumpy mum … There's a lady up the street who is a dumpy mum. She's got twin boys [and] all she does is complain … 'Oh God, I'm so tired, they were awake at 5 o'clock.' And she just goes on and on and on … She never reads a paper, she never sees a film. You can never talk to her about anything other than her kids because she just doesn't know about anything else. That makes me think, 'So that's it. You have your kids and then there's nothing else, nothing other than that.'

(The powerful influence of a few) Good men

Despite Jacinta's numerous and severe reservations about motherhood, she has come close to deciding that she will have a baby. Key to that decision is her husband Ron's determination to become a father, and willingness to share — or even take the bulk of — the burden contemporary parents bear:

> I've always said to people, 'We're not having kids … no, that will never happen.' And Ronald's always [said] … 'We're going to have six' … He brought it up, and I said, 'I'm 33, so if we're going to have a baby, we'd better have it sooner rather than later.' … And sometimes I think, wow, that's fantastic, but sometimes I think, yeah, I'm really neither here nor there about it.
>
> *Me:* What was your reaction when he brought it up?
>
> It really changed my ideas about it, because I was really touched that he thought it would be a good thing to do … I'm happy to have a child because I know that Ron will be fantastic and really supportive, and it will be a really nice thing to do together. If it wasn't for him, then probably not … because I don't feel like a really maternal urge to get pregnant and have a baby or anything … [and] I'd like to keep working … Not because I love work so much but because I … want to keep another interest up. Money's an issue for me and I'd like to still know that

I can earn ... So we've tossed around the idea of me going back to work, and him spending more time at home looking after the baby.

But while Ron is willing to pull his parental weight, 29-year-old Bethany is not so lucky. Her husband Jack is in banking, and his refusal to modify his long hours or even commit to changing the occasional nappy/diaper has led her to shelve her parenting plans until his attitude changes:

> I think I will have children ... I would probably like to watch a child, or children, grow up. [But I know that] I will play a bigger parenting role. I know that because Jack's told me that he will still be going to work, and he will pretty much be doing what he's doing now. So it will be up to me ...
>
> *Me:* Are you happy that that is the way it is going to be?
>
> It is hard to know what it will be like. He says at the moment how he finds babies disgusting and one vomited on him the other day and he thought it was foul, and he was just really grossed out by the whole thing. And he says, 'I don't want to come home and change shitty nappies after I've had a long day at work.' We had a conversation a while ago and I was saying, 'You know, it would be nice if you would come home and change one nappy at least', and he felt the whole thing was a bit ridiculous because it was not happening now.

While a man both able and willing to pull his weight is critical for waiters and watchers with partners, having a decent man in the first place is absolutely necessary (though definitely not sufficient) for the single gals I spoke to before they would even consider motherhood. Samantha, a 32-year-old graphic artist living in the inner city, explains:

> I brought up the issue of being single, because I can't actually look at [being childless and being single] separately ... I have no doubt of my capacity to love my own child, I truly don't. But I'm not the person who melts with delight at the sight of a pram. You know, like for some women, it's everything. And for me it's that vague sense of, oh yeah, it could be good. So for me it's really tied up with an idea of a relationship. I imagine part of a relationship would be to have children ... I think if I was with someone who definitely didn't want to have a child I could deal with that ... because I don't have this huge drive to have a child ... [although] it's something that in the last couple of years I've really moved towards thinking I would love to do. But I don't feel strongly enough about it that I'd do it by myself ... It's not such an overwhelming need that I'd just say, 'Bugger it, I'll just do it myself.' And I would do it if I felt the need, because I've always made my own way, but I don't feel that need.

Jocelyn is a single accountant in her early thirties. While she always thought that one day she'd be married with kids, for her there is no question that without the man, there will be no motherhood:

> I'm quite traditional in the sense that I wouldn't have children without [being in a relationship] with someone who I wanted to have them with, and to

spend time with [myself]. So without having that person in my life, it's hard to imagine having children.

Me: So you're not that sort of person who would think about having them on your own?

Nope.

Me: No question about it? So if I were to come back and speak to you when you were 38, you're quite confident that if no-one special had come into your life you wouldn't be pursuing children?

I don't think so. Children to me are part of a relationship, and not just a thing in themselves … There [would need to be] an understanding between me and a man: that with him I wanted to have children. The children on their own aren't something that you have for the sake of having children.

Options open

Waiters and watchers are the sort of women who neither make important decisions impetuously, nor admire those who do. Their hearts and souls firmly in Libra, they are first-order weighers and balancers: extremely concerned to make the rational and considered decision about childbearing that they hope will protect them from the regret and unhappiness they fear could be their fate. This is Jacinta:

I wonder whether I could possibly be a mum. I don't know if I'm cut out [for it]. I don't know if I'm equal to the task … because there is so much involved. People seem to take it really lightly. It really amazes me … Can I cope with all of the demands of my life that I've got now plus a baby? [Am I] equal to the task in terms of, it's a lifelong thing. It's not like you say you're going to have a baby and then in three years, no. It's over. It's the rest of your life sort of stuff.

Barbara has struggled with the serious and irreversible commitment motherhood entails — indeed with all serious and irreversible decisions — for most of her life. It's not that she *wants* to up and exchange her life as a successful lawyer for a waitressing job in Santorini. She just wants to know she *could*:

> I've always had this thing in life: wanting that ability to get up and go, and change my life at any time. And now I've really come to terms with the fact that I can't necessarily do that, and it pisses me off ... Because I've got a very successful practice ... and I'm married and I adore my husband, but the idea that I can't get up and go and be a waitress in Dublin or Santorini ... [is] very hard ... It terrifies me that you make a choice in life that then immediately sets off a whole chain of events that then limits your choice. That if I had a child, I then could not pursue my career — stuck! Trapped! The idea of being trapped is the most — I hate the idea of being trapped. Of making choices that are not reversible.

What Jacinta and Barbara seem to be saying here is that they are afraid. Afraid they won't be up to the demands of parenting, or that having parented for a while, they'll find themselves over it, and wanting to give the baby back. The aversion of such women to risks, according to demographer Peter McDonald, explains why many will never have a child or will limit the number of children they have:

There is a risk that children will disrupt the relationship between the parents. There is a risk that children will follow pathways that cause parents considerable anxiety. There is a risk that some harm will come to the child. There is a risk that the relationship will break up and the mother (or sometimes the father) will be left alone to support the child. There is a risk that the social trend towards child-unfriendly societies will continue. There is a risk that public support for families with children will be rolled back. People, particularly women, can avoid all these risks by limiting the number of ... children [they have].[38]

But while it seems clear that it will be in some women's natures to worry and therefore to be more aware of, and affected by, the risks associated with children, a number of the risks that McDonald cites can be — to use his phrase — 'smoothed out' by a well-developed welfare state in which job loss is covered by social security arrangements, services for children are costless or subsidised and unforeseen health risks are covered. This is unlike the current situation in Australia where the risks and costs of children are passed back to families, and away from the state.[39] For our purposes, the take-home message is clear: waiters and watchers are women who are risk-averse; they are likely to delay or forgo motherhood because of anxiety over parenting 'what ifs'. While childbearing and raising children involves some unavoidable uncertainties, some of the uncertainties currently attached to parenthood in Australia are unnecessary. Removing them would remove one of the constraints on contemporary Australian women's freedom to choose motherhood.

Is motherhood a rational choice?

Waiters and watchers are women who worry that a decision to have children doesn't make sense. Given the importance to these women of the Three Cs of the motherhood decision (careful, considered and correct), their preoccupation with the rationality of the decision should hardly be surprising. But they are far from alone. A philosopher I know, himself childless by choice, recently expressed scepticism that a decision to have kids was ever rational. 'I can understand making an irreversible commitment to a partner — at least you know them,' he said to me at a staff party. 'But how can you make a decision to love and care for someone you don't even know?'

Is motherhood a rational decision to make? In the final chapter of this book, I will answer one part of this question: whether a decision to mother can be defended on coherent, consistent and logical grounds. Here I will look at why, given how long women have been doing the motherhood thing, such a significant subsection of them has suddenly become so determined to justify the decision on rational grounds.

One reason is obvious: it is only recently that sexually active women gained some control — through modern forms of contraception such as The Pill — over whether and how often they would become pregnant and give birth. Without such control, musings about children of the 'should I/shouldn't I' variety were moot, and consequently of little interest. Indeed, such control has been the prerequisite for what researcher Marian Faux argues is a dramatic shift in the contemporary female rite of passage. While once it was the experience of motherhood that was seen to signal the passage of girls into womanhood, today it is the decision all women must make about whether or not to mother that is seen as a significant marker of maturity.[40]

Once motherhood becomes a decision rather than a biological inevitability, the need for reasons — and good reasons at that — to choose it cannot be far behind; this is the very logic of decision making and choice. One of the most fascinating and totally unexpected findings of my research was how totally flummoxed women were when I asked them to tell me what, in general or for them, was a good reason to have children. Talk about blank looks! Strangely, related questions did not prove nearly as hard. For example, women had no difficulty explaining why they *wanted* to have children; perhaps because this question asked about feelings, and they saw feelings as having no obligation to conform to rational principles or rules. In fact, a handful of women believed that just wanting children was a good reason to have them. As far as they were concerned, desire was a perfectly adequate motive, and they were perplexed at my insistence on probing the matter further.

However, the vast majority of women thought the question, 'What are good reasons for having children?' made sense, and they did try to answer it. But for nearly all, the struggle was in vain. In the end, only three women managed to mumble anything at all, and only two of them really made any sense. The remainder just drummed their fingers on the table, fondled their chins reflectively for a bit, before shamefacedly confessing that they wouldn't have a clue.

I'm sure you must be on the edge of your seats by now, so without any further ado I present the two good reasons women arrived at to have children (drum roll, please):

1   To be an extension of you and your partner; and
2   To enjoy watching them grow into good people.

Bad reasons for having children, on the other hand, were an entirely different story. Here, women had heaps to say: they came up with nine poor justifications for a decision to have kids. In no particular order, they were:

1 When you don't really want them;
2 To quell boredom;
3 To remedy dissatisfaction at work;
4 To do what everyone else is doing;
5 Because time is running out to have them;
6 So you won't be lonely when you're old;
7 To hold your relationship together;
8 To feel like a 'real' woman by experiencing pregnancy or mothering; and
9 To fulfil your own need to give, or to love.

It's little wonder that with so few good reasons to have children, and so many good reasons not to, many women concluded that a decision to mother just didn't make sense! This is Sharon:

> If I look at it rationally, I [have to] say [that] having kids is going to screw up my comfortable existence … And it really puts paid to lots of notions of career … I'm in a job where I work 50 to 60 hours a week. And there are people [in my office who are] trying to bring up young kids and work at the same time. And you have to be there at work, otherwise you're not being serious, but with young kids, there is this guilt that you should be spending more time with the kids … Yeah, so on that rational level, it's making a decision that goes forever. I don't usually make decisions like that. And physically it's hard, and financially it's hard. You can think of a whole heap of reasons why not. And I'll write a list of pros and cons. And there are

masses and masses and masses of cons. And the pros are like, 'Well, I want to.'

Barbara also thinks that when you look at the pros and cons rationally (which she adamantly believes all women should), you have to conclude that motherhood is exclusively for gals with their heads screwed on backwards:

> [I am] someone who regards the bringing of children into the world as something you really need to consider very carefully from a rational perspective: about how that fits into your life, your lifestyle and your life choices, as opposed to, 'I want a baby.' Because I honestly think most women want a baby. It is a … literally gut-wrenching urge to have a baby … I don't think women think, I won't have a good night's sleep for years. I will never have a weekend alone with my husband again. I will have to compromise in my work … I'll never go to a folk concert again. I'll never go to a rock 'n roll [concert]. I can't just go out whenever. Women don't think about it.
>
> *Me:* Do you think they should?
>
> Yes! Absolutely!

Despite this, both Sharon and Barbara want to have children. To many, this might seem odd. How can women who damn motherhood as a life decision made only by fools want to choose it themselves? The answer, according to both women, is that their biology makes them want to do it. Their maternal 'instincts', 'hormones', 'drives' and 'clocks' compel them to desire motherhood, and to pursue it despite the odds and against their better judgement. Here is Sharon again:

I [said to myself], 'Come on, you're intelligent. You must be able to think of some good reasons [to mother] …'

Me: What do you think is a good reason?

Well, because I want to. I'm trying to break that down into why, and that's where I come back to, I think it's a sort of biological thing … it's physical or it's emotional … It's really hard for me to say [why I want them]. There are these emotional, irrational reasons for having kids that are actually much stronger than the rational ones.

The fact that motherhood doesn't make sense on rational grounds also leads Barbara to conclude that the only reason women do it — and why she wants to do it — is the irresistibility of the maternal 'urge':

I know that if I had a child my first responsibility would be to the child and not myself, and that's the deal … Now in my work I've always put my clients first, my clients come before my husband, my personal time, my private life, my recreation. It's a responsibility. But I can always manage that responsibility. I can cancel the appointment. But with a child, you can't … It has occurred to me that this urge to have children is a physical thing. Men don't have it … Well look, if women didn't have a maternal urge, why would you have a baby? Why would you?

The conclusion of women like Sharon and Barbara — that it is female biology that drags them towards motherhood while their rational brain begs them to hang back — raises a number of interesting questions. Among them is whether or not what women see as the irresistible and illogical pulls of their physicality are, in fact, biologically based urges at all. The short answer is that there is no way to know for sure, though the weight of the evidence argues against biological compulsion, and in favour of the critical influence of women's very early social experiences.

What Barbara, Sharon and the other women who felt compelled to mother despite their rational assessment that having kids made no sense tended to have in common were childhood experiences in which they learned that mothering was a necessary feature of a good and meaningful life. To say this is not to suggest, as is commonly believed, that because women's desires aren't sourced in their natures they are not powerfully felt. Indeed, it is precisely because women's early experiences so profoundly shape their imagined future and identity that it is so hard for them to revise their plans and sense of self when unforeseen circumstance throws them a curve. Experiential explanations account for the depth of feeling; there is no need to resort to the sort of 'in the genes' type of explanation that implies (quite insultingly) both that women who don't want to mother are abnormal or deficient in some way, and that yearnings for (or aversions or indifference to) motherhood are fixed in the stone of our natures, and consequently impervious to change.

But it is not only early childhood experiences that influence what researchers call women's 'baseline' attitudes to motherhood. Particularly for ambivalent and undecided waiters and watchers, later experiences are key. The take-it-or-leave-it baseline attitude of waiters and watchers to motherhood means they pay assiduous attention to bad parenting conditions and are willing to revise any plans they have to parent in the face of them. Among the social conditions steering such women away from motherhood is the absence, in both Australian and American society, of what philosophers would call a normative account of motherhood, and what others would describe as a 'feeling out there in the ether' that motherhood is a wise and sensible thing to do.

The source of the 'feeling out there in the ether' that motherhood is for fools

Remember the list women provided of bad reasons for having kids? Notice anything familiar about it? You should, because about 35 or 40 years ago, this list wouldn't have been of bad reasons to have children; it would have been a list of good — or at least totally normal — ones to parent. Back in the bad old days, it was expected that all 'normal' women would have, and would desperately yearn to have, children. If you were infertile you were pitied, and the childless by choice were simply stamped 'deviant'. To get pregnant and mother in order to express your femininity, or simply to do what everyone else was doing, was just part and parcel of the good old Australian and American way. At a time when divorce was far less accepted than it is today, having children in order to try to save a failing marriage was also more or less *de rigueur*, as was the expectation that adult children would and should look after their ageing parents.

Most of these norms were scuttled by feminism; the rest were simply drowned by the rising tide of individualism. I'm not mourning their loss: times have changed, and for the most part they have changed for the better. My point is that as old reasons for having children have disappeared, no new ones have arisen to take their place. The absence of a list of good reasons to parent is the reason women started spluttering and stalling when I asked them about it. It is also a partial explanation for why increasing numbers of women — particularly the more hard-headed of the waiters and watchers — are postponing parenthood, or forgoing it altogether. When motherhood is a choice, women need reasons to choose it, and many waiting and watching women just can't see the point.

The militant childfree

The rise of a strident and not very community-minded childfree political movement has also contributed to both the demise of age-old reasons for having children and the failure of new reasons to arise to take their place. Of course not all childless people are members of militant childfree organisations, and not all members of such organisations are supportive of all the claims made by the groups on their behalf.

This is a good thing, because it is hard for someone who works in ethics (namely me) not to find some of the beefs and demands of the militant childfree totally repugnant. Among the most offensive is the insistence that all parents are mindless fools: a conclusion that follows logically from the movement's baseless — yet continually asserted — premise that anyone who really considered the issue of parenthood intelligently would end up choosing childlessness. Smug childfree couple Susan and David Moore, authors of *Child-Free Zone*, note:

> The best outcome we can hope for from this book is for more people to *think* before deciding to have children. A frightening number of people neither think about it nor make an active decision — they just have children.[41]

The militant childfree also have a host of charming names for the parents they seem to see as their enemies: Breeders, Moomies and SITCOMs (Single Income, Two Children, Oppressive Mortgage). They modestly dub themselves, in contrast,

THINKERs (Two Healthy Incomes, No Kids, Early Retirement). But the arrogance and classism inherent in such a title doesn't end there. In *Child-Free Zone*, the Moores propose that 'irresponsible breeding' is due to a downward-spiralling 'stupidity vortex' that sees the 'less educated and less intelligent' having more children (who then go on to have more children themselves) while their 'well educated middle class counterparts' have fewer children (who will eventually reproduce less themselves). Leaving aside the fact that current evidence flatly contradicts the theory's predictions of climbing birth-rates and declining IQs, stupidity vortex claims also have a eugenic whiff around them that is repellent.

The militant childfree also regularly assert that people who parent are selfish. Unbelievably, they insist that it is those who *have* children who are guilty of thinking only of themselves, and that it is those who abstain from 'breeding' who are seeking to benefit society as a whole. The classic example given is of overpopulation: few childfree websites don't have links to population panic ones, as well as to ticking global population counts. Parents, the argument goes, freely choose children despite problems of overpopulation and with little concern for the way their personal decision compels the childless to sacrifice all sorts of things — from the global environment (due to the high environmental costs connected with producing and getting rid of disposable nappies) to ease in daily life (they are forced to tolerate child-safe lids on prescription drugs and crying children in restaurants). The childfree, on the other hand, make thoughtful choices not to have children based on their civic-minded concern not to overburden the planet or their fellow citizens.

Factually, this claim is incorrect. Few, if any, of the voluntarily childless choose against children because of population worries. As one childless by choice woman put it:

If I don't have children … there's more room for people from other parts of the world to come here. But … I'm not enough of an idealist to say that if I wanted children I wouldn't have them because of the population problem. It just fits with my philosophies.[42]

Such imagined parental selfishness may be what, in the mind of the militant childfree, justifies their unrestrained animosity towards parents. On one website, parents are referred to without embarrassment as 'irresponsible addle-head shit-sucking morons', while on another a series of rants against parents is each concluded with the mantra 'breeders suck'. There is also plenty of righteous indignation from the childfree about their tax dollars going to support, and again I'm afraid I quote, 'spawn squirters' and their 'ankle biting brats'. For Leslie Lafayette, founder of the *Childfree Network*, this means opposing insurers covering the cost of infertility treatments such as IVF. For organisations like *No Kidding!* it means lobbying for tax rebates for the childless to compensate them for the payments they make to services that are disproportionately used by the 'child-burdened', such as schools and various health services.

Elinor Burkett, author of *The Baby Boon: How Family-Friendly America Cheats the Childless*, puts the hard-done-by case for the militant childfree this way:

Parents get more than nonparents. Every childless person can tell you exactly how much money their compensation package is worth versus the person sitting next to them. If I worked for [a company that offers subsidized childcare, I would be getting] fewer benefits that are relevant to my life. All this talk about how you have to have all these benefits to take care of the morale of working parents? What about my morale? Every time someone takes off for that sick child or that school conference, then someone else has to pick up the extra work. And the supposition on the part of management almost always is that the person without kids is more able — and it's true — to do that than a parent. And it happens again and again and again. After a while you're doing two jobs for one salary.[43]

The selfishness of parents, and the unseemly way they impose on the childfree, is also the subject of Australian author Tom Nankivell's forthcoming treatise, *Having Their Kids and Eating Out, Too*:

'Equal pay for equal work' was once the proud demand of the feminist movement. But like the pigs in Animal Farm, these days some women (and some men) seem more equal than others Those with their snouts in the trough are working parents who, under the guise of 'family-friendly policies' are demanding — and receiving — special treatment ... The discrimination against childless workers takes many forms, some small and subtle, others blatant and big. When mum leaves work early to collect the children from [childcare], or when dad takes 'carer's leave' to look after junior, it is the childless workers left behind who are invariably expected to finish the job ... When a business provides on-site childcare facilities, the quid pro quo of lower wage rises comes out of the pockets of the childless employees as much as the pockets of the parents who benefit from the facilities ... If successful, the current push for widespread maternity and paternity leave will only exacerbate workplace discrimination in favour of workers who choose to spend their time and money on a family lifestyle, at the expense of those who do not.

Nankivell is dismissive of those who would defend what minimal support society does give to parents:

> People who leave the workforce for lengthy periods experience slower career advancement … [because] they do not develop the same skills and experience as those who remain. Accordingly, one of the costs of motherhood — and of fatherhood if the parents decide that the male should take some years off to care for the children — is some retardation in career. But this 'cost' is simply one aspect of a family lifestyle choice: a choice that most parents would agree brings them substantial net benefits overall. Why, then, should parents get compensation?

Nankivell concludes his rant as follows:

> Overall, the pork-barrelling of parents … has gone on for too long … Whether in the workplace or elsewhere, it's time parents stopped squealing about the costs of their lifestyle choices and started focusing on their responsibilities instead.[44]

Greedy little piggies and squealing: my word! It also amazes me that anyone could title a book that is meant to be about the oppression of the childless by parents the way Nankivell has. His title makes it clear that what really gets his goat is that parents might get even a crumb of the cake that a two-income responsibility-free life makes it so much easier to scoff — and then go back for seconds — every day. And it is unseemly (to put it mildly) for those who acknowledge that they are among the most fiscally privileged and time-rich of all citizens in the Western world to spend their energies whining about how terrible it is that they don't have more.

In the final chapters of this book I will address the red herrings in the rhetoric of the militant childfree, with a fair bit more respect for the childless than they show to parents, I hope. I will not only point to the key fallacy in their contention that a decision to have children is the same sort of 'lifestyle' choice as the selection of a station wagon over a sedan, but also demonstrate the rationality of a decision to parent for anyone wanting to live a good and meaningful life.

For the moment, however, I will stick to my point about militant childfree rhetoric, which is that it is contributing to the stunned-mullet expression I saw on so many women's faces when I asked them to name some good reasons for having children. Given all the blah-blah-blahing the militant childfree do about the stupidity and selfishness of a decision to have kids, is these women's confusion surprising?

Moaning mums and whingeing writing

It is not only the militant childfree who are contributing the 'feeling out there in the ether' that having children is for fools. Inadvertently, mothers are, too. Not all mothers, of course, but certainly the painfully honest, stunningly witty and terribly amusing ones who write newspaper articles and books such as *The Mask of Motherhood* and *I Don't Know How She Does It*: books that go on at great length about how damn difficult it is to parent well in contemporary Australia and the United States.

Journalist and young mother Sian Watkins' contribution to the op-ed pages of the *Age* (during the regrettably brief period where the paper was actually regularly publishing women on so-called women's issues like motherhood) is typical. The mother of a one-year-old, Watkins lamented the trials of new motherhood, but instead of demanding more of the support that would make her life easier, went on to describe the desires of those who don't want children as possibly 'selfish', but definitely defensible:

> Men and women now have choice about the way they live, and a growing minority would prefer to live independently, with money, nice clothes and good holidays (how selfish, you say, but none of us are immune from these desires), rather than in tracksuit pants wiping Weetbix off walls every morning. All perfectly understandable.[45]

A similar rant against the loss and exhaustion motherhood entails, Allison Pearson's *I Don't Know How She Does It*, does attempt to show the structural impediments to women working, raising small children and remaining sane. But unfortunately, her fictional hero Kate Reddy's solution to the problem (taking a less demanding part-time job) is a personal rather than a political solution. The book was a bestseller even before book doyenne Oprah Winfrey declared it 'the working mother's bible', and was soon followed to the top of the charts by journalist Cathi Hanauer's *The Bitch in the House*, a similar tale about the toxicity of working motherhood to women's aspirations in every area: health, wealth, romance, work and mothering. All this just a few years after Maushart took the lid off what she contended was the silent pain of contemporary mothers in her bestselling tome *The Mask of Motherhood*.

There is absolutely nothing wrong with mothers telling the truth (or, more precisely, their truth) about motherhood. Such books are necessary, important, and at times extremely enjoyable forays into women's complex experiences and emotions as they struggle to forge new ways of living, ways of living that were unimaginable even 30 years ago. What I worry about is balance — or the lack of it — in the growing 'gripe' literature. Sure, there is plenty for contemporary mothers (and fathers) to complain about these days, but no matter how unnecessarily hard society makes parenting, there is still much joy to be had in bringing children into this world and nurturing them to adulthood. When mothers whinge about their burdens, they hope for empathy from their fellow parental soldiers, and for the sympathetic ear of decision makers with the power to make things different. What they forget is that childless women, more specifically the waiters and watchers, are listening too — and, given all the bad news coming from parent central, reconsidering their options. As I argued a few years ago in the *Age*:

> We working parents never cease complaining about the hardships of sleep deprivation, and the trauma of finding great childcare at affordable prices, and then leaving our kids there, [but] ... the deep and profound love we feel for our children (a love that is at the centre of and gives meaning to our lives) ... remains our dirty little secret ... [Our complaining and silence send the clear message that] you'd have to be crazy to become a mother. Only women who are losers or who have fallen victim to their 'biological clocks' have children. Women who evaluate the maternal cost/benefit sheet dispassionately will delay childbearing indefinitely, or remain childless.

It is not true that most women who have children regret it, or that only the thoughtless or irrational choose to have kids, and it breaks my heart to think that childless young women and men believe that the whingeing writing is warning them to steer clear of parenthood as overly risky and downside heavy. Yes, parents must continue to tell it like it is, but surely it is also time we shared our dirty little secret — that in addition to the trials and tribulations parenthood offers great joy and satisfaction.[46]

The other problem with some of the whingeing writing is its total disregard for the historical and social context that is making parenthood so hard today. There are sacrifices intrinsic to the parenting project, of course, but not nearly the number that contemporary parents currently bear; nor is there anything inevitable about women having to pay most of those costs. When moaning mums fail to emphasise that it is the social conditions within which women mother, rather than mothering *per se*, that are the source of the problems they face, they unwittingly support militant childfree assertions that the costs of children are high and unchangeable (and can therefore only be avoided by avoiding parenthood altogether). They also give unwitting support to the militant childfree insistence that there aren't now — and there never will be — any good reasons for having children, and therefore that choosing motherhood is an irrational decision for a woman to make.

Economic man and the 'irrationality' of motherhood
A few years ago childless feminist Germaine Greer grabbed headlines in Australia with her views on motherhood. Greer opined that infertile women's 'obsessive' yearnings for babies were pathological, and that their belief that children would 'fulfil' or give meaning to their lives was 'irrational'.[47]

Ah Germaine, brilliant one moment, attention-seeking the next. But Greer was right about one thing: many women do believe their desire for children is irrational. Insulting infertile women, however, will do little to help us understand the source of these beliefs, or how they can be challenged.

The dominance of market-driven ideas about economic man helps explain why women think as they do. In contemporary Western societies, rational behaviour has largely become synonymous with self-interested behaviour. Economic man (EM for short) is the rational man of the moment in this world: the 'individualistic and maximising consumer'.[48] EM's goals are simple: to mediate all his highly contingent relationships through contracts drawn up with other EMs, and to do whatever maximises his personal autonomy and freedom, and enables him to buy more stuff.

In a world that not only openly espouses such values, but also puts them into action, those who fail to act like good EMs will be tagged as irrational. And who is it who engages in these irrational, non-consensual, interdependent and permanent relationships that restrict their personal independence and their disposable income? A whole heap of reflective and perfectly sane people, thanks very much. Choosing to live a life that reflects values such as responsibility, commitment and interdependence doesn't make people irrational; it just makes them a bit like salmon swimming against the normative tide. In fact, every woman and man with a child is such a fish, because even in societies that provide equal and adequate support to both parents to raise their kids, some of the intrinsic (that is, unavoidable) demands of parenthood run against the EM's rules for a good life. Parents the world over create dependents to whom they make extensive, long-term emotional and fiscal commitments — no ifs, buts or ands about it.

Parents need to recognise that the values behind their decision to parent are ones that importantly and fundamentally challenge EM's vision of a good life. So far, however, this simply hasn't happened. The upshot of this for the circumstantially childless is that when they are thinking about mothering, all they will hear are the militant childfree banging on about mindless Moomies and parental snouts in the trough, and the whingeing writers moaning about being stressed-out mums. There is a deafening silence from the other side: parents willing and able to defend the values that led them to decide to have kids, and to enjoy the process of raising them.

The pure relationship ideal and the irrationality of motherhood

Anthony Giddens is one of the most influential thinkers in the contemporary Western world. A British sociologist, currently director of the London School of Economics and Political Science, his writings have been influential across the social sciences, as well as in history and philosophy. In the academy, to put it bluntly, Giddens is a theoretical god.

Giddens thinks that the wise and with-it contemporary gal does, and should, pursue what he calls the 'pure' relationship. A pure relationship is one that is not based on emotional or financial need, but on interpersonal fulfilment. Such relationships are what Giddens calls 'contingent' — and what I would describe as 'disposable'. That is, the moment one partner stops feeling 'fulfilled', he or she must drop the other without delay and begin searching for a replacement capable of providing greater satisfaction. When a pure relationship flowers, something called 'confluent love' is its fruit: an active love in which both participants make themselves vulnerable to the other by revealing their concerns and needs, and in which reciprocal sexual satisfaction is essential.[49]

All very fine and nice, as far as it goes, but insert children into the pure relationship and it's not hard to conclude, à la Grover in *Sesame Street*, that one of these things just doesn't belong. It isn't so easy, in other words, to dispose of an unsatisfactory partner when he happens to be the father of one's children, and a father the children would prefer to have around. As British legal scholar

Carol Smart has wryly observed, 'Children stop confluent love in its tracks.'[50]

Women are all too aware of this, but while the elusive nature of confluent love may lead those already married with children to remain in less than sterling relationships, the ideal has a different impact on women who haven't had kids. Namely, it leads many to see motherhood as a highly irrational decision to make. After all, if what they *ought* to be doing is seeking a pure relationship, then having the children that will make it hard to ditch a less-than-pure one seems a poor tactical move.

Children undermine confluent love in other ways, too. Rather than sharing the intimacy created by the mutual disclosure that Giddens describes, couples with very young children only rarely have in-depth discussions about anything other than the colour and consistency of poo, and the most effective teething gel. Instead of sexual satisfaction being at the top of their to-do lists, it is task sharing — of the 'who got up last night' and 'who changed the last dirty nappy' sort — that tends to be uppermost in tired parents' minds.

Relationships recover, of course, though experts disagree about how well — some argue that the post-child relationship trajectory is a U-bend, while others point to only a J-curve revival. My beef is with the pervasive glass-half-empty assumptions of the Giddens worldview: assumptions that children function only as a negative when it comes to intimacy, rather than as a force that both *modifies* existing relationships and provides new sources of relationship satisfaction. There is no doubt that children change a marriage, and that in the early days the change is definitely for the worse, as is nearly everything in life compared with how it was before (sleeplessness, and the weight of new responsibilities, will do that to you). But once parents are through the early years (many date their liberation to the first day they exited the house *avec* kids but *sans* nappy bag) things improve rapidly. Sure, wading through the shit together, literally, tends to kill that giddy flushed 'I can't wait to get him in bed' feeling, but let's be honest: except for the lucky few (and I reckon they're lying), that newly wed feeling dissipates around the three- to five-year mark in any case.

But it isn't all downsides. Experts such as Relationships Australia's Lyn Fletcher say that after the excitement of the 'discovery' phase winds down, all couples have to find a way to deepen their intimacy — by revealing the 'essence' of themselves — or risk disintegration (through affairs or divorce) anyway.[51] Children provide parents with a built-in opportunity to forge and deepen their unique bond: a bond grounded in the love they feel for, and the shared work of raising, the new human beings that they've created together. Even the most fractiously divorced couples find the joy of talking about the progress of their children unavailable with a new partner, no matter how beloved. I know a number of divorced parents who have only one regret about leaving their partner: the loss of a shared life with someone who knows their children as well, and loves them as much, as they do.

Children themselves also provide a new source of relationship intimacy and joy. For many parents, nothing beats the way their offspring approve, trust and love them so unconditionally; nor the way — and the intensity with which — they feel all those things for their kids. That Giddens got away with writing an entire book about intimate relationships without even mentioning the parent–child bond is testament to the depth and breadth of parental silence in the United States and Australia on the joys of, and reasons for, having kids.

The cant of the militant childfree, the moaning of mothers, and the silence of parents and relationship researchers on the joys of parenting: it is any wonder waiting and watching women hesitate to take the plunge?

Regret

If I had a penny for every time a woman expressed her fear of regretting her decision to remain childless, I'd own several islands by now. Regret — or more specifically, fear of regret — was a mega-issue for the women I spoke to who were considering not doing parenthood. Not just waiters and watchers and the thwarted mothers, but some among the childless by choice too.

Midwife Janine is profoundly worried that she will regret missing out on motherhood:

> [I worry that I'll regret] never having that bond, that love that I think only a mother and child can have. Never having the sensation of a human being growing inside me, never being able to breastfeed.

Sharon worries that regret about not having children will turn her into a bitter, unhappy woman:

> I've got a bit of a fear that, you know when you've got two incomes and no kids, both professionals who earn a lot of money, it's possible to get very insular in some ways and think the world revolves in a certain way, because you can order most things in your life. Whereas you can't order having kids ... They operate on different timetables and have different needs and basically you've got to deal with disorder ... I know quite a few women in their mid-forties who haven't had kids and they can be pretty narrow and bitter and selfish.

Sometimes fear of regret is so powerful that it can tip a childless woman who is to-ing and fro-ing over a decision about kids over to the motherhood side of the fence. This was the case for Mary, who, after her first marriage broke up, was seriously tossing up her plans for motherhood:

> If I didn't have children then I'd always have heaps of money to get by. I [could] go and travel anywhere I want, and there are still a few places I would love to travel to. And I think it's probably a bit more carefree and easy a lifestyle, and more spontaneous; you can just do what you want to do. So I sort of [thought about] that, [but] always in the back of my mind I [kept] thinking, would I regret it later on? And I [never got to the] stage where I could comfortably say, 'No, I don't want to have children, and I'll never regret it.' I [never] got to that stage.

Despite early signs of fertility difficulties, Hilary has also been spurred on to pursue motherhood out of fear that she'll regret a decision not to have kids:

> Others ... have the dog or the cat, they have something that they acknowledge [is their] baby, and that's enough.
>
> *Me:* So why isn't that enough for you?
>
> ... Because ... I might regret not having a baby.
>
> *Me:* What do you fear you'll regret?
>
> ... Missing out on something. Not the actual labour or anything like that. But the pregnancy, what it's like to be pregnant, and then more than that, what it's like to have a little person to mould, and to ... know what [my husband's] son or daughter [would] look like.

The truth is that women's worries about regret cannot be dismissed lightly. Research suggests some women do regret, or at least feel discontent about, not having had children. One American poll, for instance, found that 60% of childless women wished they'd had children. Another study, of 90 childless women (the vast majority of them childless by circumstance), found that nearly all had regrets about not having children, and that for some, these actually became more profound as they grew older. In Australia, a survey of men and women aged 45 to 54 found that 25% said they had fewer children than they wanted. This number rose to 30% among those aged 65 and older.[52] One older woman's reflections on being childless were typical:

> I don't think that I ever had time to think about it. I was always busy. I never truly regretted it when I was in business. I never [regretted not having children then] but now I do, I do.[53]

I lay out such sobering facts about regret in the hope that they will shock complacent national decision makers into action to reduce our climbing rates of circumstantial childlessness, but I am also aware of how devastating they may be to women whose time for childbearing is nearly, or already, past. There is, however, no need to despair. First, it is important to recognise that those at greatest risk of regret are likely to be the circumstantially childless. Women who have actually chosen their childlessness are less likely to be affected. Second, while women do worry that they'll regret not having children, it's important to remember that when they are young, they also worry that they'll regret missing out on other important aspects of life if they have children too early. Said one young woman interviewed by Anne Summers:

I want to live my life, because as soon as I get married and have a kids and then a mortgage, I am not going to be able to just take off and travel ... If I do everything I want to do now, later on I am not going to regret anything.[54]

What this means is that women who are worrying that they will regret missing out on motherhood need to keep in mind that if they had dropped everything and pursued motherhood before they were ready, they might now be regretting other things. Third, even among women who desperately wanted to mother but missed out, disappointment and regret did not always translate into discontent and unhappiness. As researcher Grace Baruch has pointed out, unhappy women can't be identified by their status as either mothers or non-mothers, or even by the degree of choice they exercised over their parental status. Rather, happiness (in relation to childlessness) is determined by the way a woman frames, or comes to see, her childlessness, and her capacity to accept the finality of the outcome and then move on and find other sources of meaning and satisfaction. Childless women can live and enjoy their lives, in other words, while at the same time wishing that the circumstances that led to their missing out on motherhood had been different.

Are waiters and watchers 'selfish'?

All childless women have, at one time or another, found themselves at the sharp end of the selfish barb, but waiters and watchers are particularly vulnerable. This is because, unlike thwarted mothers, waiters and watchers are (to greater and lesser degrees) ambivalent and undecided about having children, and do little to disguise the evidence-based way they pursue a resolution to their quandary. It is this uncertainty about whether motherhood is really worth it and whether they can or even want to cope with what Jacinta describes as 'all the demands my [usual] life ... plus a baby', that makes waiters and watchers more vulnerable to criticism by others as selfish, as well as to intrusive attempts at persuasion by those who are parents. This latter group is far less noisy than it used to be — indeed, many childless now report that one of the most common responses by parents to their 'choice' is envy — but some still do stick an occasional beak over the fence to loudly worry about a childless friend's future loneliness or regret.

Luckily, the waiting and watching women I interviewed were also the least likely to be concerned about the 'selfish' barb. In fact, many of them had a pretty good stab at reclaiming the word, in much the same way as AIDS activists reclaimed Hitler's pink triangle as a symbol of gay pride. For these women, being 'selfish' means having a normal interest and investment in one's own career and personal growth; an approach to life they see as much more sensible than a 'selfless' one that would see them marry and parent at a tender age.

Jacinta is happy that she and husband Ron have the freedom to be 'selfish':

> I've thought that ... Ron and I have such a fantastic relationship [that] I don't want ... a baby to come in and spoil what we've got ... Got a good little life ... We spend so much time together and we just seem to be so well matched. We are selfish, but I'm not critical of the life we have. I've heard people say there is an element of selfishness in not having kids, but it always seems to me to sound like a negative thing. We can do whatever the hell we want. If we want to take off on a weekend, if we want to sleep in until 11 o'clock, yeah we can do that.

Museum director Martine was one of a number of women who determinedly dedicated their youth to 'selfish' pursuits — travelling, educating themselves and advancing their career. Following her mother's advice, she determined that marriage and children would have to come later:

> The people I grew up with who got married and had children, they did it in their early twenties, so their whole life is completely different to mine and has been for years and years ... I look at them and I'm reminded of my Mum and Dad's concerns, the house in the suburbs, and ... they behave like them in some ways ... That's my expectation of it actually. That the woman ends up bearing the brunt of the physical and the emotional work and whether she does it because he foists it on her or ... because she pulls it away from him, it just happens and there's no escape from it.

Bethany is young and content enough with her life with Jack to be 'horrified' at the thought of the sacrifices that mothering — particularly the way Jack seems determined to force her to do it — will demand:

> The whole thought [of childbearing] absolutely horrifies me ... What [children do] to your lifestyle and how that changes a relationship. And it's obviously very theoretical for me now because I haven't experienced it so I don't know what is it like. But I know that at the moment I'm not ready to go and see what it is like ... I know that most people who have just had a baby, and even for quite a long time afterwards, much of their time is occupied with the children. And I know that I have to feel that I can take that on, and be prepared for it, and I just don't feel

like I could do that at the moment … I quite like the way things are at the moment, and I feel like I haven't had enough time with Jack, just the two of us, to hang out together and stuff. And I'm not prepared to give that up at the moment and I don't know if he is either.

Not only are waiting and watching women happy to wear the 'selfish' badge in explaining their indecision about motherhood; they are largely non-judgemental about other women donning it too. This is 31-year-old Mary, born and raised in the country:

Lots of my friends have no intention ever of having children. A couple of them would probably like to if they had the opportunity and were in a good relationship, which they are not at the moment. But one of them is adamant that there is no way she ever wants children. I've known her for 15 years, and she's always been the same. I think that's just her. I've probably talked to a few people too, since I've been weighing it up … They say, 'I've got no interest in having children. I don't want to give my money to anyone else. I just [want to] spend it on myself, enjoy life.' Another girl said, 'Oh, I'm too selfish to ever have them because I like my lifestyle.' She works on and off and plays golf and travels.

Me: What do you think about that?

I don't have any problems with it … They probably just like things how they are in their lives and don't want to change them … [And] I don't think that every woman should grow up, be married and have children. And I don't think that every woman who is in a relationship should have children.

It is these last two sentiments of Mary's — that not every woman should get married and have children, or have children if she is in a relationship — that go the heart of the matter. Back in the 1950s, when the prevailing moral view was that every woman should marry and have children, it is likely that many women who felt ambivalent and unsure about whether marriage and motherhood (particularly the apron-wearing, stay-at-home-in-the-suburbs type that was the norm for the middle classes) were for them were swept up in the pro-picket fence fervour of the times, and ended up doing both anyway. Some of them may have become valium-popping victims of what the experts at the time dubbed 'housewife's syndrome';[55] others may have become desperate and guilty Laura (*The Hours*) Brown-type runaways from a maternal role that was irreconcilable with their intensely individualistic natures.

Today, thank heavens, women who definitely don't want children, or who are ambivalent and undecided about childbearing, have more options. And if there is one thing we should be thankful about, it is that our society now offers women who don't want to mother the freedom to just say no. Indeed, the willingness of women to be open about their waiting and watching orientation is testament to our society's changes, evidence that feminists have largely disentangled motherhood from womanhood, and freed young women to imagine themselves and their futures without motherhood.

In fact, one can imagine that as the fruits of the women's revolution continue being institutionalised in Western thought and day-to-day life, as generation after generation of women grow to adulthood with a clear view of motherhood as optional (read: subject to prevailing social conditions), the number of women with a waiting and watching orientation towards motherhood will grow. In the future, there are likely to be greater numbers of women willing and able, should they judge the social conditions wanting, to give motherhood a miss with little angst and few regrets.

This is not to say that waiting and watching women don't want to have kids, but rather that they only want to mother if the conditions are right. If Mr (wants to have children) Right arrives to catalyse her desire to mother, and states his willingness to share the work and sacrifice involved, and if she feels confident she can raise children while maintaining the career or outside interests that prevent her becoming a 'dumpy mum', then most waiting and watching women will hop off the fence and say 'yes' to motherhood. It is only in a world that forces them to choose between a self-sacrificing and self-abnegating motherhood and a 'selfish' desire to maintain a life of their own that they will, however regretfully, say 'no'.

The time has come to stop talking in generalisations and get to down to specifics about the roadblocks in the way of circumstantially childless women having the children they want. The first stop? The myth of motherhood.

Chapter 4

THE FERTILITY CRUNCH I: THE MYTH OF THE 'GOOD' MOTHER

I asked a Mother what she thinks a 'good mother' is.

'A good mother is nothing like me,' she said. 'A good mother always knows what to do, and does it well, without complaining, without yelling, without manipulating anyone. A good mother uses her power to protect her children from all harm. A good mother has healthy, happy, wonderful children ...'

'You're describing a faery goddess and a machine,' I interrupt.

'Yes, maybe I am. But I think that's what a good mother should be.'

From the diary of American writer Phyllis Chesler, 1978

Before I was really old enough to understand what being a woman meant, I already understood that the world of women was divided in two: there were proper mothers, self-sacrificing bakers of apple pies ... and there were the other sort. At the age of thirty-five, I know precisely which kind I am, and I suppose that's what I'm doing here in the small hours of 13the December, hitting mince pies with a rolling pin till they look like something mother made. Women used to have time to make mince pies and had to fake orgasms. Now we can manage the orgasms, but we have to fake the mince pies. And they call this progress?

Fictional working mother Kate Reddy, in Allison Pearson, *I Don't Know How She Does It*, 2002

'You're your own worst enemy,' my mother used to say to me when I was a teenager, forever moaning about my nonexistent bloated tummy, my imagined greasy hair and the fabricated blemishes on my skin. Years later I grew up and wised up enough to see that she was right. No-one was ever as unrealistically tough on me as me.

It's the same with women who are mothers — they are their own worst enemy when it comes to the standards they set for how women should feel, think and act in order to earn the 'good mother' stamp of approval. Harsher still is the way they judge and punish themselves, and each other, when expected standards aren't met.

But what does 'good mother' mythology have to do with childless woman? Quite a lot, as it turns out, though sadly it is rare for the connection to be made. Good mother mythology contributes in important ways to the growing problem of circumstantial childlessness.

The (frustratingly enduring) myth of the 'good' mother

The myth

I'm not going to spend too much time on good mother mythology, because most of us — mothers or not — pretty much know the drill. There have certainly been enough books written on the topic. From Susan Douglas's *The Mommy Myth* to Diane Eyer's *Mother Guilt* to the sell-out theatre sensation 'Mum's the Word', these days there is a mini-industry dedicated to persuading mothers to abandon their 'good motherhood' guilt.

So far, it hasn't worked. Good mother mythology has the longevity of gum stuck to the bottom of a shoe: it sticks forever in the cracks between how women are exhorted to live and how they really do. Largely unchanged since the 1950s when the standards were first proclaimed, the power of the myth persists despite reams of feminist protestations and — more impressively — a rapidly changing social landscape that means the day-to-day reality in which young mothers parent today bears little resemblance to the environment in which their grandmothers raised kids. So despite the fact that the majority of mothers with kids under two work outside the home, such women are still driving themselves to bake homemade mince pies for the Christmas fête, to be at home by 3:30 to meet their little angels after school (perfectly lipsticked mouth curved in a gentle smile) and to never, ever lose their temper no matter what the little angels do or say.

No, I kid you not: this is the 'good motherhood' job description that mothers today swear by in the same anxious, sweaty-palmed way their maternal predecessors did. Good mothers, these poor guilt-ridden souls tell researchers time and time again, are those who provide unconditional love, are ceaselessly patient, endlessly nurturing and totally responsible. It's as though when it comes to motherhood, normally sensible generations of women suspend disbelief and begin babbling about maternal responsibility like a squadron of well-drilled Stepford Wives. How else to explain women's relentless expectation that when they have a child, even the most intolerant will develop saintly patience, the most assertive will develop dutiful passivity, and the most intellectual and ambitious will wake each morning abuzz with excitement at the prospect of another few hundred viewings of the Teletubbies? Hello, it's motherhood; not alien abduction!

If pregnancy, labour and birth did cause this sort of personality replacement, all would be well. But it doesn't. Instead, what happens is that mothers remain more or less the same people they were when they were just plain women: armed with the same strengths, and debilitated by the same weaknesses. The only difference is that they now also have a child in tow. Most of them get little help raising it from their man and the society in which they live, and to cap it all off, they acquire a permanent backache from bending double each day under the weight of the guilt that they are not, and never will be, good mums. As married couple Tony and Anne Morton put it:

> We prize our individual autonomy and identity and at the same time chide any woman who refuses to renounce it as soon as she becomes pregnant. Little wonder that women, given the choice, are doing what men have always done and opting out of child-rearing altogether.[56]

The point the Mortons are trying to make is actually two-pronged. First, they are scathing about a dogma that reduces mothers — upon pain of being labelled callous, selfish or just plain bad — to 'mere instruments to [their] child's wellbeing'. Not only does compelling them to be stay-at-home mums (or superwoman-type paid workers pretending to be full-time mums) make mudpies of their identities, but it plays havoc with the careers in which they've invested so much time and effort. Which brings the Mortons to their second point: where the hell is the father in all this?

Good fatherhood?

The answer, according to the Mortons, is, 'at work.' This is because despite paying lip service to the importance of children and their desire to be more hands-on fathers, the reality is that men 'are unwilling to accept the loss of independent identity that has been women's lot ... rightly perceiving that with its loss goes a loss of [self and others'] respect'. There is more than a little truth in this observation. We humans are social creatures, and as such, our self-esteem will always be at least in part dependent on the esteem others hold us in. And we in Australia and the United States have the added bonus of living in patriarchal societies, in which, claimed researcher Andrea O'Reilly in a recent conference speech, both 'motherwork' and those who do it are critically undervalued. The institution of motherhood, she argued:

> give[s] women all the responsibility of raising children but no authority from which to enact this responsibility ... we don't make the rules, we just are expected to follow them ... We are expected to perform this monumental task [of mothering] alone, isolated, usually exhausted/overwhelmed, without support, time off, or validation ... The ideology of motherhood is impossible to fulfil in our actually lived lives ... and the discourse puts us all under surveillance and mothers who are not the so-called good mother of this ideology are judged as bad mothers and treated accordingly. Motherwork [is] not valued, but more significantly, [it is also] not seen as work. In particular, [it is] not seen as a practice with profound cultural significance and political import.[57]

Not surprisingly, such a job description doesn't tend to hold much attraction for those who have other options — rich women and most men.

But the good motherhood myth's exclusion of fathers is more all-encompassing than this. Essentially, society defines good mothers and good fathers as polar opposites. While to be a good mother, women must abandon work when their child is born and never prioritise it again, a good father's job description is the mirror opposite: it compels men with kids to centre their lives around paid work. Good mother mythology makes women nurturers to the exclusion of all else, and good father mythology makes men breadwinners to the exclusion of all else. Consequently, when children are born, researchers continue to find that women temporarily retreat from the workforce, while men dive in face first. One study concludes:

> Becoming parents chang[ed] women's and men's work *motivation*, in opposite ways. Women were less emotionally involved with their work for a while … By contrast, many fathers felt an additional impetus to make it in their jobs — the need to work more, to be an especially good provider.[58]

Making good fatherhood about breadwinning is a losing strategy for countless reasons. First, as I'll discuss in detail in the next chapter, rapid economic change is quickly making historical mincemeat of this role. More importantly, making what the goose does totally different from what the gander does once goslings come along deprives both sexes of the full range of life experiences they need to feel fully human. When women do nothing but nurture, they miss out on the sense of mastery that comes from meaningful and valued involvement in the work of society (not to mention the independence and autonomy that comes from earning). In contrast, endless time at the office for men means they miss out on the pleasure that comes from being intimate with their partner and kids.

While it used to be only women who complained about this, increasing numbers of men are now jack of it too. Indeed, I would argue that the new generation of men, those now in their twenties and early thirties, barely question that hands-on caring work is part of the responsibility of a good dad. Respected social researcher Hugh Mackay agrees. In his book *Generations*, he says that men born in the 1970s:

> appear to understand gender issues more readily and comprehensively than their fathers or grandfathers did, and they appear to be sincere in their assertions that men and women should have equal opportunities and should take equal responsibility for parenting.[59]

Such profoundly changed attitudes are not just down to many of today's young men having been raised by feminist mothers (nice work, girls); they are also down to the growing influence of the men's movement. Men's movement guru and bestselling author Steve Biddulph, for instance, argues that breadwinning is no longer a father's primary role. Instead, his central responsibility is to spend time with his kids, and to care:

> Men show their love by working hard and long. And they do not get appreciated for it — since it is their presence not their bounty that is hungered for by their children.[60]

Respected Australian researcher Don Edgar agues that the powerful ideology of motherhood oppresses not only women, but men too. By 'driving men' away from 'an equitable sharing of the childcare and housework tasks' described by the good motherhood ideology as 'the natural domain of women', motherhood has:

> destroyed fatherhood as an interpersonal status and substituted for it the role of 'breadwinner', the absent but important provider now so vilified ...[61]

Defining fatherhood as about caring rather than earning is not a job for sissies, says Edgar. Only the most masculine of men have the confidence needed to rework the father-as-breadwinner role into the father-as-carer role. And the only ones who will succeed in reclaiming their paternal 'right' to spend time with their kids will be those 'confident in their own masculinity [and] unconcerned at any jocular mockery that may come from their "mates"'.[62]

John Q Public's view of the good father, and correspondingly of the good mother, is also changing. There is growing community acceptance of fathers as competent carers of young children and, correspondingly, of mothers as earners. A 2001 Gallup Poll found that of those Americans who believe the ideal situation is to have one parent working at home or part-time outside the home, 69% think it doesn't matter which parent works full-time and which provides the care. This is a significant change from ten years earlier, when only 55% were indifferent to who did the breadwinning and who did most of the childcare.

While there has been little evidence so far that redefinitions of fatherhood have subverted the uncompromising requirements of good motherhood mythology, I continue to live in hope. Surely the interconnectedness of male and female social roles, and definitions of masculinity and femininity more broadly, make it inevitable that positive changes to the way good fatherhood is defined will lead to positive changes in definitions of good motherhood.

The blame

But the fact that things *are* changing doesn't mean that they *have* changed, and the truth is that not all men are feeling relaxed and comfortable about the changing social roles of men and women, and the changing parental roles of mums and dads. Some men, particularly the older and less educated ones, recognise that they're on a pretty good wicket, and would like to retain as much of the unfair advantage in the divvying up of employment and family-based responsibilities as possible, thanks very much. Who can forget the moral panic in the United States several years back when Hillary Clinton dared suggest that baking cookies and serving teas were not required of those laying claim to the good wife and mother seal of approval?

In Australia, the tender feeling many men continue to have for the most oppressive tenets of good motherhood mythology was demonstrated a few years ago in a Newspoll published in *The Australian*. The survey found that 81% of men, compared with only 70% of women, believed that if women had their children's best interests at heart, they wouldn't return to work until their kids were at school. In addition, 68% of men (compared with only 48% of women) believe that stay-at-home mothers have a better relationship with their children than do mothers who work. And while these figures look slightly less scary when men are grouped according to education (the more educated the man, the more progressive his views), there is still a significant fault line between the views of educated men and educated women on home and hearth. For instance, when 7682 Australian households were polled about their agreement or disagreement with the (tragically grammatically unparallel) statement, 'It is much better for everyone involved if the *man* earns the money, and the *mother* cares for the home and children', only 42% of men with Bachelor degrees or higher qualifications disagreed, compared with 56% of similarly educated women.

Australia, sad to say, is also burdened with political cartoonist Michael Leunig, who has done more to undermine progress on the gender equity front than a pope on cocaine. In his cartoons in the *Age*, Leunig regularly laments changing parental ideals that not only seek to grant full personhood to mothers, but implore fathers to do more:

The thrust of Leunig's argument, if I must dignify it with that term, is that *only* mothers can care for babies, and 24/7 maternal care is essential for child development. Women who fail to provide this sort of care are selfish. The supposed need infants have for their mother's constant care not only rules out women being mothers and employees simultaneously, but puts a serious crimp into what many would see as their basic human right to be mothers and human beings simultaneously (a charge to which Leunig replies, 'I'm sorry, it's the baby's feelings that are important here, not the woman's'[63]). More self-servingly, the Leunig theory of parental obligations to infants (which, it has to be noted, garners little support from recent early childhood education literature) leaves men entirely out of the picture. Conveniently, in the world of Leunig, men can be good fathers without having to do anything for their children; oh, except one thing. Good fathers do, the cartoonist concedes, need to defend the 'right' of mothers to parent in the way that serves men like Leunig best. 'I feel it is natural for a male to be protective of mothering,' Leunig explains breathlessly. 'It's an act of fathering in the cultural sense to be concerned about this.' 'Oi va voy,' as my grandmother would say. 'With friends like these …'

I'm not telling you this just for the fun of scaring you witless about the fact that not only does a man like this still exist in the 21st century, but is regularly honoured as a national treasure. I'm telling you this to remind you that despite being far past its use-by date, the debate about what good mothers and fathers look and act like is still very much alive. Indeed, it is the continuing potency of good motherhood myths in contemporary Australian and US cultural conversations that explains how these myths have the power to influence the lives of women who mother, and women who don't.

The requirements of pre-motherhood: childless women up the moral ante

Couples are key

As it turns out, women's fervent desire to parent in accordance with contemporary 'good motherhood' standards begins long before they gaze down lovingly at their brand new bundle of joy. It even begins before they're pregnant. In fact, it starts at the point where the perfect relationship with Mr (wants to have children) Right is just a twinkle in a woman's eye, because for most childless women, finding and establishing a stable relationship with He-(or She)-Who-Is-The-One is a big part of what good *pre*-motherhood is about.

When I interview 32-year-old Lori, she makes her 'first comes love, then comes marriage' standards clear from the outset, although like most of the women I speak to, she is careful to apply them only to herself:

> I've never [believed] … that's it's OK to be on your own; that's it's OK … to raise kids on your own if you want to raise kids without a husband and … all that. I don't believe in that at all. [I believe in] having the normal thing. Meeting someone, falling in love, and having kids: the old traditional concept … I don't want to [provide for a child on my own]. I don't even think about it.
>
> *Me:* How do you feel when other women do that?
>
> No, I don't frown on that one bit. If that's what they want, that's great. But I can't imagine having a child [that way].

Blair, a 34-year-old lesbian tennis pro, is no less strict about the proper order of events if kids are going to be a part of the picture:

> Definitely one of the more important things for me to have a child would be a stable relationship. I feel that in order to bring a child into this world, you have to have a certain stability. And in my life right now, I don't have that.

For some childless women, preparations for good motherhood don't just involve finding and establishing a rock-solid relationship with Mr or Ms Right; they also mean making a vow to stick with it — even if things get rough — once kids are involved. This is 31-year-old Kylie, the former model who left the husband who didn't want kids to marry recently divorced Paul:

> I don't [regret that my ex-husband and I have] split … [but] I don't think that you should split if you've got kids. I really don't. Looking at the pain that this husband's been through on the whole thing, I don't think so. And looking at [his] kids' pain and their tears, it just breaks your heart.

Other childless women, such as 35-year-old Darcy, have more temperate views on the marriage-is-for-life issue, but remain convinced that good pre-mothers have their kids in the context of a relationship they believe is going to last:

> I feel very strongly about having two. Sure marriages and couples split up every day. What I'm saying is I'd like to start off on the right foot. And if we don't work, well then OK, we don't work. But I'd actually like to start off with giving my child two parents.

All the women I spoke to, without exception, agreed that good pre-mothers have their children, when at all possible, in the context of a stable relationship. However, after this point the women broke ranks. While most didn't care whether the stable couple were or were not actually married, or were a straight or gay pair, others had firm opinions on these matters.

Latisha, aged 32 and working as an administrator in her husband's business, was mildly disapproving of the trend — particularly in Australia — of unmarried couples having kids:

> I think love and marriage, horse and carriage, marriage and children. But then again, you don't have to be married to have children these days. [But] I think it's probably a better way to do it.

Lori also feels strongly that marriage must precede kids, at least for her:

> *Me:* Have you ever tried to become pregnant?
>
> Absolutely not.
>
> *Me:* Why 'absolutely not?'
>
> Because I'm not married. My whole thing is that you don't do one without the other.

Only two of the women I spoke to were pursed-lipped about lesbian couples trying their hand at parenting. The first was 35-year-old Darcy, who states her reservations in her typical clear and no-nonsense fashion:

> There are issues out there about gay women having children. I don't think that fills the role at all, to have two women. I think you need the male and female,

that the child should have the influences of the female and the male.

The other woman worried about lesbian mothers was Judi, a 28-year-old Texas-based public servant:

> Intellectually, there's no problem when two women raise kids. But I think that, to be perfectly honest, there's a little part of me that [feels it is not] the most natural thing, or that there is something you lose in not having a man around ... Intellectually, I think that it's much better to have two loving parents, be they females or males ... than one stressed out, economically distressed parent. But I do have to say that I don't know.
>
> *Me:* Can you put your finger on what is important to you about there being a parent of each gender?
>
> Well, just the obvious stuff ... Physical anatomy lessons ... different things a guy would probably expose the kid to. Not to say that you don't have two women who have different interests. But the sexes are different. And just for a boy child to identify with. I don't know if all that is true necessarily. But those are the sort of things that I would [consider] ... Also, homosexuality isn't that well accepted, and if I look at it from the kid's point of view, they'll probably go to school and have some difficulty there.

But being firmly strapped into a good relationship with forever potential is only the start of women's pre-motherhood requirements. The childless women I spoke with had other requirements as well. They included having their children at the right age and at the right time in their relationship.

Getting the timing 'right'

Once childless women are in a solid relationship, they turn their attention to the next item on their pre-motherhood to-do list: getting the timing of the first child right.

Many childless women who want children, particularly those who live in the cities, face a series of very tight deadlines. Most wish to complete high school, experiment with a variety of relationships and jobs, go overseas, get more training or a degree or two or establish a career, find Mr/Ms (wants to have children) Right and spend a bit of time with them before having two children: and all before the menopausal gong is struck.

Researcher Anne Summers also found that while motherhood was definitely on the wish list of nearly all the teenage Australian girls she spoke to, it always came last:

> These young women knew exactly what they wanted to do with their lives: 'Travelling, then get married, and have a career and then have kids. In that order.' This was a remarkably common answer ... As teens, life is bright with possibilities and promise. Everything is up for grabs and they want it all, travel, careers, husbands, houses and kids. But they are very clear about the order in which they want it and kids come a very definite last on the Life To Do list of Australian teenage girls today.[64]

Why don't young women want to travel with a partner or to be tied down in a permanent relationship while attempting to obtain a degree or establish a career? Because youth is a time to be alone, to experiment with different relationships and enjoy one's freedom: the time to do all the things a steady relationship and kids will one day make impossible. 'I want to live my life,' a woman in her twenties told Summers in what was a fairly typical response, 'because as soon as I get married and have a kid and then a mortgage, I am not going to be able to just take off and travel ...'[65]

Not surprisingly, such highly scripted pre-motherhood agendas don't always go to plan. As I'll discuss in more detail later, the right man can sometimes fail to be obliging in committing to marriage or fatherhood — or even in simply showing up — in the small window of time women have left themselves to put their relationship house in order so that their motherhood plans can proceed. Minor schedule derailments lead most women to simply post revised plans. If a woman is unable to secure her relationship with a man by the time she's 33 (giving the two of them a few years to enjoy childless married life before launching into the first pregnancy at 35), she may simply decide she'll have to attempt her first child at 36, or 37, or even 40.

Darcy's story demonstrates this flexibility well. While she, like most of the women I spoke to, had wanted her early thirties to be the time when she put her motherhood plans into action, when her now ex-boyfriend Gregory refuse to oblige, she revised her deadlines for becoming a mother upwards:

> I've always known I would have children ... [Gregory] ... was the first person that I would consider having as the father of my children ... I said to him, 'We need to have a look at this. I want to know if we are committed to one another, because I want to start looking at a family. Because if we are not committed, we shouldn't be together. We are not in our twenties. I don't see any point in us wasting our time' ... He bottled up, and basically we ended up splitting ... [Even though I'm now 35] ... I don't have any urgency [about having kids] ... [But] if I was 40 and I was sitting here talking to you and I didn't have any children, I would be feeling pretty lousy, I think ...

People say that the older you are ... the harder the birth will be. Well, I'll just have to put up with it, because what can I do about it? Nothing.

In a few cases, however, bungled timing led women already tilting away from motherhood to shelve their plans for good. When Ivan continually forced Kelly to delay her plans to mother, she eventually found herself past her personal cut-off date, and with one more reason to give motherhood a miss:

There is definitely a cut off. I feel that if I waited until I was 40 or plus, I'd be cheating the kid out of a bit of parent time. I wouldn't have the energy like I would have had when I was younger: to run around, do things with them. And what would I do on their 21st birthday when I'm 60? I can remember going to school with a girl, she was obviously a 'change of life' baby, and the generation gap was just huge. For her, it was like growing up with her grandparents. And I just remember thinking [that] if I had kids, I wouldn't want to do that to them ... If I was going to do it, I always thought that I'd have two ... So [I'd have had] one at 35 and the other at 38. All out of the way by 40, nice and tidy.

For the most part, women's beliefs that a 'good' mother had her first child no later than age 35 was based on their understanding of the increased difficulties they were likely to have after that time conceiving a first pregnancy and carrying it to term (this is another piece of evidence that strongly suggests that Virginia Haussegger's ignorance of her biological limits is one not widely shared among Australian women). However, some women's focus on the mid-thirties as the cut-off date for first-time motherhood was also based on a belief that older women are unable to parent well and that having kids too late will make it harder for the women to enjoy their eventual retirement.

While 28-year-old Bethany is happy to accede to her husband Jack's desire to delay parenthood at the moment, she makes no bones about her desire to avoid being an 'old bag of a mother':

> I don't want to be an old bag of a mother. I know that sounds really harsh, [but] I don't want to be in my late thirties and having my first baby ... I don't want to be having to deal with a young child when I am that age, and then growing older and still having a teenager around the house and having all these sorts of pressures when I [will] probably be dealing with menopause. Having to deal with some ratty teenager and menopause and all those sorts of things doesn't sound very appealing, or ideal at all, so I sort of thought that if I could start early ... Jack is a bit older than me. But his father had his first child at 40. And he has no memories of his father being too old or not being able to go outside and play ball with them or anything like that so he doesn't ... feel that 40 is getting old to be a father ...

Hilary, 35, agrees that one important reason for starting early is to finish early, so she can get on with her life:

> If Johnson and I are going to have children, we'd better have them soon, because if I have a child now, that child will be a teenager [when I'm] 50. And that's a worry ... I don't want to be coping with teenage trauma and puberty and crap like that when I'm 50 years old. Maybe I will [cope], maybe I'll take it in my stride, [but] I just imagine what a 50-year-old wants to

do with their life. That's maybe when they're thinking about the world cruise, or something like that. Or lying back and relaxing. So Johnson and I are prepared to work really hard for the next twenty years and then reap the benefits after that so that in our later years the hard work should be behind us.

Women's own age, and that of their partner, is not the only thing occupying their thoughts. Many are the children of divorce, and are highly sensitive to what they see as the requirements for getting a partnership off on the right foot, and keeping it working well. For many, this recipe includes enough time together to build a shield that will protect them from the relationship wear and tear they know the early years of parenthood will bring. This is 28-year-old Kristina talking about her partner Martin, who had unceremoniously ended their relationship several weeks before we spoke:

> Martin always loved kids … It is hard to say, but I imagine we would have eventually had kids. I think we probably would have done a lot of stuff before we would have had kids … I guess it depends on the age when I get married, but I would really like to have a marriage without children for a while. I think you need time for the two of you before you bring kids into it. We could have travelled. If we had ended up together we could have done a lot of that stuff together, and then settled [down].

Part of the reason Hilary waited until her mid-thirties to start trying for kids was that she strongly believed that financial and emotional stability within the marriage had to be established first:

I [didn't want to] have a child until I was financially and emotionally prepared for it. A lot of material things do need to come first. And emotionally, being in a good relationship and really knowing my husband and things like that ... So now financially we are ready, and emotionally I think we are both ready.

So while timing is an important aspect of good motherhood planning, it is also fairly open to revision in the face of a non-compliant reality, and thus becomes a less critical pressure on pre-mothers — that's until women begin veering dangerously close to menopause. However, other aspects of the good motherhood myth aren't so flexible, and consequently play a greater role in pushing childless women away from parenthood.

Good mothers don't work

It's no exaggeration to say that good motherhood mythology scares the bejesus out of most childless women, particularly the wary and pragmatic waiters and watchers. This is because, as Leunig's cartoons so graphically illustrate, the myth's key demand is that women must either give up paid work outside the home (at least until their youngest goes to school) or become society's favourite whipping-girl. As most of the childless women I spoke to are working women who either get satisfaction from their jobs or value their financial independence — or both — the thought of making motherhood their 'career' (in a way that men are never expected to make fatherhood theirs) leaves them cold, or at least seriously anxious. Many of these women are extremely intimidated by the prospect of having to totally reshape their personality to conform to the 'paragon of self-sacrifice' that is incorporated into the stay-at-home part of the good mother rule book.

For some childless women, the easiest solution is to simply give up their plans to mother. Having accepted without question such good motherhood standards, and decided she'd be almost certain to make a 'bad' mother, 37-year-old Lorne decides that remaining childless is the only possible way forward:

> I believe I'm not the correct person [to be a mother]
> ... I figure that means that I'm just not into sacrifice,
> or [I'm] selfish and all those things, so I guess that's
> just bad luck, if that's the way I am. But I'm also not
> into pretending. I wouldn't be able to pretend ... I just
> think mothers are just absolute angels, they're on such
> pedestals — but it's a pedestal I've never wanted to sit
> on myself. But I think they're just incredible. I mean I
> see them all around me and it just never ceases to
> amaze me what they do. And it's all just quietly done.
> And the husbands I see, who are all fantastic guys, but
> if they do something like sweeping the floor, they
> expect three million gold medals ... I know for a fact,
> I would be out with the moccasins, ten-ton Tessie, the
> fags, I'd go right into it ... off with the Valium. I
> would just fall right into the pit of the fat, numb,
> housewife thing.

Blair, the 34-year-old tennis pro, also sees herself as being the wrong type to parent well. Her acceptance of the requirement that good mothers stay home full-time, coupled with her certainty that she could never hack being a full-time parent, has led her to rule herself out of the motherhood stakes, despite having a strong desire for kids:

> I love kids ... [but] I just don't think that I am the
> type of person that would be a good parent ... I like

being with children, playing with them, working with them at their colouring or school things or doing crafts or whatever it happens to be. But I don't think I could do it full-time. I like my own time, I like my privacy. I don't know if I'm the type ... I [am not saying] I don't want [children]. I just know that I don't have the type of personality I should have.

Ironically, walking away from motherhood and embracing childlessness is the easiest way of dealing with the horrifying conflicts good motherhood prescriptions force women with children — and those thinking about having them — to confront. In other words, it's not much sweat for a woman who is not going to mother to nod her head vigorously in agreement at the social demand that mothers give up paid work before she charts a course to Childfree Island, where paid work remains every person's right and responsibility and women are still expected to behave as individuals rather than Robo-mums.

The lives good motherhood mythology is really wrecking (apart from those of mothers) are those of the childless women who are, despite the odds, bound and determined to mother. This is because for these thwarted mothers, there is simply no alternative but to confront the challenges the myth poses to their current lifestyle and value system and find some way of reconciling the conflicts.

One way women try to reconcile the conflict between good mother expectations and their own needs and desires is by employing what I call 'imaginary thinking' (and what your average kindergarten teacher might describe as 'pretending'). Women do this in all sorts of different ways. Some pretend the conflict isn't really so big, or say that it makes no sense to worry about it now when it might be different or even solved by the time they have a child. Others arrive at (often startlingly unrealistic) 'solutions' to the conflict that enable them to put the issue out of their mind and continue chugging on towards their maternal goals.

I know this is what women do not only because they told me, but because I was an 'imaginary thinker' myself. A thwarted mother type with a leap-first and look-later personality, I was still switched on enough in my early twenties to notice the trauma and conflict working women faced when they had children. But did I worry that I'd face the same problems? Nah! I simply pushed it all out of my mind, vowing to worry about it 'later'. In any case, I had what in retrospect is a touching sort of faith that 'feminists' would have sorted the whole mess out by the time my turn came to mother.

Many of the childless women I spoke to adopted similar approaches, and this led to a pattern developing in many interviews. My questions would inevitably lead the woman to an acknowledgement of the obvious clash between her views about what a good mother is and does, and her career ambitions. I would ask her how she intended to negotiate this conflict and after a brief pause during which her eyes would squint and her brow would wrinkle, she'd briskly inform me that she didn't see any reason to worry about it at this stage, since it wasn't happening now. Then she would try to move the conversation on. Interestingly, there also seemed to be a tendency for men to put off difficult conversations with their partners about precisely what they (the men) would be responsible for once Junior arrived in similar ways. This was certainly Jack's response to waiting and watching Bethany, who was trying to nail down how much of the hard work of motherhood was going to be seen as hers alone:

> We had a conversation a while ago and I was saying, 'You know, it would be nice if you would [help a bit

with the baby]' and he felt the whole thing was a bit ridiculous because it was all not happening now.

But by far the most common solution childless women proposed to the conflict between 'good' motherhood and paid work was that it could be easily solved by any woman armed with a can-do attitude and good planning skills: a woman, to be precise, who'd set herself up to work from home.

It would be hard for me to overstate the amount of faith childless women put in home-based work as the solution to all the conflict contemporary motherhood brings. Like drowning souls grasping at straws, women hold to their belief that home-based work is the answer to the good motherhood/paid work conflict with a tenacity born of desperation. The working-at-home picture they paint is an uncanny match with my favourite photo of the happy home-based working mum. Posted on an internet site dedicated to small business ideas, it shows a woman typing away happily at her computer while her children cluster, smiling, around the keyboard.[66]

Kylie was among the most fervent believers in the power of home-based work to solve her dual goals of having her own project (and thus income source) and of being a 'good' mother who cares nearly exclusively for her own children:

> [Working is] fine as long as it doesn't cut across the kids ... where they suffer ... I suppose because I had the environment where my mother was there, and Dad would get home at six o'clock and off we'd go ... That's what I would like to have for my children ... They're not being dropped off at childcare and then picked up at six o'clock. With the carers seeing more of the children than what the actual parents do. I don't necessarily agree with that ... I'm not career-

orientated, at this stage anyway. Maybe in a few years I will be, but at this stage I'm not.

Me: So what are your work plans when you think about … getting pregnant?

Ideally, something like work from home. That would be great … [because] you have your own area of interest and your own income source … You've got something going on, but the kids are there, as a part of that thing. Or you know, at some stage … they [might] get dropped [off] or whatnot. But not where it's a regular thing that they're in childcare … I have never really ever been in a situation where I've had somebody else pay for me … I don't quite feel comfortable with it. Only because I've never actually turned around to somebody and said, 'I need some money. Can you pay for blah de blah?'

Darcy has firm ideas about being the sort of hands-on mother she never had. Yet she also says she is someone who 'couldn't not work'. The solution to this apparent conflict? You guessed it — working at home:

[When I was a girl my brother and I came] home to an empty house. We didn't have a mother to come home to. We had housekeepers who came and went. My father was a builder, so he'd be gone by seven in the morning … I think that having a mother in your life, to put a bandage on your sore, to kiss you and tell you everything is going to be all right and that they love you very much, is a really important thing … That's why I will always remain self-employed. So I have the freedom to work the hours that I want, and

to have the time that I need. I will always have a
career, but I will always tailor it around family …
I will always be working. I couldn't not work. But
I will not be a mother that doesn't exist for children.

Given the great store circumstantially childless women set in
home-based work, it's worth asking a few hard questions about
how effective this solution to the good motherhood/paid work
conflict actually is. Studies are few and far between, but there is
some evidence that firstly, the vast majority of employees who get
the chance to work at home are executive males, not mothers.
However, when women do get a guernsey, some do find that
home-based work works for them: in particular, these are women
with what Kylie calls low 'career-orientation', women who simply
want to keep their foot in the workplace door and take the edge
off their economic dependence by earning a bit of money. This is
because while home-based work gives women the necessary
flexibility to deal with school holidays, illness and the range of
unexpected events that become a regular part of life with
children, it also squarely deposits them on the circular tour called
the mummy-track, at the end of which there is no pot of gold,
but rather reduced pay, and inferior conditions and opportunities.
Working at home is a trade-off, in other words, that only solves
the good mummy/paid work conflict for women who are content
to wait out their child's early years on the career sidelines.

Women who are more career focused or financially strapped
may be less content with the reduced work quality and income
that home-based work delivers. As well, they are likely to feel
frustrated by the limited benefits and promotion opportunities
offered to those at home. Like part-time workers, home workers
— and no surprise, they are nearly all women — aren't taken
seriously unless and until they get back on the full-time, present

in-the-office track. The point is that telecommuting (as the Americans call it) is a limited, short-term solution that does not go to the evil pulsing heart of the work/family problem. Rather, it focuses on driving the consequences of the problem out of sight by pushing women who are grateful for the opportunity to do more for less behind closed suburban doors.

But what about running their own business, which is clearly what someone like Darcy had in mind? Does this work-at-home solution provide a real answer to the good mummy/real life crunch? Again, a glass-half-full answer is possible here. When a woman runs her own business from home, she is no longer at risk of the employer-imposed reductions of pay and conditions that are part and parcel of the usual discrimination against home-based workers. At the same time, she can put the control she has over her time to good use managing the schedule-free demands of her children.

But (you knew there had to be a 'but') the fact is that working at home is a useful tool for managing the good mummy/paid work conflict; it is not a solution for it. This is because despite Kylie and Darcy's high hopes about all they can accomplish while caring for kids at home, the reality is that *no-one* — I repeat, *no-one* — can do paid work *at the same time* as they're doing an even minimally decent job of looking after kids. The happy brood clustered around Mum's keyboard, in other words, is a myth. Notes one mother who participated in an email discussion I set in train a few years ago about the costs and benefits of working at home:

> [While it may be possible to] vacuum the porch while talking to children, it is impossible to do research, make cold calls, draft documents, code programs, handle customer complaints, or add numbers while adequately attending to them.

A number of government reports and websites support this conclusion, warning employees not to view home-based work as an alternative to paid care for their dependants.[67] The upshot of all this is that women can't be traditional good mums — the sort that stay at home full-time and are always there to bandage boo-boos — *and* be productive paid workers. If they want paid work (inside or outside the home) they'll need to organise their husband, parents or a paid carer to look after their kids. Home-based work may smooth out the pointier edges of the good mother/paid work conflict, but it does not eliminate it.

There were two more solutions childless women proposed for the good mother/real life conflict. One was getting their bloke to stay at home and behave like a traditional good mum while they take the absent father role, and the other was to start asking some searching questions about how workable or fair 1950s-derived specs for good motherhood are at the start of the 21st century.

Jacinta and Ron intend to solve Jacinta's worry about becoming a 'dumpy mum' (and her consequent refusal to mother) with the daddy daycare solution. Ron will stay at home, while Jacinta will heigh-ho her way to the office each day:

> work … I've always been the one that has held down a steady job. So we've tossed around the idea of me going back to work, and him spending more time at home looking after the baby.
>
> *Me:* How do you feel about that?
>
> I feel really good. He's a fantastic carer. He's actually worked in childcare centres before, over the years, so he's really great with kids …

While daddy daycare won't work for every couple, it is the work/family solution of choice for an increasing number of couples. Somewhere around 16% of American preschool-age children are primarily cared for by their fathers.[68] Another set of figures has nearly a quarter of married American women ticking the primary wage earner box on the Census form, up from 16% in 1981 (though, interestingly, their fathering partners were more likely to describe themselves as studying or running their own businesses rather than as stay-at-home fathers).[69] The UK Office of National Statistics identifies 155,000 British men as stay-at-home dads, while in Australia 16% of men are out of the workforce, with 10% (up from 4.5% in 1994) citing the desire to care for their kids as their main motivation.[70]

Dollar signs drive the change in many cases, with household decisions about who will participate in the paid workforce, and who will care for the kids, coming down to who is making more when baby is born. Sadly, in the vast majority of cases, this still tends to be the man (which makes true parental choice when it comes to selecting care options for their children yet another good argument in favour of pay equity). In Australia, women make 85 cents to every man's dollar for the same work; in the United States that figure is just 77 cents. Indeed, Edgar sees pay inequity, and the resulting lack of choice it gives individual couples in dividing up work and caring responsibilities, as just one of the many ways societal structures and practices around parenthood are 'stuffed':

> Paid work still confers more status than unpaid caring work [and] boys are still brought up to seek self-worth and confirmation of their social value in work; rather than in family concerns ... There is [also] still the obstacle of women's lower wages making 'choice' a useless construct in deciding who will stay at home.[71]

The upshot of all this is that entrenched pay inequity is a decisive factor in why the responsibility of caring for children remains women's work — and work they largely do alone, due to the long hours their partner spends at the office.

Of course there is another option for women seeking to resolve the conflict between society's demands of good mothers and their own needs for a life and an independent income: they can reject all or part of today's good motherhood standards and draw up their own definitions and requirements for what a good mother is and does.

One of the women who did this was Bethany, though her questioning of good motherhood ideology was extremely limited. She planned to give up work once she had kids and to care for the children, more or less full-time. What Bethany was after was some brief daily relief from the daily drudge of solitary care: relief she didn't expect to be provided by her husband, but by her husband's money:

> Jack earns enough money for us to be able to have someone to help, which would be good. I don't ever see myself as being a career person. I'll probably always do bits and pieces just to earn a bit of money, but he'll principally be the supportive person financially ... I might have someone who helps me so [I can have] a bit of time to myself ... It would be nice to have someone a few hours a day or something like that during the week ... [I] think that I would go mental without any time to myself.

Bethany is willing to question the good motherhood edict that women must abandon all they need and value as people when they have kids. What she doesn't question is the notion that the hard work of parenting is woman's work. She accepts that if she isn't going to provide full-time care, it is up to her to organise someone who will (and presumably to worry and feel guilty about whether or not that care is adequate). Not only does this presume that Jack has no obligations to provide such care or to take some of the responsibility for organising someone who will; it also lets the wider society — which benefits from women's free childcare labour and the citizens of tomorrow produced by it — off the hook.

The same can be said of Tina, who is looking to marry wealth in order to escape the heavy and solitary burden of good motherhood:

> I want quality of life [so I need to] marry somebody who doesn't spend his whole day sitting in front of the TV set. I need a husband who has some sort of capacity to earn relatively well, so that I can actually organise a nanny, or I can send my children to crèche, so I can have a bit of both. I'm not prepared to say, 'I'm now going to have children, I've got to give up the gym, I've got to give up all my activities, we can never go out to dinner.' I want to be able to … get a nanny [and say,] 'Please look after the children for the next week, my husband and I are going on holiday.' That's what I want, so I've got to find somebody who's making a little bit of a living.

While it is great to see contemporary women aware of their very human need for 'quality of life', it seems unfair to restrict the capacity to pursue that quality to those who can pay. Bethany and Tina's solution to the tyrannical edicts of the good motherhood myth, in other words, is one only wealthy married women can afford.

It was left to 38-year-old Laney, a single woman who if she did mother was almost certain to be doing it on her own, to directly challenge the most fundamental aspects of good mother mythology. She challenged the claim that to be a good mother a woman has to give up her career and her hard-won individuality and identity:

> Just because I'm a warm nurturing person doesn't mean I'd be a good mum, I don't think.
>
> *Me:* What do you think it takes to be a good mum?
>
> I think it is being very sure of yourself and being free within yourself … Women in their thirties are working towards finding out who they are. And I certainly know who I am much more than I did when I was 30 … I would [want to] feel that I would be strong enough not to get swallowed up by motherhood. [My friend Carol] has this jibe, 'Well, Laney, if you have a child, you'll know what you're in for. No-one would be able to say that they didn't tell you.' Because I've watched so many of my friends have kids.
>
> *Me:* Have you seen them getting swallowed up?
>
> Yes, but I think some have been able to maintain their own lives more than others … I identify more with their ability to maintain a sense of themselves for themselves.

It's been said that motherhood radicalises women: raising their consciousness of the injustice and cruelty of gender-based inequality to which they were previously blind. But what the above suggests is that it's not just motherhood that radicalises women: the *intention* to mother does, too. When women don't intend to have children, they can simply give oppressive contemporary good motherhood standards an approving pat on the head, wipe their hands and walk away. But when women really do wish to mother (and particularly right before they take the plunge), they have to wrestle with the identity-stealing and autonomy-stealing social expectations of good mothers, and to forge soul-saving solutions of their own.

But as hard as women find it to peer through the smoke and mirrors of good motherhood ideology, they find proposing the sort of radical solutions required to extricate them from the corner into which they feel this ideology has painted them even more difficult. Home-based work, daddies doing daycare and expensive nannies can all mitigate the conflict, and make life easier for the lucky few, but they fail to challenge the antiquated ideas and misogynist social realities that lie at the problem's dark heart. Only by challenging what is being asked of mothers, and of mothers alone, can women begin to break down the imprisoning tentacles of the good motherhood myth, and begin forging their own ideals for how responsible mothers and fathers should act.

The power behind the myth

Mothers, particularly new mothers, on whom the myth exacts the highest toll, find this hard to do. A woman's vulnerability after her first birth largely explains why. Shocked, exhausted and frightened by the swaddled bundle of screaming responsibility she still can't believe the authorities have gone off and left her to care for — unsupervised — such women are what anthropologists call 'liminal': caught in the temporary purgatory between their old identities as pregnant women and the new ones they wish to have as good mums. The myth capitalises on women's weakness at this time, exploiting their expected eagerness to jump through whatever hoops are set before them to prove they've got the right stuff. It proposes austere and self-denying standards of maternal worthiness and proof, including the expectations that good mums won't use pain relief, no matter how torturous their labour, that good mums breastfeed no matter how bad their mastitis, and that good mums never give dummies, no matter how much they might aid them in getting a decent night's sleep. It is these sorts of demands that build extreme selflessness — what experts would call self-abnegation — into a woman's earliest ideas about herself as a good mum.

But explaining why good mother mythology has such a hold on women doesn't reveal why the mythology has been crafted as it has. Why has extreme selflessness come to be seen as the central test of good motherhood? Why do we use a woman's commitment to putting her own needs second as a measure of her maternalism — her very *womanliness* — when self-abnegation is not and has never been a test of paternal competence or achievement? Ah, my little ducks, prepare yourself for an answer that is only slightly more ancient than it is depressing.

Of powerful men in smoky rooms

It comes down to power, and to questions of social control. The plain and simple fact is that civilisations, including the current Western one, are built on women's unpaid labour. Without the work women do in caring for the elderly, children and the house, as well as all the onerous tasks of what Susan Maushart calls 'wifework', men wouldn't be able to march off to the factory or office and put in a full day's work — these days, often much more than eight hours — free of worry or responsibility for matters domestic. Indeed, of all the patriarchal privileges that powerful men are struggling to hold on to in the 'post-feminist' world, the one valued most is the pervasive and powerful assumption that, to quote Australian Institute of Family Studies researcher Irene Wolcott, 'employees are free from family and other commitments that are unrelated to the workplace'. The belief that each worker is in possession of a 'wife' who raises the kids and takes care of the home shapes everything from the location and rules of our workplaces to the length of the school day and the opening hours of shops.

Only when this (usually false) belief — that there was in the past and should be from now to eternity a little woman at home tending to all matters domestic — is defeated, will the way be open to refashion fundamental institutions like workplaces and schools so that they accommodate the two-earner family. Some blokes would be more than happy for this to happen, but unfortunately, such gorgeous sorts tend to be situated mid-way or lower down in the power hierarchy (perhaps because they've been passed over for promotion because they leave work at 5:00 pm, or refuse to attend crack-of-sparrow's-fart breakfast meetings because of family commitments).[72] The blokes at the top of the pecking order, though — that is, those holding the social reins — have wives at home whose unpaid labour has been indispensable in getting them where they are today, and they know it. These guys have no intention of giving up without a fight.

Indeed, as Edgar has pointed out, any government or workplace policies that try to even things up — between women and men and between active and absent dads — make breadwinning power-lords nervous. This is because they see such reforms as a 'direct threat to their own jobs and career advancement prospects', and as an 'indirect threat to the stability of their own marriages'.[73] Why? Because if hubby starts to fall behind in a gender-neutral race to the top of the career ladder, and his partner has considerable opportunity to achieve in paid work, she is likely to start questioning the sense of her decision to make all the stay-at-home sacrifices, and to insist that he share more of the domestic work as well as the opportunity to excel and earn outside the home.

Do the powerful blokes *admit* to any of this? Oh come on, of course not. Who's going to raise his glass at some corporate function and say, 'I am where I am today because I have chosen to accept society's invitation to exploit my wife economically — honey, stand up and let everyone see you — and to use every bit of the unfair advantage this has given me over all the working mums at the office, and those few working dads struggling to split the work and sacrifice required to raise children more fairly with their wives.' No, what they do is use all the power they have, as newspaper editors, politicians, religious leaders and corporate CEOs, to reinforce the outdated definitions of good and bad mums (and dads) that have been so integral to their own success. As Summers noted in *The End of Equality*, 'few of today's CEOs have partners who work outside the home. They are not, therefore, in a position to understand or even empathise with the struggles of corporate women and men who lack such support to juggle their lives and their jobs.'[74]

Indeed, the smear job on childcare and the mothers (never parents, always mothers) who choose it has been so successful that despite the evidence — which nearly all experts agree shows that high-quality care does no harm and may even benefit children's cognitive and social skills[75] — many Australian and American mothers have abandoned full-time and even part-time paid work, re-latched the gate in the picket fence and returned to caring for their kids full-time. Indeed, in the United States the return of educated women to full-time motherhood has become a sort of born-again movement for the well-heeled, as such women are shrugging off economic independence in favour of marrying wealthy men who will support them. Danielle Crittenden, author of *Amanda Bright@Home*, and the unelected spokeswoman for this new army of 'good' suburban mums, says these women aren't really interested in careers because they believe that if they leave their baby and go to work, they won't 'really' be the ones raising them (to which the interviewer responded, 'Amazing how often the same thing is said about working dads.' Not!). According to Crittenden, the idea that men might do their fair share of the childcare and domestic work so that women can do more paid work is 'dead'. Instead, what women want is for their husbands to be 'manly' men who 'go to work and make a lot of money so [they] can stay home and be with [their] children'.[76]

Maternal 'choice' is classist waffle

Frankly, the class overtones and indifference of such retro-ideology make me feel ill. Simply because Crittenden's hubby, former White House speechwriter David Frum, makes big enough bucks for her to afford to 'stay@home' to care for her kids, this makes it the 'choice' of the good mother? Were Ms Crittenden to make the same stay-at-home decision but not have a wealthy hubby to support it, I guarantee you no-one would be calling it a 'choice', nor praising her as a good mum. Instead, she'd be labelled a lazy, shiftless welfare mum, and before she could say 'middle-class double standards', she would find herself levered into work, and her kids into childcare.

The same class-ridden double standards about good motherhood are rife in Australia. In 2000, the Howard Government endorsed the McClure Report, which examined models for welfare reform that included defining single women with school-age children on benefits as dole bludgers and proposing mandatory job-readiness programs for them at the same time as it was expressing unequivocal support, often backed up with money, for middle-class stay-at-home mums whose husbands were supporting their 'choice'.

The point here is that female 'choice' about paid work is a choice for only some women. Most women need to work, either to keep their sanity, or to keep their households fiscally afloat, or to keep their future options open. Making the choice about work one of the tests of good motherhood is simply not fair. This is not to say that societies shouldn't have standards for good parenthood. They should, but such standards should be gender-neutral (what makes the goose a good parent should apply equally to the gander) and attainable by all parents, not just those with fat pay packets. They should also, if I might be so bold as to suggest it, be based on facts about the relative outcomes for children of different care arrangements, not on ideologically driven fiction. The truth is that a wide variety of family and non-family care arrangements can turn out happy and well-functioning children. It is true that different childcare arrangements seem to foster different strengths and weaknesses (kibbutz-bred children, for instance, who were once raised largely in children's houses, were disproportionately represented in senior levels of the Israeli Army because of their superior group-management skills; and children in quality daycare tend to score higher on tests of language, memory and social skills than those in full-time maternal care). However, the facts so far suggest that only very young children who spend very long hours in centre-based care, or children in low-quality care — whether provided by parents, grandparents or childcare workers — are at serious risk of being unhappy, poorly adjusted kids.

Bum-biting attitudes and policy

In the mountains of words dedicated to the conflict between middle-class working mums and those who stay at home (a.k.a. The Mummy Wars), it hasn't just been the classist nature of good motherhood definitions that has been overlooked; the impact of such unreasonable and unrealistic definitions on women who aren't yet mothers but are considering becoming them has also been ignored. While conservative support for antiquated definitions of good motherhood, coupled with public policy that has made it more difficult for women to achieve a balance between work and family, has succeeded in chasing some wealthy women back behind the picket fence, it has had the opposite impact on many women considering having children.

Let me repeat that. Conservative social policies may return short-term gains (to conservatives) in terms of increased numbers of women staying home full-time to care for their children, but they are likely to lead to a reduction in future birth-rates. The very attitudes and policies that may succeed in getting some working mothers to abandon their jobs and return home to care for their children may also ensure that there are fewer mothers to force back into traditional roles in the future. And herein, and oh so ironically, lie the seeds of the myth's ultimate demise — or at least its severely weakened future hold. For if there are fewer women in the future who are mothers, there are fewer women vulnerable to the coercive impacts of the good motherhood myth; and fewer women who will have any need to drop out of the workforce to care for their young ones the way good mothers do (not so coincidentally easing the way for the wifed-up daddies to snaffle all the plum positions at the same time). Let the powerful cigar-puffing blokes put that in their pipes and smoke it!

Torching, or at least weakening, the hold of the good motherhood myth is an essential part of any strategy aimed at reducing circumstantial childlessness. This is because it is the waiters and watchers who pay closest attention to unreasonable social expectations of mothers and who are likely to respond to them by deferring a decision to mother. Making it clear to women that they can be — and can be considered — good mothers and good women if they lose their temper occasionally, or share the care of their child with their husbands and paid carers while they work and otherwise have a life, is a necessary part of any package designed to convince such ambivalent and uncertain young women that saying 'yes' to motherhood would be a rational decision.

But this isn't all that's needed, because it isn't just society's ideological unreasonable demands of mothers that lead some childless women to baulk at having kids. It is also the real-world clash between the practical demands of motherhood and the capacity of only-human women (and men) to meet them. It isn't just society's unforgiving and unreasonably high expectations of how motherhood ought to be done, but the difficulty women (and a few good men) have — in our child-unfriendly world — providing even minimally 'good enough' parenting. This means that even if the world increases the reasonableness of the moral demands it makes of mothers, and mothers (and those who intend to be them) lighten up on themselves, there are still significant forces afoot in contemporary Australian and American society that can capsize the childbearing plans of all but the most determined women. In the next few chapters, we will have a look at them.

Chapter 5

THE FERTILITY CRUNCH II: THE TROUBLE WITH MEN

So he says to me, 'So why haven't you got any kids?' And it just makes me so mad. So instead of answering, I ask him, 'So, have you got any kids?' And he says, 'No. I'm not ready for that yet.' So I say, 'You're the reason I don't have any kids. I keep dating men like you.'

Conversation overheard between two women in a café

Female Seeks Male. Are you 30+ wanting to start a family? I'm an attractive woman who is seeking a man with the same priority in life. Finc secure, poss long term r'ship. No time wasters, genuine callers only.

Ad in Australian local paper

In the last 35 years, young women's job description for Mr Right has altered radically. Back in the old days, it was the size of a man's pay packet, and his willingness to share it, that was the essential criterion for a woman looking to marry. After all, having tied the knot, young wives became dependent on their husband's incomes to survive, as there were few work opportunities for working wives, and relative to men, their pay and conditions were extremely poor. As a consequence of their powerlessness in the world of paid work, women were compelled to ensure their own economic security and that of their children by exchanging their unpaid domestic and childcare labour for a claim on their husband's wages. In Australia, the breadwinner trade-off was the basic wage provisions enshrined in the 1907 Harvester judgement in the Federal Court of Conciliation and Arbitration. Underlying the judgement's key assumption — that a worker's rate of pay should enable him to live as a 'human being in a civilised community and to keep himself and his family in frugal comfort' — was a very particular vision of the connection between home and work life:

> Young men would enter work after leaving school, work full-time, retire and then die. Women would initially work and then, following marriage and the birth of children, would leave the workforce to care for husbands and other dependants on a full-time basis.[77]

As researcher Ian Watson and his colleagues explain, this view of what a normal family was explained why the Justice deciding the case assumed that 'women were not breadwinners, and set their rates [of pay] at half those prevailing for men'.[78]

Few Australian women now expect, intend or desire that female role in the breadwinner arrangement. As Anne Summers says of the Australian teenagers she interviewed for *The End of Equality*: 'none of them saw themselves as stay-at-home mums'. 'Too boring,' they agreed. In speaking to young women in Australia today, countless other social researchers — myself included — have had similar responses. Today, nearly all educated young women want, train for, and expect to participate in the paid workforce for most — if not all — of their adult lives. These same young women find the idea of relying on a man to pay the bills old-fashioned and at least mildly distasteful. Indeed, if the women I spoke to were any guide, the idea of *needing* a man for anything was seen as a somewhat quaint and faintly nauseating historical relic: like key parties and hair-washing with mayonnaise. Instead, many contemporary women, able to supply a fair whack of the income they'll need to live and raise their kids on, have begun scanning the available pool of mates for life partners and soul mates. They are looking for men who are willing to embark on (to use the most up-to-date sociological lingo) a 'pure' relationship: a collaboration and equal partnership based on deep emotional wants, not practical financial needs.

Even for less well-heeled women, the breadwinner contract has fallen out of fashion. Not because such women are necessarily as confident as their better-educated sisters that they'll be able to make their own way, but because of the struggle they know many men now have to earn a decent amount of money.

How men contribute to circumstantial childlessness

It's important to get one thing clear straight away. Women still want men. They still want to partner with them, have children and raise those children with them. They want men who will love, cherish and partner them for the long cha-cha of life. Men still matter to women, as much as they ever did. Perhaps even more.

The 'male problem', as many of the childless women I spoke to saw it, was that there weren't any around. Or, to be more precise, there were no *useful* sorts around. Sure, there were a fair number whose entrance into any room is accompanied by red flashing lights and a nuclear facility-type announcement of 'Danger! Danger!': the no-hoper, terminally damaged ones thwarted mother Shaney opined had been left on the shelf 'for a reason' and the ones whom women like Catherine, the heroine in Sophie Cunningham's novel *Geography*, chase throughout their fertile years, winding up only with the 'scar' of childlessness as a memento of their 'misguided obsession'.[79] There are also plenty of men in the partnering pool who happily confess to wanting to have children 'someday', but are either ignorant of, or indifferent to, the Big Ben-like bonging sound of the biological clock of the woman sleeping fitfully beside them. There is also a plethora of available guys who are all too happy to father as many children as a woman wants, as long as the women counter-commits to making all the sacrifices necessary to raise them.

Where the man shortage *does* exist is among that better-quality sort of bloke: the sort who doesn't hurl at the thought of love or even commitment, but looks quite capable of pulling off both should the need arise. The sort of bloke who is interested in dating for a bit and then, if things are going well, setting up house together or maybe even (gasp!) marrying. There is a critical lack of the sort of men who, without being asked, simply pitch in as equal partners in child-related tasks such as finding a decent boy's name, decorating the nursery, arranging for paternity leave and getting their as-yet-unborn baby's name down on the local childcare centre's waiting list. In other words, there is a veritable dearth of men who are both capable of parenting and keen to do it, and who don't see the fatherhood role as wallet-based or mere window-dressing, but rather as a hands-on job critical to their own and their child's development. Such men are rarer than a size 8 at the end of a shoe clearance. 'Men?' The women I spoke to asked me in exasperation. 'What men?'

Educated women and the truth about the man shortage

Jocelyn, 33, has a history that is typical. Slim and extraordinarily pretty, she earns a tidy sum as an accountant and has plenty to say for herself. But despite this, Jocelyn simply can't find a decent man to date — never mind one to marry:

> I was living in a college up at uni and met a guy there. Then ... his mother was diagnosed with cancer and he just broke it off ... I was really upset by that. Then I was living in a house with a bunch of people and ... one of them said, 'Well, what about it?' So we went out for a couple of years. Then he moved back to Adelaide ... Then I ended up meeting someone who I got along well with. He was probably the person I felt most comfortable with ... we spent a few months in Spain together. Then I came back early and ... when he got back he said, 'I'm not that happy.' And I said, 'But you just got back, how do you know?' But it wasn't that happy. So that was that. And then I didn't see anyone for probably about a year ... Then I went out with a fellow. He'd just come out of a relationship with someone. And I think I was wanting too much too soon ... More recently I met a guy through some friends who on paper seemed really nice. He was very interested in music and theatre and all the things that I was interested in. And you know, a great cook, and handsome and well dressed, and blah blah blah. But he turned out to be quite intense and depressive. But I

thought I've been on my own too long; that maybe I should give it more of a try … So I tried. I said to him, 'You've got to take it really slowly … But I'm willing to give it a go.' And after three months he said, 'Well, I'm not willing to give it a go any more.' Notice in writing that he dropped round, effective immediately. He's a lawyer, handed me an envelope with all these writings in it and said, 'It's self-explanatory.' And rode off on his bicycle into the sunset.

Brenda, 28, has found the search for Mr Right equally trying:

[My last boyfriend] was a Libran [and] just couldn't commit. I deserved better, but that was it. When I first met him he'd been living with a girl for five years. They'd bought a house together and she'd walked out on him because he didn't ask her to marry him. He was just procrastinating on that, didn't realise that's what she wanted. I was going out with him about three months after she'd left, and by the end of our relationship nothing had changed between them. They still had the house together, they still had the same car together and you know he couldn't commit to me. He finally said, 'Well, really we're at the stage in our relationship where we either have to get engaged or split up. So we're splitting up.' I was trying to force him to [commit], but … the ball was definitely in his court, because he was the one with the past history and the baggage.

Since her divorce from David, Tina has searched energetically for the 'perfect guy', but to no avail:

My energy has gone into looking for that perfect guy. And God, that takes a lot of energy … I've been on that many blind dates … And me the idiot goes, and I'm quite happy to meet people. But as far as compatibility with a suitable husband, no I think I'll actually have to have him made … I want to meet someone and think, well, he's nice. Not necessarily, he's absolutely stunning. But I want to feel physically attracted to him, and I want to feel mentally attracted to him, because I need someone who I can feel stimulated by.

There is a good news story and a bad news story for educated women searching for Mr Right. First, the good news. Remember the hysteria a few years back when a Harvard-based study claimed that a college-educated female aged 30 was more likely to be hit by a bus than find a mate? Well, as Pulitzer Prize-winning journalist Susan Faludi found when she looked into it, it was all backlash malarkey: not a word of it was true. Just another beat-up in the endless quest to prove to women that 'feminism' has cost them more than they have gained. The truth is that a 30-year-old college-educated American woman had a 58% to 66% chance at marriage, and that at age 40 her chances declined to 23%: far better odds than those of a motor vehicle calamity. In fact, as Faludi discovered, a 30-year-old educated woman was *more likely* to marry than her less-educated counterpart.

The same is true in Australia. In 2001, university-educated women aged 35+ are more likely to have married than their less-educated sisters. Indeed, since 1986, it has been women *without* degrees whose chances of marriage have steadily declined while the chances for more-educated women have either levelled out or increased.[80]

The bad news is that the man-drought bedevilling middle-class women in their thirties is not a figment of their imagination. The dearth of good men is real, and the reason for it comes down to the kind of men women like Jocelyn, Brenda and Tina want and expect to date. Though they don't say it, when educated women picture their Mr Right, he is holding a degree — not a spanner or a dole cheque — in his hand. For better or worse, educated women have the same sorts of ideas their mothers had about the importance of setting their dating and marrying sights up, rather than down: they want to partner with a man who is either as educated, or more educated, than they are.

Unfortunately, such men are in short supply, and they are fielding offers from a wide range of eligible gals. In 2001, 21% of 30- to 34-year-old Australian women had bachelor degrees or higher, while only 18% of men this age were equally well schooled. Among 25- to 29-year-old women the gap was worse: 25% compared with 18%.

To make matters worse, educated men, while happy to partner with similarly educated women, don't feel compelled to do so, and less-educated women — like their more-educated sisters — are more than happy to 'marry up'. What this combination means is that while educated men have an abundance of choice when shopping for Ms Right, the partnering options for educated women, given their expectations, are not nearly so expansive.

Woeful men

It's hard to know what's worse. Searching in vain for a decent fella, or dealing with the commitment and basic growing-up issues of the one you've got. Mary's husband Troy agreed early in the marriage that they'd have children. But after numerous delays, Mary realised he had little intention of honouring his promise:

I always thought I would have children ... I would have loved to have had a child when I was 25 or 26. I talked about it with my husband ... and he said, 'Why don't we keep working? We'll just pay off [the house] first.' [But] I felt, I'm old enough now [to have a child]. Then we got to the point where [he said], 'You only have one more year and then you get long service leave. Why would you throw that away?' He was never really as keen to have children as I was ... and all that time I'd been led to believe that he was ... We started to argue all the time ... [During one argument] he said to me, 'There is no way I'd ever have children with a person like you' ... I thought I could never trust that he would ever have them now ... It really scared me.

Shaney hadn't been with Prentice long before she was delighted to discover that she was pregnant (she eventually miscarried). Prentice, however, was far from happy at the news:

We went out for two years, though it was a fairly volatile relationship ... because of his fear of commitment. His mother died when he was seven, and he's never really dealt with that. We'd broken up once and he'd had the big realisation that he couldn't live without me and came back on bended knee. But it only lasted for a few months before he started pulling away again, at which point it was too late because I'd fallen pregnant by accident ... He was mortified, [but] I had been putting a bit of pressure on him. I wasn't stamping my foot, but I said [to him], 'You do have to make a commitment sooner or later here. And I'd rather it was sooner.' But he wasn't sure I was 'the one', so wouldn't make a decision. Eventually he arranged that we would have a part-time relationship. Which basically meant that he would catch up with me when he felt like it, and the rest of the time he would do what he wanted.

Shaney's experience with Prentice, and the dating agency, has led her to conclude that women looking for Mr (wants to have children) Right have their work cut out for them:

> It's not easy at this age to meet a man you can create a partnership with. They're just not around. [I] tried lots of things … it just doesn't seem to happen … There's just not that many people around. After 30 there were a reasonable number of people around until I was 35, but the crowd was getting thinner by then. And the fellows that were left were left for a reason, shall I say.

Women childless by relationship
Men who won't have kids

Some men won't partner, some men will, but having done so, won't father. Particularly as women age, this latter sort constitutes a profound obstacle on the road to parenthood. In the title song on the *Nick of Time* album, singer Bonnie Raitt describes what the world looks like to ageing women whose partners refuse to father:

> A friend of mine she cries at night
> and she calls me on the phone
> Sees babies everywhere/and she wants one of her own
> She's waited long enough she says/but still he can't decide
> Pretty soon she'll have to choose/and it tears her up inside
> She is scared/scared to run out of time.

In the past, partnered women who end up childless because of father-reluctant partners — those I would call 'childless by relationship' — have been classified by qualitative researchers as 'voluntarily childless'. The (always unstated) assumption seems to be that no matter whether or not a woman wanted children, if she stands by her I-don't-want-to-be-or-act-like-a-daddy man, she is childless 'by choice'. But if you have a good listen to the stories of these women, it soon becomes clear that no matter how resigned to, or accepting of, or (eventually) even happy they are about being childless, the choice to miss out on motherhood was definitely not theirs.

All childless by relationship women have at least a vague plan to be a mother one day. Sharon, aged 35, for instance, was raised by her third-generation farming family to believe that after she had had an education and a career, marriage and kids would follow:

> It was always assumed, but not discussed, that we would have kids. The model definitely was you grow up, you go to university, you have a career, meet someone, get married, and have children … So as a child, definitely, I assumed that I'd grow up and get married and have kids.

When they discover that their partner is firm in his opposition to parenting, these women decide, however reluctantly, that their only option is to accept a childless fate, and they set about re-imagining their future without kids, and with a non-maternal identity. And it's just like breaking up: many women find it hard, sometimes extremely hard, to do.

Sharon, much to her surprise, really struggled with it. In fact, she found it so difficult to reconcile herself to a future without kids that she packed her boyfriend Martin off to therapy in the hope that he might deal with his fatherhood 'issues':

> My partner is not very interested in having kids. So we're having this huge debate at the moment, and it's been going on for about a year and a half about having kids and not having kids, and it's a nightmare ... We went to see someone at Relationships Australia because we got to the stage where we just couldn't talk about it. I was just getting upset all the time. She was quite good, and she talked us through a few things, and then ... suggested he go and see a psychologist and actually talk through some of this and figure out what's going on. So he's doing that and I'm trying not to create too many scenes for the next few months ... I can't quite imagine what I would do. And it's really funny, because you know, [when I was younger] it was like, 'I'm not going to have kids, I'm going to do all these things.' And now I can't imagine what I'd do if I didn't have kids. It's like this bizarre twist.

Kelly, aged 39, was so sure she'd hear the pitter-patter of little feet one day that she chose a job she believed could be done at home:

> I decided that ... I want[ed] to be a mum who stayed at home. But I knew that I'd still have to work. Because I knew I'd go spare if I had a little baby talking gibberish to me all day. I'd go nuts without other's people's adult conversation and input. So I actually structured all of my work so that I could work from home if I needed to.
>
> *Me:* What kind of work were you doing?

Desktop publishing. So I could be home with my [computer]. Could have my fax machine. Could have my modem. It could all just happen. If I needed to, I could just pick up the kid, put it in the car, drive off, deliver. You know, it could mainly be at home.

But Ivan, Kelly's true love, had other ideas. Despite her certainty that she'd be a mother one day, by the time we spoke, Kelly had succeeded in re-imagining her future as a non-mother. However, as she explains, the journey was long and arduous:

I always imagined [I would have kids but] Ivan ... didn't really ever show much interest in other people's kids ... So I started talking to him about the possibility of it. Because he's [a few years] younger than I am ... and I think he'd always been a little bit wary of the whole thing ... So the subject would come up every now and again ... [And I'd think] oh well, another year, it'll be OK ... But then I'd suddenly go, 'Oh, gosh, well I suppose if I'm going to do it I'd better start thinking about it again.' Then I'd resurrect it. He'd be sort of like, 'I don't know if I really want to do it' ... So I think I got through to about 33 and then, just all of a sudden, I'd see a woman with a baby. And I'd find myself wanting to cry. Or I'd see something, like an ad on telly, read something in a magazine, and tears would come ... [But] now I wouldn't have a baby. I don't see myself being a mum.

Kelly's story leaves little doubt that it was Ivan who put the kybosh on her mothering plans, even though it was clearly her own ambivalence and indecision about motherhood that led her to pick Ivan as a partner despite his having made his lack of certainty about the parenting project clear from the start.

Kelly is not the only woman facing such 'limited' choices when it comes to children. Recent research for the European Commission found that approximately one-third of couples disagree about whether or not to have a child (or, if they already have one, about whether or not to have another). Women, either driven by their own internal goals regarding motherhood or their ticking biological clocks, are nearly always the ones to initiate discussions about children and to continue to press the issue as the relationship progresses. Men, on the other hand, are nearly always the ones putting up obstacles. While many are vaguely in favour of becoming fathers, they decide that 'one day' is 'now' only when the relationship is firmly established and travelling well and they feel economically secure:

> Female motives are mainly based on individual emotional attitudes ... motives [that] may be present with the woman already a long time, even before the durable relation[ship] with her partner. Very early in the relation[ship], the man may share with the woman a positive attitude towards having children, but his desire to have children usually grows during the relation[ship], lending an ear to the female desire already there. *The woman will usually wait until the partner gradually comes to agree on the issue,* rather than pushing the matter to satisfy her feelings; nevertheless the woman tends to raise the issue more than the man when [the] time has come ... Starting later may be due to the desire, especially with the man, to secure practical external conditions (housing, paid work) ...[81]

Some men never give the green light, and their veto — or 'blocking' power — is a critical factor in whether or not their loving partner will ever become a mum. Indeed, it is women's ultimate willingness to acquiesce to the man's wishes regarding children that is the basis of the childless by relationship phenomenon:

> No doubt the decision for parenthood is in the first place a decision for motherhood (by the mother-to-be). Fatherhood takes somewhat more time: not so much for the decision to become [a] father one day (most men do not doubt this either), but [because the] decision to become a father [requires], in a number of cases, careful preparation … Male power in decision making therefore seems to be mostly *blocking power* (or postponing) power.[82]

A woman's response to her man's 'blocking' power depends on when she first twigs that he isn't just dithering, but is deadly serious about living a childfree life. Men who do want to parent 'one day' and those who are sure that they don't may not look all that different to a woman who, in the early years of the relationship, is in no great procreative rush either. Most couples, believe it or not, never openly discuss their childbearing desires and plans, relying instead on hidden or 'implicit' understandings. Such 'communication' strategies (such as they are) leave ample opportunity for women like Kelly to see their partner's opposition to childbearing as temporary hesitance rather than a serious resistance to parenthood that will increase, rather than lessen, over time.

Having realised that he's serious, a woman who wants to mother is left with a variety of age-related replies. She can leave in search of Mr (wants to have children) Right, a strategy often adopted by younger thwarted mothers, or if she loves the man passionately or has left the leaving too late, she can reconcile herself to a childless future.

Interestingly, one recent survey suggests that many young adults believe that if things are otherwise happy, breaking up because of disagreements about parenting is the wrong thing to do.[83] Women who are childless by relationship tend to agree, though their belief in the power of love over motherhood is peppered with a strong dose of age-related realism. All the childless by relationship women I spoke with were in their late thirties: old and wise enough to know that a good relationship is hard to find, and therefore unlikely to be discovered, under pressure from a ticking biological clock, with a Mr or Ms (wants to have children) Right.

By the time Ivan impressed on Kelly the depth of his lack of interest in children, she was in her mid-thirties. Kelly had loved and lost a number of true bastards in her time, which made her really treasure what she'd found with Ivan:

> I knew about the second day that I was with him that this was it ... I'd found the person ... One of the things that makes me know is the relationship I have with Ivan. It's very precious. Very, very precious ... There's a very dear friend of mine who lives in Italy, who is 75. She met her husband in the Resistance ... [Ivan and I] went to Italy when I was 35 to visit her ... And I said to her, 'Did it ever bother you that you and your husband didn't have any children? Did you ever feel like you missed out on anything by not being a parent?' And she said ... 'I will tell you something that has helped me enormously in my resolution about this ... He was my lover, my best friend, my husband and my child. There was nothing that I could add to this relationship that would make it any more perfect than it was.' And I thought, she's right. And I do feel like that about Ivan ... That's how I feel about him.

Sharon clearly loves Martin, but her rocky relationship history and advancing age means that if he doesn't come around to the idea of fatherhood, she's likely to stay with him anyway:

> I hadn't been in any long-term relationships until this one. I'd been in lots of short relationships … But if I don't have children [soon] I might not have the opportunity [because] I'm getting older …
>
> *Me:* At what point will you start feeling you're too old?
>
> Well, it's creeping up all the time. I mean two years ago if I hadn't had my first child by the time I was 35, it was too old. I just shifted the goalposts a bit … [Now] I wouldn't want to be having children after 40 … But if he's absolutely convinced he doesn't want to have kids, do I go and find someone else, do I have kids by myself, or do I stay in this relationship? I mean, I want to stay in this relationship … [and] I don't really relish the idea of going out there trying to find a partner to have kids with … So I'm actually trying really hard, and I haven't ever said, 'We have kids or I go.' [I've said], 'Let's work through this together [until] either you convince me or I convince you, so that we can both still stay together and be happy about it.'

Men (and lesbian partners) who won't parent

Sometimes women's partners can put an end to women's parenting prospects not by refusing to become a parent, but by refusing to participate in any of the parenting work once the baby arrives. Janine, 38, a midwife who has only recently come out as a lesbian, and whose orientation towards motherhood is more thwarted mother than waiter and watcher, has nonetheless reluctantly abandoned her plans to parent. Why? Because her partner, Cathy, has stated point blank that she wants no part of the responsibility of raising the child, and Janine doesn't feel she can manage things on her own:

> [My partner] doesn't want to be a parent, and she said to me, 'If you do choose to have a child, you need to know that the responsibility would be all yours … You need to go in thinking that it's your decision [and] it's your child, if we ever split up.' I think she's sensible about it really, and she would be a fantastic mum, she's fantastic with her nieces and nephews. Children just love her, but she's not prepared to be a co-parent … She's 43; she says she's too old now. She likes her sleep and likes her lifestyle, and children would be a major inconvenience.

Perhaps the fact that Cathy's reluctance was the crucial factor in Janine's decision to miss out on motherhood was what led Janine to insist, as I was arranging the interview with her and later when we spoke, that my analysis recognise that not all women without children chose — in the full and classical meaning of the term — to be that way:

> I can reject … [motherhood] with my head, but with my heart I think that's what women are designed to do, and it's a little bit sad to think that I'll never experience it. Perhaps in years to come that will be something that I'll have to learn to live with — my decision … I've spent a lot of years around women and birth and babies and I've been present at deliveries and helped a lot of babies into the world … I often go away from a delivery thinking this is something that I will never experience now. And maybe it could have

been different. But it's a choice. But it's not really a free choice … It's a limited choice.

Janine's story also reminds me of Bethany's. Remember Jack, Bethany's high-flying partner, who finds baby spew 'foul' (I love a dollop of it on toast, myself), and has no intention of reducing his hours or committing to changing even one nappy after a hard day's work? While Bethany's waiting and watching orientation towards motherhood means she won't leave him because of this, despite probably having time — she is only 28 — to do so and re-partner, she does want children enough for there to be grounds, should she wind up childless at the end of the day, to sheet some of the responsibility for this to Jack's unwillingness to do little more towards the fathering project than donate his sperm:

> [I want to have children] because of my own family. I've got such a wonderful family and I really like it … and it's not always going to be there … people die … and my brother and my sister may not have their own families … I find the family experience a really wonderful one … I see [it] as a very important thing.

Women like Janine and Bethany — those fighting the uphill battle to motherhood against partners for whom 'share and share alike' is just so much Greek — are far from alone. A recent study by Australian researcher Lareen Newman suggests that the attitudes of women's partners lead some women to not only delay having kids, but also to plan on having fewer when they do get into gear. It also leads women who, having ventured to have that first child, have found themselves — literally — left holding the baby, to seriously rethink their plans for further procreation. This is particularly the case, Newman says, for mothers who had previously enjoyed equal partnerships with work-oriented men. Such women are shocked, and not a little bit resentful, to discover that after the baby is born their partner's previous commitment to equality disappears, and he simply refuses to share the work of caring for the child or the daily logistical acrobatics required to balance work and family. As one mother told Newman, she just couldn't see herself mothering again with the woeful level of support she'd got from her partner the first time.[84]

Why staying isn't choosing

Qualitative researchers nearly always consider women who are childless by relationship to be childless by choice, despite the fact that many women in such studies make no bones about the fact that they'd certainly have mothered if they'd married a different man.

Among the reasons researchers have for lumping such women in with the true childless by choice are their assumptions about the range and usability of the reproductive options available to women at any given time. Put simply, the thinking is that if she 'chose' to stay knowing he wouldn't consent to having children, or to help raise them, then she 'chose' to be childless.

This is idealistic rubbish that wrongly assumes first that most women uncover their partner's deep and abiding aversion to kids early in the piece, second, that they think nothing of dumping a partnership (particularly a marriage) with a person they are truly and deeply in love with in the trash, and third, that if they are prepared to do this, they are well placed to locate another great bloke to share the rest of their life with (who *does* want to parent) before their biological clock chimes midnight.

This is fantasyland. The real way it works is this. Girl meets boy. Girl marries boy. Girl divorces boy. Girl waits for another boy for ages and ages and is 37 before finds boy again. Girl fears raising the issue of kids for fear of scaring Boy off, and by the time she does and Boy agrees, she's biologically past it. Or perhaps it is Girl meets Boy, but Boy is a prick. Girl stays with Boy for way too long, finally leaves him, and needs a few years by herself to rebuild her life. By the time Girl is ready to meet new Boy, there are no even vaguely passable Boys around. Girl becomes menopausal. Or how about this: Girl meets really, really ace Boy and falls madly in love. When Girl raises issue of children, Boy reassures Girl he does want kids one day, but doesn't feel 'ready' yet. Girl forces issue in her late thirties, and Boy reneges. Girl stays with him because she loves him and figures she's too old to find someone else who would have kids with her anyway. This one might sometimes also end with Girl becoming so distressed that Boy — citing her over-demanding nature — leaves Girl high and dry. Several years later Boy marries much younger Girl with whom he has, and devotedly helps raise, several kids.

Academics Jim Franklin and Sarah Chee Tueno, authors of a recent article on the partnering challenges faced by contemporary women, might propose an additional scenario. Smart Girl decides to do postgraduate work and so doesn't have a chance to focus properly on relationship with Boy until she's in her early thirties. By then available Boys are either married, insolvent or commitaphobes. Right Boy marries younger Girl with less HECS debt.

Get the picture? The executive summary is that women today are running their lives on extraordinarily tight schedules. By the time they have travelled, got their education and established themselves in a career — all of which they want to do, and all of which they want to do first — they have only a few years left for the three-step program:

1   Find Mr (wants to have children) Right;

2   Get him to commit to a long-term relationship; and

3   Produce one or two children.

Delays in any of these steps (and as we have seen, some gals struggle with all three) can lead a woman to slam into her own personal fertility wall and — simply because she's failed to beat the whistle — end up childless. This is a tale of modern Western women compelled to adjust and readjust deadlines to deal with unexpected snags in their progress towards motherhood. A tale of women dealing with disappointment and settling for what they can get. It is not, by any stretch of the imagination, a tale of women who are childless 'by choice'.

Women who are childless by relationship make their decisions about remaining with Mr (doesn't want to have children) Right or even Mr (doesn't want to have children) Approximate against this background of snags and disappointments. They make their decisions in light of the availability of other viable options, and use the time they have left to, in management-speak, 'action' them.

This is not to say that women who do decide, for a variety of reasons, to stay with a man who doesn't want children are pitiable or passive victims of fate. Not at all. Nearly all decisions in this world are made in the context of some constraints. This neither makes them non-decisions, nor renders them unworthy of respect. What it *does* do is raise questions about the nature and degree of the external constraints that are present, and whether those limits are nice, fair or even wise for society to impose.

I'm also not trying to say that in the silent depths of their hearts all women who are childless by relationship are desperately unhappy about missing out on children. Some are; those whose basic orientation towards motherhood is more thwarted mother than waiter and watcher and who consequently struggle to reorientate their identity and imagined future to childlessness when it becomes clear that kids aren't on the cards. But others — more waiter and watcher in basic outlook than thwarted mother — are likely to take the particular twists and turns of their life in their stride, and to make excellent headway in the 'moving on' stakes. The good news is that even those who are really miserable about ending up childless will recover in time. Kelly, for instance, now speaks excitedly about her new clothing enterprise and how she can't ever imagine herself as a mum anymore. Yet, this was a woman who spent her entire 33rd year fighting off tears every time she saw a woman with a baby.

I don't want to drone on dirge-like about the miseries of women childless by relationship, or indeed of any woman childless by circumstance. Rather, I want to acknowledge that while circumstantially childless women will eventually survive and thrive, questions need to be asked about a society that moans endlessly about declining birth-rates and waxes lyrical about the importance of reproductive choice, yet does little to reduce the constraints on women's childbearing options, and their freedom to select among them.

Men and women apart

Women respond to the obstacles — er … 'challenges' — that men create in the childbearing arena in numerous ways. Some doggedly pursue Mr Right and only turn to Mr (wants to have children) Approximate when time runs short. Others aren't motivated to mother enough to leave their Mr (doesn't want children) Right so they stay, while others stay with Mr (doesn't want children) Right or even Mr (doesn't want children) Approximate because they feel too old to meet with success if they returned to the dating scene.

Some women judge themselves young enough abandon Mr (wants to have children) Approximate for the chance to have it all — a fulfilling relationship and a child — and a small thwarted mother-type group of women are game enough, in the absence of anyone even vaguely suitable, to go it alone.

But no matter how women decide to deal with the challenges men pose to their childbearing plans, there is simply no way around the fact that male immaturity, recalcitrance, fear, insecurity, sexism, or whatever it is that makes them do the infuriating and exasperating things some of them do, is partly responsible for the growing number of women who will end their days childless by circumstance. *Age* journalist and single childless woman Sushi Das makes this point in her discussion of the reason for declining birth-rates, or what newspapers like to refer to as the 'baby-bust':

> Some young men are too self-absorbed, too career-oriented, or stuck in a sort of ill-groomed, selfish immaturity, for a woman to feel they would be able to provide a stable and loving environment in which to bring up children. Put bluntly, some men just don't measure up ... Being equal does not just mean women are free to pursue careers. Being equal also means we expect men to shoulder some of the responsibility for having children at a time that is safe and sensible for women.[85]

You said it, sister. The question is, where did it all go wrong?

Once upon a time ...

Back in the bad old days, women needed men considerably more than men needed women. Yes, men have always needed women to bear the children who will carry on their name and inherit their property, but women's reproductive power has, until recently, also been the main source of their sexual and political repression. This is because until the recent arrival of DNA testing, ensuring his woman's 'sexual purity' was a man's only way to guarantee that the squalling offspring disturbing his sleep and otherwise draining his resources was really 'his'. Whether this was done through passing laws allowing women accused of infidelity to be stoned, or by securing their wife's chastity by lock and key, men have always made sure that society was organised in ways that gave them control of the means of reproduction while providing little to women — in terms of power or money or independence — for services rendered.

Women, for their part, were not in any position to complain. Indeed, in what was perhaps the original Faustian deal, Susan Maushart claims that women in early human groups relinquished their sexual power and economic independence to individuals or small groups of men in exchange for their protection from other violent males, particularly during their most vulnerable moments: when pregnant, and when nursing young, says Maushart:

> The provision of a wide range of caretaking services was how females persuaded males to stick around, to share resources and to provide protection to offspring — generally from the marauding of other males.[86]

Thus, according to Maushart, the answer in evolutionary terms to the age-old question 'what do women want' is 'a mate to protect and provide for them and their offspring, at least until those offspring are off their hands'.[87]

Fast forward to one of the most critical developments for marriage and family functioning: the industrial revolution. The shift of production from individual households, where it was shared among all family members young and old to factories saw the end of the acknowledgement of middle-class women's and children's economic value as contributors to household survival. The creation of such 'separate spheres' has, over the years, given rise to quaint notions such as 'domestic science', and to fundamental shifts in thinking about children (essentially, the idea of childhood is a 20the century creation). But most importantly of all, the industrial revolution kick-started the recasting of women and children from independents who pulled their own economic weight to people 'dependent' on the wage of the 'breadwinner' for their very survival. The whole arrangement hung on the thin thread of marriage: the legal basis for the woman's claim to enough of the man's wage to support her and her children.

Right up until the 1960s, when women's social freedom and economic opportunities began to expand, the most important game in town was convincing men that it was in their interest to marry. Maushart argues that what she calls 'wifework' was women's attempt to sweeten the deal, while George Gilder, the conservative author of *Men and Marriage*, believes society pressures men into accepting the confines of marriage for its own benefit: to civilise what he calls the 'barbarians' — young men and boys in their teens and early twenties — and induce them to undertake the 'disciplines and duties of citizenship'.[88]

But sociologist and respected commentator Barbara Ehrenreich disagrees. In *The Hearts of Men*, she argues that no matter how shiny her floors or tempting her meatloaf — or how insistent the powers that be were that men got married — men smelled a rat. By the end of the 1950s, says Ehrenreich, it was male discontent with the breadwinner bargain, not female discontent with their dependent lot, that instigated the unravelling of the gender compact:

The collapse of the breadwinner ethic had begun well before the revival of feminism and stemmed from dissatisfactions every bit as deep, if not as idealistically expressed, as those that motivated our founding 'second wave' feminists.[89]

Among the people egging men on was the young Hugh Hefner. From the first issue, Hefner's mouthpiece *Playboy* argued (to those who read the articles) that rather than undertake lifetime support of the female 'unemployed', a bloke would be wiser to buy his food from restaurants, wash his clothes in a laundromat and spend the remainder of his salary on a swinging bachelor pad where he could lure buxom beauties (of the sort the magazine featured) for decidedly unmissionary sex. In the 1950s, the definition of manhood included being heterosexual, married and a hard worker. In the same way that feminists would later try to extricate the definition of 'woman' from that of 'mother', Hefner saw his task as eliminating 'husband' from the normative description of 'man'. Says Ehrenreich:

> *Playboy* charged into the battle of the sexes with a dollar sign on its banner. The issue was money: Men made it; women wanted it. In *Playboy*'s favorite cartoon situation an elderly roué was being taken for a ride by a buxom bubblebrain, and the joke was on him. The message, squeezed between luscious full-color photos and punctuated with female nipples, was simple: You can buy sex on a fee-for-service basis, so don't get caught up in a long-term contract.[90]

Despite the flaws in Hefner's case — he ignores the issue of children and the vital inheritance function they play — many men were sold, and began either flying the coop, or seriously considering it. By the time the contraceptive pill entered the picture in the late 1960s, the male revolt and feminist responses to it were well underway. Combined with shifts from an industrial to a post-industrial or service economy, the family wage — and the family form that it underwrote — came under unprecedented pressure.

The world in which men exercised ultimate control over the terms and conditions in which women and children entered and remained part of their lives was coming to an end. Life would never be the same.

Exit breadwinner, enter ...

The reason men don't hold all the cards when it comes to marriage and forming families at the start of the 21st century is that while women still want them to be in on the game, they no longer *need* them to be. Reliable birth control and increased access to safe abortion both took the social heat out of the good girl/slut distinction that contributed to shotgun marriages, and allowed married women to avoid childbearing as long as they liked in order to pursue opportunities in the labour market. Increased educational opportunities paralleled the expansion of job opportunities for women, making marriage a choice rather than an economic necessity for many. Even having and raising a child alone, from the get-go or after divorce, is now a viable choice, because of the end of the harsh social stigma attached to being an 'unwed' or 'divorced' mother (or the child of one), and the creation of supporting payments for sole parents.

Men, on the other hand, are wearing the brunt of economic change as jobs disappear from the male-dominated blue-collar industries and flow instead into the female-dominated post-industrial service economy. In Australia, for example, the number of men aged 25 to 29 in full-time work has actually fallen: from 76% in 1986 to 67% in 2001. Similar declines can be seen among men in their early thirties. Even in the late 1990s, when the Australian economy was going gangbusters, employment rates for men of all ages fell. Faludi tells a similar tale of blue-collar 'grunts' in the United States being rewarded for their loyalty to corporate leviathans such as McDonnell Douglas or Lockheed 'with insecurity … pink slips [and] massive spasms of downsizing, restructuring, union-breaking, contracting out and outsourcing'.[91]

Indeed, the whole concept of breadwinning — in which the entire economic fate of the family hangs on the bloke's job — has become laughable as more and more positions become increasingly 'low quality': that is, part-time, poorly paid, insecure, or all three. In today's post-industrial economy both partners need to work, or at least remain securely attached to the workforce, both to achieve a reasonable standard of living and to hedge against periods of unemployment and under-employment.

Working-class man

Job insecurity affects men at the top and bottom end of the economic ladder differently. For men at the bottom end of the workforce, the lack of a secure and decently paid job is likely to mean the difference between finding a mate and being forever left on the shelf. As demographer Bob Birrell explains:

> There [is] a huge and growing gap in partnering rates for high-income men relative to low-income males, especially those not in the labour force or unemployed. For example, for men aged 30–34 earning less than $16,000, 41 per cent were partnered compared with 71 per cent for men earning $52,000 or more.[92]

As Birrell tells it, the gulf between the low paid and better paid is even greater when it comes to marriage:

> Men who are married are now predominantly drawn from the ranks of the better off. Again for men aged 30–34, 30 per cent for the low-income group were in married partnerships compared with 59 per cent of those in the higher-income group.[93]

In the tale Birrell tells, low income is a consequence of some groups of men missing out on the benefits of what, from the 1980s onwards, have been seemingly endless rounds of structural change to the Australian economy. In other words, it seems that the restructuring of the Australian economy has not been a good news story for everyone. In fact, it has produced both winners and losers, and among the losers are young men who've missed out on a post-school education and the benefits it provides: a decent job and the chance to partner and be in a position to have children. As Birrell's figures clearly demonstrate, the partnering rates of 'other' men were below those of their more educated counterparts in 1986.[94]

As Birrell is at pains to point out, better-educated men always fared better in the marriage stakes than their poorly educated brothers. What has changed in Australia since 1986, he argues, is the gap between the two:

> The proportion of this 'other' group of men aged 30–34 who were partnered declined from 68 per cent in 1986 to 57 per cent in 1996 and to 52 per cent in 2001. This is startling drop. If this pattern continues, a majority of men could soon be unpartnered.[95]

There are a few theories as to why less educated and consequently less well-off men are losing out in the partnership stakes. One is that they are reluctant to take on the responsibilities of a wife, mortgage and kids when they lack the financial wherewithal to meet such commitments. This lack of capacity comes not solely with being unemployed but also with being employed in low-quality jobs. In fact, the vast majority of jobs that have been created in Australia since the 1980s are either part-time or full-time casual and consequently tend to lack security of tenure, predictable hours and income, and basic job protections that people need if they are to feel confident enough to take on significant and ongoing responsibilities like house repayments and children.[96]

Another theory about the unmarriageability of such men is that those women who would have been in their prospective partner pool in the past — those with similarly poor levels of education and employment — are no longer interested in taking them on. There are a number of theories as to why this might be so. Birrell argues that unlike their more educated and higher-earning sisters, who are in the market for a collaborative-type relationship defined by 'confluent love' and by an expectation that both paid and domestic work will be shared equally, less-educated women are hoping to find a traditional breadwinner to support them in exchange for their commitment to keep the house and raise the children. Birrell argues that such poorly educated women disproportionately fill the ranks of low-paid, boring 'pink-collar' service and sales jobs that most would be more than happy to leave — at least for a few years — to raise kids:

> For women leaving school at age 17 or 18 and not continuing in any post-school studies, work is not likely to present much challenge or excitement since for the most part it will be at the routine level in service occupations such as sales assistants or office

workers: "pink-collar" occupations where the majority of jobs are casual and offer neither security of employment, predictability of hours or basic job protections. For the women in question, employment is unlikely to offer strong counter attraction to partnering and homemaking roles.[97]

However, Pam Bone, now an editor at the *Age* but once a low-paid factory worker, insists that no matter how dull or repetitious, paid work offers working-class women the financial independence that most dearly treasure:

> For three seasons, from January to April, along with several hundred other women, I did the 6 pm to 2.20 am shift … There I was, aged 28, four children (the oldest aged five), rushing off each evening to work in a noisy, steamy factory and liking it … You were out of the house, and at children's bed and bath time, the worst time of the day. You had lots of people to talk to as long as you could raise your voice above the noise of the cans. No worries about the children, because they were being looked after by their fathers (do them good to see what it's like for a change). And money! To have money you didn't have to ask someone else for! … There are some boring and menial jobs around, for men and women, but it's patronising to assume that only middle-class professionals enjoy and take pride in their jobs. As a member of the 1970s working class, I must say that feminism suited my aspirations very well … Working-class women understood well enough that a job gave them an identity and an independence they couldn't get as the non-earning partner in a marriage

... The old adage that 'he who pays the piper calls the tune' was and is true.[98]

Bone's claim, that nearly all contemporary women have a strong attachment to the workforce, is backed up by findings of the Australian Longitudinal Study on Women's Health which shows that 91% cent of women aged 18 to 22 intend to engage in paid work on either a full-time or part-time basis. Only 4% were hoping for a future in which they worked full-time in the home (with the remaining 5% wanting some other unspecified work option).[99] This commitment to paid work, whether such work is well paid and glamorous or casual and menial, is strong and in part reflected and reinforced by the 74.5% of women who said that by their mid-thirties they wanted to have more educational qualifications than they did currently. Consequently, the argument would run, the vast majority of women are seeking 'collaborative' relationships with men, relationships in which the responsibility for earning and for domestic and childcare work is shared and unemployed or low-paid, insecurely employed men don't fit the bill.

Such a dispute is, in any case, largely academic, because whether less-educated women are rejecting marriage offers from men because they fail to fit either the breadwinner bill or the collaborative partner one, what is patently clear is that in the eyes of such women many of the men currently on offer fail to measure up. This is particularly the case when such men turn out to have traditional sexist attitudes — of the me Tarzan 'I want a beer'/you Jane 'Go bring me one'-type. Indeed, as Summers tells it, only a handful of the married women she interviewed from across Australia agreed that their husbands did their fair share of the work around the house.[100] As one 30-year-old working mother explained:

I was still looking after the child, looking after him, looking after the family and making sure there was food on the table and getting the clothes in and giving baths, doing everything and working as well. Having the partner is just having an extra person to look after.[101]

The cold hard truth is that when women have, or are capable of achieving, some degree of fiscal independence, they are voting with their feet and saying 'no' to marriage with men who will contribute little to the bank balance but much to the domestic load.

This is not to say that women see no use for such men. While they may not wish to partner with them permanently, there is evidence that they are happy to let them stay around long enough to father children. Fertility rates for unpartnered women in Australia have climbed in recent years, and while many among the lone parent ranks were once married, an increasing number have never tied the knot. In 1986 the proportion of never-married single parents was 17% while in 2001 it was 42%. For single parents aged 25–29, the proportion who had never married increased from 37% in 1986 to 66% in 2001. Statistics from one state in Australia suggest that in 2001 approximately half the unmarried mothers were living with a man in a de facto relationship at the time their child was born, and half were not.[102]

According to anthropologist Sarah Blaffer Hrdy, such figures are exactly what you'd expect in an environment where a woman's potential male partners are unable to provide enough protection and provision for her and her children to make mating with him monogamously and for life a wise strategy:

For monogamy to benefit a mother, her mate must be in a position to protect her or to reliably provision her. Demographic rates and sources of mortality are also important. High adult survival rates among men make

it worthwhile for [women] to invest in relationships ...
[but] where males are poor providers, likely to die young
or when resources are unpredictable — then mothers
are far better off polyandrous — if they can be so safely.
A woman's children may be better off with several
fathers than with one inferior or unreliable one.[103]

The reason why when things get tough for men, women may
be better off mating — or even partnering short-term — with
several blokes rather than just one, is that while men will only
intensively or extensively invest in children they are sure are
genetically theirs, if they think there is a chance a child is theirs,
they may contribute something in terms of time, food, protection
or money. Here Hrdy gives an example using monkeys, but she
says the argument applies to humans as well:

Any male who provides exclusive care to an unrelated
baby, and ... fails to sire children of his own, may find
many satisfactions. But he does not increase his
reproductive success ... But what about assistance
divisible among a number of babies? What if care is
only intermittently required? ... Such fathering is
divisible ... among many recipients. The important
point is that the male need not be certain of paternity
to proffer paternal-like assistance...Such fathers may
divide their time between many possible offspring. If
an infant is possibly theirs, and intervention is not too
risky, these scattershot fathers can afford to be less
than certain.[104]

Whatever the reasons for the rise in single motherhood, Birrell
reminds us that without the fertility of Australia's single mums,
the nation's birth-rate would almost certainly be languishing

around the level of Spain's and Italy's, where the business of childbearing is left strictly to married women. More importantly, to my mind, is the fact that at the start of the 21st century the sole parent's pension that has made single motherhood possible ensures that women's fertility aspirations aren't tied to the availability of adequately paid and securely employed men, and the willingness of those men to commit to a stable partnership.

The top end of town

The main difference between well-educated and less-educated men is that the former find it easier to find work and, consequently, to pull chicks. But while compared with their working-class brothers such men are doing well, they too are finding no shortage of challenges in the post-industrial job and marriage market.

While educated men find it easier to land a job, their current and future employment prospects are also highly insecure. Many see their late twenties and thirties as the time to put in heaps of hours and significantly advance their career in order to achieve the income and job security they believe are necessary before they embark on parenthood. Tim Wooster, aged 27, is a research scientist at a top Australian university, but his contract runs for only three years. The decline in tenured positions in the higher education sector means his chances of getting permanent work in the future — the sort of work he feels is essential if he is to have a husband-and-fathering future — are dim. Despite this, Wooster regularly works 60 to 70 hours a week, trying desperately to make a good impression on his senior colleagues in order to get ahead.

The story is much the same for Andrew Price, a 27-year-old chef making $44,000 a year. He too wants to have kids but feels he needs to protect his future employment and earning prospects by first making executive chef. This involves working up to 70 hours a week, often on night shift. It's a roller-coaster pace and schedule and recently led his latest girlfriend to disembark in search of a safer and more predictable ride.

Greater responsibility, longer hours and no guarantees that your job will still exist at the week's end. This is the job market better-educated men face at precisely the time ticking women need them to ante-up to marriage and start talking parenthood. For many blokes the prevailing economic climate simply makes it the wrong time, leading them to start babbling about 'someday', and edging towards the door.

There are men willing to tie the knot, or at least move a few pieces of clothing in and 'see what develops'. Invariably this sort wants a girl who earns. This preference doesn't mean most are closet feminists, but rather that they are able to do their sums. In a post-industrial economy where hours are increasing (from 1982 to 2002, the proportion of men working 50 hours a week or more grew by 22%), work is getting harder (through understaffing, a reduction in rest times, and an increase in simultaneous demands and the pace of work) and job security is declining,[105] the best hedge against poverty, stress leave and possible unwanted stretches of unemployment or under-employment in the future is a dual-salary household.

Experts call relationships where both partners assume that the other should and will work 'egalitarian' or 'collaborative'. The data suggests, however, that few blokes who sign up for the collaborative deal have given any — or more than passing — thought to its full specifications. Namely the bit in the contract that says, 'in exchange for the female's acceptance of her share of the responsibility to earn, the male will share all domestic chores — including child-minding — equally'. As Australian researchers Birrell and Virginia Rapson put it, 'Some men give lip service to the idea [of sharing the domestic load] but fail to put it into practice.'[106] Instead, many middle-class guys these days seem stuck in the 1970s: forever patting themselves on the back for 'letting' their wives work 'too'. The tension between what men say they believe and what they actually do can lead to marriage breakdown. Tina's divorce from David, on the grounds — among other things — that he wasn't ready to change a nappy or otherwise share the work of raising a child, is a case in point. Men's failure to share the domestic load may also lead to childlessness, as Bethany and Janine's stories vividly demonstrate.

While truly collaborative relationships are still pie in the sky for most women, feminism and changing economic realities have significantly revamped their job description for Mr Right. While economic dependence and social repression forced their grandmothers to take whatever hubby dished out as long as he handed over his pay packet come Friday night, contemporary women are now free to make their own way in the world. They want to partner and raise children with a man, but they no longer have to marry or mother. More than any other generation of females, women today have other options.

These options give women, perhaps for the first time in history, the upper hand when it comes to marriage and motherhood. As already noted, this is not to say that women don't want to partner and have their kids within that partnership or, to take the point further, see no advantages in doing so. They know that the income of a well-educated man trumps a sole parent's pension when it comes to bearing and raising young children, and they appreciate that a stable partnership provides easy access to sperm from a known donor, as well as an on-site father for their kids. But the existence of the pension, and at least some sperm banks willing to help single women achieve a pregnancy, increases women's power in the marriage bargain (and thereby explains conservatives' opposition to both). It is women's newfound social and economic power that has enabled them to rewrite the job descriptions for 'good' husbands and fathers, and to insist that men measure up. And it is the gap between what many women now want from men — as partners and fathers — and what men are able or willing to provide that explains the trouble so many women are having finding and securing a relationship with Mr (wants to have children) Right before time runs out.

Where has all this left men?

Men have had the rug of longstanding definitions of masculinity pulled from beneath them: how do you think they feel? Some are angry, more are resigned or resentful. But no matter how they appear, beneath the surface most are wondering the same thing: what do they have to do these days to feel 'masculine' and — if they are straight — to impress the women on whom they depend for both their emotional and physical wellbeing and their chance — when they're ready, of course — to get into the fathering game?

To get a sense of how extraneous to women and female family plans many contemporary men are feeling, one need only recall the hysteria that surrounded Leesa Meldrum's quest to become a mother. Meldrum, infertile and desperate for motherhood, used the courts to challenge the state law denying her access to treatment because she was single. While feminists strongly opposed the discriminatory law restricting Meldrum's reproductive options, male politicians and opinion leaders supported her exclusion from treatment programs. Why? Because as they saw it, she was denying the importance of men in the forming of families and the rearing of children. From Prime Minister John Howard's insistence that children had a 'fundamental right' to 'the care and affection of both a mother and a father' to the Catholic Church's insistence that children were entitled to 'know and be cared for by both parents', men and male-dominated institutions across the nation shrilly resisted what they saw as the implication of Meldrum's pursuit of single motherhood: that men were no longer a necessary, or even desirable, feature of family life.

While I fully support Meldrum's right not to be discriminated against because of her marital status, and to gain access to the treatment she sought, I think it's important to hear and respond to the collective male anxiety that women are increasingly willing and able to 'go' parenthood alone. Let's face it, being in a relationship and having children are among the most important and satisfying experiences in life. Given how long the women's movement has spent trying to convince men of this fact, and that they matter on the domestic front, it shouldn't be too surprising that men get scared and angry when they are told, or feel they are being told, that they are surplus to requirements.[107]

The reporting surrounding the birth of the first fatherless mammal said it all. The animal, a mouse created from two separate eggs, made headlines around the world. Several weeks later, however, news services were pumping out reassuring copy about the importance of men in the reproductive endeavour. 'Here's proof,' ran one headline. 'There is a need for men after all.' 'Men can breathe a sigh of relief', noted another. Scientists now realise that men play 'a more vital role in procreation than they may have thought'. 'Men are not obsolete,' Wayne University scientist Stephen Krawetz concluded sagely. '[They] do have a function.'[108]

Working-class man

When we last left working-class man, poor labour market prospects and his own outmoded sexual politics and ideals saw him locked in hand-to-hand combat with the sole parent's pension for the role of husband and dad. In many cases, he was losing.

While increasing numbers of working-class women view less-educated men and their dirty socks as a poor second to the reduced domestic labour and nominal economic independence government payments can provide, many working-class men disagree. These men feel they are taking it from all sides: watching women snatch the lion's share of jobs being generated by the new post-industrial economy and then, as a consequence of their own declining economic fortunes, having those same gals snub them as partners.

Their responses to this vary, in type and extreme. Some feel they've been tattooed across the brow with a giant L (for Loser), and have retreated to the pub to nurse their sorrows. Others head for the internet to browse among the endless sites advertising 'beautiful', 'feminine', 'sincere', 'faithful' and 'passionate' brides who 'know how to take care of a man' and cause far fewer 'hassles' than 'modern Western women'.[109] Others, say journalist Tom Morton, resort to 'threats, abuse, harassment, violence [against] or murder [of women]' to try to turn the power balance back in their favour.

Some angry working-class types fall into gangs, insulting women as slags and making 'exaggerated claims to potency' that some academics see as a protest against their 'desperate disadvantage in the labour market'. By beating each other up, engaging in petty crime, tooling around in souped-up cars and taking a 'fuck 'em and leave 'em' attitude to 'bitches', 'whores' and 'pussies' (and I do indeed quote), such men make a claim to power that they don't and aren't likely to ever really have.[110]

Using the classic male strategy of claiming a corner of public space as their own and fiercely defending it against 'enemy' incursion, some angry working-class blokes have even begun pissing in corners of cyberspace. Angry-men websites offer such disgruntled men a venue in which they can rant about the evils of particular women and feminism in general while taking absolutely no responsibility for their personal trials and tribulations or those confronting their sex. My favourite is www.angryharry.com, which covers a wide range of gender 'issues' that bear no relationship to one another other than that — in the demented mind of the site's creator — they 'prove' the pathological evil of all womankind and the inherent innocence of her vulnerable male 'prey'. The following is a reply Harry posted to a woman who had the temerity to be offended by his site:

> You exhibit exactly the behaviour that I often describe in women: hostile insults and false accusations. You're pathetic. You have absolutely nothing of interest to say to me. You're even stupid enough to give me exactly the kind of evidence for my website that proves my point concerning the mindless and vindictive way in which many women nowadays behave. Indeed, there is not one phrase in your entire email that is even suggestive of an intelligent comment about anything that I have written. Not one. I suggest that you look at your own spiteful behaviour and try to recognise what it says about you … Basically, you're a typical western female who actually believes that her gender alone entitles her to be abusive and insulting whenever she feels like it and that it will also protect her from retaliation. Well. Those days are rapidly coming to an end, my dear. And you will soon discover that you are not as superior as you think … I doubt very much that there is actually anything that you can do better than me — apart, of course, from attracting sex-starved men and having babies … I tell you what. Go and have a pout somewhere and pretend to cry. I'm

sure that some Neanderthal desperate for sex will eventually turn up from somewhere to caress your over-inflated fragile ego. You'll feel a lot better then.[111]

There is no doubt that 'Harry' has a screw loose, and I am not suggesting that all or even most men who feel they've lost out in the post-industrial economy and gender relations become this pathologically angry. However, I do think Harry's ravings provide an insight into not just the humiliation experienced by men who have lost out in postmodern economies and politics, but also the way (in a phenomenon well recognised by sociologists) they reply with either verbal insults or physical violence to counter their humiliation. Luckily, 'Harry' is locked away in cyberspace where he can't hurt anyone, but there is no shortage of examples of retaliatory working-class man violence. However, the Montreal massacre in 1989 of 14 women 'accused' of being 'feminists' by the young, unemployed and very angry Marc Lepine shows what can happen when such men gain access to guns in real life. So too does the murder in 1996 of Jean Majdalawi by her estranged husband outside the Family Court in Sydney and failed serviceman and sacked plumber Shawn Nelson's rampage through San Diego's well-populated streets in the M-60 tank he stole from the National Guard armoury after his wife left him. In popular culture, verbal face-saving rage can be found in the misogynist lyrics of working-class rap singer Eminem, who regularly 'disses' women as cheap, superficial and manipulative whores who, when they dare to profess love for him, merit having their 'drunk ass' left on a runway. Australian cartoonist Michael Leunig's all-too-pointed rant against single women (or was it really just a certain single woman who obviously found him wanting at some point?) is also a case in point. In Stephen Biddulph's bestselling *Manhood*, published in 1994, Leunig writes:

So, you're one of those single women, 30–40 years old, who can't find a good man and think that men are too stupid to appreciate what a ravishingly brilliant creature you are; who think that men are too dull and cowardly to engage your vivacious, intelligent spirit, your proud confidence, your sheer excellence and the awesome richness of your experience and achievement. Don't despair. The answer could be quite simple. For instance, has it ever occurred to you that you might be too pompous? Or just too greedy and brattish; or too sanctimonious and hypocritical: just too up yourself and full of bullshit? Or have you considered that you might not presently have the capacity to recognise a good man even if you saw one and that a good man mightn't want to go near you with a forty foot pole because you are such a screeching nasty scolding tyrant; a pain in the neck, a crashing bore and a sly, ruthless megalomaniac?

The top end of town
Though they are arguably less trigger-happy and blatantly disrespectful, better-educated men are also far from sanguine about the alterations that changed social and economic circumstances have made to contemporary definitions of manhood. According to Morton, their sense of dislocation and intimidation has been made worse by the contraction of their social and economic power at precisely the time women's opportunities are expanding:

> Women's range of choice in life has expanded dramatically as their economic dependence on men has lessened. It's this perception of choice that gives women greater bargaining power in their

relationship with men, power that some men find deeply threatening.[112]

As the breadwinner family model dies a slow and agonising death, middle-class men are increasingly bewildered about what it is exactly that women want. Morton again:

> But what will replace [the breadwinner role]? How will a man keep a mate if being a good provider is no longer enough? Will he have to become a raunchier, more skilful, sensitive lover? A better communicator? A sparkling conversationalist? Will he have to participate more in childcare and homemaking?[113]

Terrified of not knowing, or fearing that they lack the goods, men — some of whom are on the shelves that fertile single women are scanning — have turned tail and fled. Middle-aged John Birmingham, author of *Leviathan* and *He Died with a Felafel in His Hand*, trembles:

> I find myself surrounded by them — forbiddingly intelligent, attractive women, witty, forthright, driven and alone in the world ... [Over] beers ... with my secret stash of available guys, I broached the subject of why they'd never made any serious attempts on our mutual friends, the überbabes. Through a stream of drunken, barely articulate responses came a moral certainty: they were scared of them, and of what they would demand.[114]

Norm, from the American TV sitcom *Cheers*, tells a similar story, though far more succinctly. 'Boy meets girl. Boy drinks beer.' According to Canadian journalist and relationship guru Wendy Dennis, North American men are similarly distressed, depressed and confused about what it takes to attract a woman these days. Many claim to be as keen as mustard to pair up with the right woman and to (one day) have kids, but they feel unsure how to persuade her that they'll be a useful, or at least a satisfying addition to her life. Says one sad fella:

> [Men] can't kid themselves that they're superior to women anymore. All they have to do is look around them and see how successful women have become … They can't fall back on any of the traditional ideas about being a man — those ideas just don't hold anymore … I think men look at women these days and they start asking themselves what men are good for anymore … Lots of women give them the feeling that they're not good for much — except maybe to romance them when they're in the mood, or take care of them, on their terms, or fuck them once in a while.[115]

Other things bothering men

It is impossible to truly get to the bottom of why men behave on the relationship front in the way they do without understanding the impact of relatively recent changes to the laws governing child support after divorce. In both the United States and Australia, an unflattering history of male behaviour when it came to backing up sperm deposits with paternal support led to radical changes to the child support system in the 1980s. The intent of the changes was to put an end to the happy-go-lucky days when men could boast — as some did, according to one Australian family law specialist — that they didn't even know how many children they had and staggering numbers of children lived in poverty.[116]

Backed up by the DNA paternity test, the new laws make it the business of the state to track down a child's biological father and get him to start paying child maintenance. Using the taxation system where necessary, both the courts and child support agencies have been implacable in enforcing the new 'biological father pays' formula.

Much to men's consternation this has led, in both Australia and the United States, to a variety of court cases that have resulted, in the most egregious cases, to the biological father being allocated fiscal responsibility for his biological progeny even when both he and the lesbian mother considered him a 'known donor', and both parents had signed a paper stipulating that the man would have no financial responsibility for the child. In other cases, impregnating men have been told to pay up even when they had a mental disability, were unconscious, or even underage — and thus a victim of statutory rape — at the time of sexual intercourse.

For politicians, there are obvious advantages to enforcing the biological-father-pays formula: when men don't pay to keep their child/ren out of poverty, taxpayers do. Indeed, despite the fact that increasing numbers of men are paying the child support for which they are liable, 56% of Australian single mothers either never see a penny, or reap less than $3000 a year. In the main, this is because these fathers make so little money that they have no financial liability under the law. This supports figures that show that low-income men, when they do partner up — which they are less likely to do than high-income men in the first place — are the most likely to wind up divorced.[117] One report found that only 22% of fathers, those with some earning power, are making a major contribution to the sole parent's family expenses.[118]

The high cost of relationship failure is something that increasingly preys on the minds of potentially eligible men.

Among the factors reducing the desire of university research scientist Wooster, whom we met earlier, to tie the knot are his pessimistic relationship predictions and his observation of the financial hardship some men experience after divorce:

> I don't think about having children and having a marriage all the way through. One of the things that keeps me up at night is if I have children, it's likely that it will end in divorce just because of the sheer number of marriages that end in divorce, and then the financial ruin it will put me in.

This is not an isolated worry. As a recent report into the state of Australian relationships concluded:

> One background factor likely to influence men's attitudes to taking on a relationship involving marriage and parenthood is the financial consequences of failure. Most should be aware of these costs, given the media discussion of the topic and the large number of males responsible ... for [child support] payments.[119]

Ongoing financial liabilities for first families may also deter men from *re*marrying or, if they do dare to hook up with another woman, having another child with her. I know one spunky and committed father who splits the care of his preschooler with his ex-wife, but admits to being wary of a new relationship because the new woman might want children of her own and — should the whole thing fall over — he'd be liable for the time and money necessary to support another household. Interestingly, this man reports that few childless women are interested in him anyway. While he puts it down to their reluctance to mother his child, I can't help but wonder whether the commitment of so many of his resources to his existing child makes them suspect what is in fact the case: that he would be reluctant to have a child with her, and even if he did, his fiscal and emotional participation in raising the new child would be restricted because of his existing commitments to his ex-wife and existing child. Certainly the vociferous gripes by some high-profile second wives about the percentage of a man's income allocated to children of a previous marriage suggest that at least a handful of second wives (and perhaps potential ones too?) keep a close watch on this issue.

What women want and how they might get it

Despite all the angst, the answer to the question of what most women want is actually quite simple. What they want is men. And babies. In general, and I say this as a social researcher with over a decade's experience in probing women's plans and ideals when it comes to relationships and reproduction, women are quite traditional. The majority still want — when the time is right — the picket-fence dream: a bloke, a couple of kids, and the requisite number of domestic animals. Here are just a few quotes from the women I spoke to (selected from among a veritable barrelful), which express how much women want to get partnered with men and stay that way:

> I've always wanted to be in a permanent relationship. It's been a goal … One I thought wouldn't happen. At 35 I decided [that] statistically it won't happen. Statistically, women of my age do not meet the man of their dreams and live happily ever after … I had never been in a stable relationship since I was 20 until now. [Now] I'm married

and I adore my husband ... [I'm in] a relationship with the most loving and devoted — Troy is the most wonderful husband/partner. It is just extraordinary how wonderful he is and how happy we are. (Barbara)

I love my partner, we've been together five years ... I suppose I'm so happy because my partner asks for nothing ... He's got his own full life, and I have mine. And we come together and we love to chat about it all ... I mean I've said in moments of drunkenness [that] I hope we're together forever. That's what I would love. Forever and ever ... I've heard friends say, 'Oh, you know when it's the right one' and I've always thought, what a load of crap. But I do. So that's lovely ... [and] an amazing feeling. I can't believe that I've actually finally got that feeling. (Lorne)

Indeed, even the much-pilloried infertile single woman Leesa Meldrum made it clear to *Age* reporter Victoria Button that in an ideal world she would like to have a husband or be in a relationship, and that she regretted her life had failed to materialise into that 'picket-fenced fantasy'.[120]

The reality is that while marriage does not always guarantee children, the failure to marry (or to seriously commit on the partner front) nearly always assures childlessness. As childless by choice Latisha put it, 'I think love and marriage, horse and carriage, marriage and children', and most people agree.

The statistics show that the majority of de facto relationships, if they survive, become marriages. An extensive analysis of recent Australian Census figures by respected demographers Bob Birrell, Virginia Rapson and Clare Hourigan concludes that 'most young women are unlikely to contemplate having a child if they are not in a secure relationship'. This observation is backed up by those analysing the enormous Household, Income and Labour Dynamics in Australia (or HILDA) dataset:

> For all age groups, current partnering status is the most significant factor associated with predicting whether individuals expect to have children in their lifetime. The importance of partnering becomes particularly clear for men and women aged 30 years and older. The size and direction of the estimates ... show that expectations of childlessness appear to be linked to the current status of being in a relationship or not, and a measure of the stability of that relationship (crudely measured in this analysis through expectations of marriage in the future).[121]

Now as anyone who has read this far (or surfed the real world for .04 of a second) knows, it is not only knot-tying that stands between women yearning for motherhood and a babe in arms. Mary's reneging ex-husband Troy, Terri's immature David, Sharon's reluctant Martin, Kelly's adamant Ivan, Brenna's juvenile Ken and Bethany's uncompromising Jack are just a few examples of the male-centred difficulties motherhood-desiring women face after the knot is tied. Nonetheless, the non-negotiability of a stable relationship being a precursor to motherhood for most women means that stable partnerships are *necessary* for motherhood, though they are not in most cases *sufficient*. We have seen the reasons 'someday' fathers have for delaying marriage or remarriage: a lamentable cluelessness about the age-related limits of female biology and the negative impact of ageing sperm on the health of future progeny; the desire to first achieve employment security; and financial responsibilities towards existing children. However, another major reason happily partnered men are reluctant to father or — having crossed the daddy threshold once — to father again is the same conflict slowing many women down. The conflict, that is, between work and family.

Working-class man

Unemployment or low-paid work plus — at times — the sort of male chauvinist pig behaviour that sees dirty laundry morph into loungeroom art, is what makes these blokes so unappealing to potential spouses. One approach to their problem is to focus on getting them back to work that is full-time, secure and decently paid so that they can properly ante-up when bargaining with the girls (however many their number) who want breadwinners. Get that man the secure, decently paid J-O-B that will go some way towards compensating the woman who takes him on for all the domestic work he makes. Say Birrell and Rapson:

> Boiled down to its essence, a sizeable proportion of men now have less to offer on a predictable basis as providers than women can earn for themselves in the labour market ... What can be done about the situation? One answer ... is an improvement in the job market for men.[122]

How likely is there to be such an improvement? Not very likely at all. The pendulum has been on the reactionary side of its swing in both the United States and Australia for a long time, and neither government will abandon its ideological commitment to the 'lean' and 'flexible' workplaces that make working-class man's life so hard. We are currently confronted, comments Morton, with the 'perplexing spectacle' of governments that align themselves with traditional family values driving the very policies that are tearing such families apart.[123]

In the absence of breadwinning opportunities, working-class men may need to rebadge themselves as viable marriage partners who not only clean toilets and care for children, but even inventory the fridge and cupboards themselves and rectify all relevant shortages without being asked (in a process women have long referred to as 'doing the shopping'). They may need to share the domestic work, in other words, while their partners fulfil their obligations to earn some of the household bread. While this sounds breathtakingly obvious, it actually requires working-class men and women to redefine not only the gendered expectations they have for themselves, but also those they impose on members of the opposite sex. Less-educated lads are going to need to include pram-pushing and laundry-sorting in their definition of acceptable masculinity, while working-class women will need to find pram-pushing and laundry-sorting behaviour truly knicker-wetting, as well as incorporate 'does paid work' into their feminine ideals. As RW Connell rightly notes (though in the sort of academic-ese that makes me want to slap him): 'masculinities do not first exist and then come into contact with femininities; they are produced together, in the process that constitutes a gender order'. What men do and how they see themselves, in other words, is defined in response to what women do and how they see themselves — and vice versa. So if women want men to change, they can at least start the ball rolling by changing themselves.

The top end of town
Timing
The inflexibility of female biology means that women who want more than one child (and that's most of them) need to start breeding by their early thirties. As I've already discussed, given women's legitimate desires to travel, get educated, establish a

career and date before settling down, they are operating on a meet-and-greet schedule that would have taxed Princess Diana, and that has little margin for error. The high proportion of delaying 'one day, but not today' fathers, and the ever-present availability of younger still-fertile women when the time — for them — finally becomes right, only increases the difficulty.

Of course women aren't to blame for the rigidity of their fertile moments any more than men should be praised for a physiology that gives them more time to decide and put their plans into action. This simple truism, however, doesn't get in the way of the great majority of media on this topic doing just that: blaming women for the incorrect priorities or sheer stupidity that leads *them* (in the great and apparently solitary journey that is baby-making) to delay childbirth. The following, from a multi-page spread in a weekend paper magazine supplement, is a women-blaming classic:

> The truth is that there are an awful lot of women who are leaving it worryingly late to conceive. So, with feminist guns still blazing, can we admit that we have, in fact, got it wrong? ... The figures are there, and it's now generally agreed that a woman's chance of conception starts to decline at 30, or even earlier ... 'Some of this stuff is just biology,' says Stephanie Calman, 42, founder of the website badmothersclub.co.uk. 'Biology isn't sexist ... We're the generation that says about everything, "This is my right." Well, guess what? There are some things that don't respond to that. The problem is, you cannot f— with fertility. You cannot watch the egg-timer run out and think you can just turn it upside down and start it again. That's not going to happen. And that's the horrible moment when the bell tolls and you realise you've blown it.'[124]

Columnist Cathy Sherry has made a career out of blaming women for the various difficulties and misfortunes they suffer at home and in the workforce, except when she faces a problem, in which case it is the system that is to blame. But because Sherry had the opportunity to give birth before the chill winds of age-related fertility began blowing her way, she chastises women for the selfishness or ignorance that leads them to delay having kids:

> Women are most fertile during their late teens and 20s, and yet more women are delaying childbirth until their mid to late 30s or even 40s ... Most women delay childbirth in order to obtain an education, travel or pursue a career. Up to a point this makes perfect sense. Children make all of these things more difficult ... But at a certain point, somewhere in our early 30s, the advantages of delay need to be weighed up against the risk of childlessness. At 32 it would be good to have another three years unencumbered to do as we please, but is it good enough to risk not being able to conceive at 35? Many women are not aware that there are risks in waiting this long.[125]

Even when the women-blamers acknowledge that men also have a role in baby-making, and that delays may have as much to do with male priorities and schedules as with female ones, they nonetheless offer simplistic solutions for solving circumstantial childlessness: solutions that implicitly accept the gendered division of labour snd consequently belittle women's needs and concerns while letting men off scot-free. One set mocks the entire generation of contemporary women for being silly enough to believe they could 'have it all', and advises them to 'grow up' before it's too late:

We're the generation that was sold the Great Lie that you can have everything you want. You only have to ask a man to discover that this is rubbish — because men always knew that you were either at work or you were at home; you weren't managing both at the same time. It's obvious[ly] nonsense. But for some reason a whole bunch of us somehow got this fantasy that we'd be the people who could manage something no-one on the planet could ever manage. We've paid the price in various ways.[126]

Male privilege in never having to choose between fatherhood and career (and never blamed for selfishly wanting it all) is never mentioned. Another approach is to chastise women for being too fussy, and their own 'worst enemies'. This one advises them to get out there and grab a man — quick! — and get busy on their backs before it's too late.

Excuse me for noticing, but doesn't such a mercenary life-partner selection strategy raise serious ethical issues? I can just see the magazines that are currently urging women to hurry up and get on with it condemning those same women 15 years hence for the 'selfish' baby-hunger choices they made that have now ended in recriminations and divorce. More to the point, it is by no means certain that if women lower their expectations of men, the result will be increased numbers of marriages and children. The reality is that men are following their own timelines to fatherhood, timelines that are related to their own anxieties and 'selfish' preferences, and it's hard to see how a collective lowering of female standards will alter that. As author and Walkley Award-winning journalist Erina Reddan puts it:

Our body clock ensures we have to face … reality in our 30s. Men of the same age can drift on in their extended adolescence for much longer. When it hits men that they have missed out, they can marry younger women and still go down the family path.[127]

As my grandmother always says, it takes two to tango. Telling women to dance faster won't fix the fact that they're standing in the spotlight alone.

Miscommunication, misapprehension and misunderstanding

Unfortunately, while women were happy to tell *me* how interested they are in getting it on in a permanent sort of way with the male of the species, they often fail to make this raw desire clear to their male counterparts. Part of the reason for this is a desire to avoid appearing 'desperate'. Women sought to avoid desperation — and the appearance of desperation — for two reasons. First, in individualistic Western societies like ours, being seen as desperate is the social equivalent of tattooing 'failure' across one's face and strolling the neighbourhood. Second, for a surprisingly large number of women, 'desperation' was evidence of an embarrassingly unfeminist sense of pride.

To understand this, a little history is required. The second wave feminist movement — at its high point when most of my Generation X interviewees were coming of age — was firm about women's need to disentangle their sense of self from male desire, or approval. Women were advised to get their own lives and through them, a sense of identity and self-esteem independent from that earned through their roles as daughters, mothers and wives. Many of the women I spoke to took such advice to heart and were at pains to stress — à la Gloria Gaynor — how they would survive and thrive despite all relationship obstacles or lack of relationship.

Renata, aged 41, broke up with Justin, her childhood sweetheart, five years ago. However, despite being lonely, and well aware that the good ship *Motherhood* was about to sail without her, she feels angry at her mother's suggestion that she is 'desperate':

> I'm not going to slash my wrists because … [I don't have a relationship] happening currently. It's like anything; you make your life. You could sit home and close the doors and not go out, or you can get out there and be part of just what's happening and things that interest you … I'm quite happy. I mean it's hard to convince some people of it, like my mother, who thinks I must be chronically lonely and depressed … [It] took a bit of soul searching, as it does in everyone's life, but I'm comfortable with who I am, what I do … I go, I make my life, [I don't] sit back and wait for it to happen.

At 32, and well into her personal journey of self-discovery, Kaitlin also feels ready for a relationship. However, she is firm in stressing the 'completeness' of her life without one:

> I feel really ready to be in a relationship with somebody … an intimate relationship with a man who fulfils my needs, my feelings … I feel that, but I don't feel desperate, I don't feel incomplete. But that would be a lovely addition. [If it didn't work out] I think that would be very sad, because we all have needs and there is nothing more beautiful than to be held by a man. But we live in a world where women are just striving and men are not keeping up in many ways.

Thirty-four-year-old lawyer Sarah Highfield picks up this theme, arguing that it's only when women refuse to feel or act desperate that men will hoist their socks:

> I have this theory that women let men off with bad behaviour and it makes them think they can just do it. If you're so desperate to have a man that you will take anything, take any kind of behaviour, then what incentive is there for [men] to behave better or be more engaging and interesting people?[128]

Women don't just assert the completeness of their single and childless lives; they live it. Like Renata, they make their own lives, and have no intention of sitting around waiting for the phone to ring. Many travel and socialise with friends, and put significant energy into their careers.

This leads to a conundrum which a number of women are aware of. Refusing to dwell on their singleness or childlessness, they put their energy into finding satisfaction in those areas of their lives that are going more to plan and over which they feel they have more control: financial security, career and friendships. Office administrator Linda Berry, 37, who has seen a number of relationships collapse when the man realises she's serious about having kids, explains:

> I'm not a career-minded person ... if I [had] had a chance I would have had children in my twenties. I was ready to have children at 28 ... I haven't concentrated on my career, but what do you do when you haven't got a relationship? You work and buy a house.[129]

But as 33-year-old museum curator Sylvie points out, career advancement leads to being labelled a 'career woman'. This modern-day epithet not only leads men in the immediate dating vicinity to conclude that such a woman nightly sprouts the fangs necessary to eat her own young; it can also lead her larger social circle to see her highly successful career as the cause — rather than at least in part the by-product — of her being single and childless:

> People imply that I've missed out. That my life hasn't started yet because I haven't had children. In particular, artists that I work with, mainly men. They are kind of pitying about my situation [and] talk about it a lot ... Now that is particularly galling when they obviously find me professionally very good at my job ... I hate the moral judgment that goes with it: 'If you have a career you can't be a mother.' They feel like I have chosen to be a 'hard-bitten career woman' and to give up on emotionally intimate relationships ... They also seem to imply that I'm single because I work hard, so it's my fault. I've had this argument with quite a few men and I don't actually know what they are getting at. [Do] they think I should be at home waiting by the phone in case I meet someone?

I don't think Sylvie, Linda or any woman should be home waiting by the phone, or short-changing herself career-wise in order to convince men she is interested in having a relationship. I mean, to some degree, there is no other solution to this problem than to insist that men stop being so easily put off and otherwise screamingly pathetic in the face of smart, independent women. That they step up to the plate of the woman of their dreams, swing at the damn ball, and see what happens. Have a go! Ask her for a date and see what happens! This certainly seems to be the advice being offered by the almost-certainly female subeditor given the task of writing the lead-in to John Birmingham's snivelling article about 'überbabes'. Introducing the story, she writes:

> Beneath the thin veneer of his post-Lib sensitivity, the modern man is as bad as his Neanderthal predecessor, argues John Birmingham, and just as scared of his female equal. Isn't it time he got over it?[130]

But of course, and unfortunately, it is more complicated than that. Included in Kaitlin's discussion of her desire to 'be held by a man' was her assessment that many men are simply failing to 'keep up' with women. Lawyer Sarah Highfield's pointed contempt for badly behaved men is similar. The truth is that some of the demands contemporary women make of men are beyond the capacity of many men to fulfil. Today's men are falling short of today's women's requirements, and women haven't been backwards about coming forward with their complaints. Under such withering glances, is it any wonder that the boys shy away?

This, of course, takes us back to our discussion about the need for men, in a post-breadwinning world, to work out what they need to say, do, BE goddammit, to keep women happy. And the truth is that while women like Highfield have a list — most women have lists — the usually vague specifications ('attractive', 'intelligent', 'a good communicator', 'loving', 'ambitious') don't give even a bloke who's listening and trying really hard a helluva lot to go on. Nor are things made abundantly clear in critiques like those of 'Monique', a woman whose views are highlighted in one of those ubiquitous newspaper and magazine articles in which women loudly complain about the shortcomings of men:

> At my café book club there is one man and nine women. Go to Latin American dance class and there's a shortage of men. The girls have to pretend to be the guy ... [At a 50-guest party I organised] the men, to my mind, didn't put a lot of effort into their

appearance, they huddled around in groups together … but when you talked to them, it was predominantly about their work and sports. I couldn't find any other topic … I've started to feel that it would be easier to [meet a man] if I 'dumbed down' and lowered my expectations of what a mature, healthy relationship should entail.[131]

Male confusion means that change, slow at the best of times, has ground down to a snail's pace. Not to mention how hard change is anyway, even when the male changee has the best of intentions and is really giving it a shot (which is definitely not always the case). Deputy director of the Centre for Health, Sex and Society in Melbourne, Gary Dowsett, made this point in a recent discussion of contemporary sexual politics:

[The last 25 years] has been a tumultuous period in sexual politics … Women have moved tremendously in that time … [and this has put] the pressure on men … Of course, many men have not changed at all and others are too powerful to bother. But some sections of the male population have faced up squarely to the challenge of feminism and adjusted significantly. Not all men are unwilling to change, but the process of change is difficult even when it is willingly pursued.[132]

There is some evidence that fear of relationship failure is also stalling or halting partnering rates. This is an issue for both sexes. So-called 'pickiness' can result from an unhappy childhood experience of parental divorce. According to researcher Judith Wallerstein, for children of divorce, the legacy of their parents' marriage — which did not survive conflict but surrendered to it — is the false belief that any spousal disagreement spells danger, 'threatening to tear the fabric of family life, destroy ... marriage[s], and break ... hearts'.[133] Some decide that the only way to remove the anxiety that their marriage will fail as well is to pick a partner who is so 'perfect' that no conflict will ever arise between them. The outcome of such beliefs is that some adult children of divorce avoid relationship conflict, and when it inevitably arises, they cut and run (ensuring that they'll be tagged 'Peter Pan' if they're men and 'One Screwed-up Bitch' if female).

Women and men together: sharing the problem and the solutions to circumstantial childlessness

To summarise then, men contribute to circumstantial childlessness in five key ways:

1 Refusing to partner;
2 Delaying partnering;
3 Once partnered, delaying having children;
4 Once partnered, refusing to have children; and
5 Once a father, delaying having more children.[134]

As should be clear by now, some of the 'problems with men', while nameable, don't have easy solutions. Some men are, not to put too fine a point on it, emotional basket cases and must simply be put dow ... er, I mean, written off. Others, on crude measures of education and class, fail to meet the shopping specifications of the increasing number of women who are highly educated and looking to buy. Still others are dead-set against fatherhood; should an unsuspecting woman marry one of these and choose (or feel she has no choice but) to stay, then while she's by no means 'chosen' childlessness, she is indeed out of luck on the motherhood front.

However, some of the problems women are having partnering, and therefore getting to motherhood, *can* be solved, or at least alleviated. Increased biological knowledge and emotional sympathy between the sexes would go a long way towards soothing the meet-and-greet treadmill on which so many feel trapped.

If men were a bit more *au fait* about the limits of female biology (as well as about their own), they might ante up for marriage and fatherhood with their female contemporaries earlier than they do now. If women were more willing to try out a plumber or a 'chippie' for size, and to work up a bit more sympathy for how their überbabeness has freaked out and intimidated such blokes, they might have more options on a Saturday night. On the other hand, if men were less easily pushed away by women's not wanting-to-seem-desperate bravado, a bit more certain about who they were and what they had to offer as men *and* less pathetically fearful of getting knocked back every so often, they might find there are women willing to lay their careers aside for the night to share dinner and a movie.

In a nutshell, what women need is to develop some empathy for how much men see themselves as extraneous to women's emotional as well as material well-being. Given that the demise of the breadwinner template for Tarzan and Jane relations is relatively recent, they also need to temper their expectations of overnight behavioural change miracles from the Jungle Kings in their lives. For their part, men need to stop moping, get a haircut and otherwise make an effort to impress the female of the species instead of hanging around with their buddies in large defensive groups wearing clothes that either come from the homeboy school of fashion or need ironing. They need to try with women, in other words, and not behave like disappointed schoolboys when they get the occasional knockback. Losing a dating battle, it seems necessary to point out, is not the same as losing the intimacy war.

Above all, women and men need to be nicer to one another. More understanding, more open, honest, and decent. We need to consider how our behaviour might affect another vulnerable human being, because, says relationship guru Wendy Dennis: 'Let's face it — when it comes to matters of sex and love, we're all vulnerable little bunnies, aren't we?'[135]

The point, and I don't think it can be stressed too strongly, is that these are transitional times and we — women and men in our twenties, thirties and forties — are a transitional generation. Economies, workplaces and the ways of living, loving and breeding they make possible are changing before our very eyes. While demand for women in the workforce and the economic necessity of paid employment for most couples who want kids are, despite the dinosaur roars of some reactionary baby-boomers, an immovable part of the post-industrial landscape, the gender roles, partnership patterns and parenting practices that accompany these changes are still a work in progress. All of us are struggling to work out how we can mate and breed in the new world economic order. But we're either going to have to look history in the eye and spit on it together, or be dragged out to sea alone. As Dennis puts it:

> Yes, we're in a time of turbulence. But if we seize it and work it through to a more hopeful stage, we'll be okay. We can't just collapse and say we're powerless in the grip of history, lie down on our bellies and whimper and whine that it's not fair, it's not fair. We have to find a way to embrace living well, in the philosophical sense, with one another. And that's going to take some fortitude, some energy and some time.[136]

Fault shmault

What all this suggests is that circumstantial childlessness, and the plummeting birth-rate it is contributing to in most Western countries is neither women's 'fault' nor a problem that they can solve alone. If fertile women are to blame for their unwanted childlessness, then fertile men are just as responsible. Says Das:

> We cannot always have babies on cue. It's one of those aspects of our lives over which we do not have complete control. I was brought up to believe that having a child is a privilege — a privilege that is granted by the opposite sex. I think it is important not to forget that.[137]

However, as I hope I've demonstrated, it is also true that neither women nor men have as much control over the conditions in which they make decisions about partnering and children as they'd like. Indeed, the constraints are bigger than both of them: they arise from the economic and social conditions that shape the available options, and people's freedom to choose from among them. This makes recriminations against each other, feminism or God equally inappropriate and pointless. If we are going to solve the problems that are keeping men and women apart, we are going to need to work together.

We can do this first by ignoring backlash social commentary that blames the women's movement for women's and men's current dissatisfactions with their partnering and parenting options and outcomes. The implied solution offered by such commentary is to turn back the clock to the social relations of the 1950s, when women were relatively powerless and men were relaxed and comfortable. Not only would such a retrograde step be unfair; it would be impossible, given the absence of the economic structures on which such strict gendered divisions of labour were based.

Second, we can increase our collective reproductive freedom by seeing the opposite sex not just as fellow travellers in the charting of new relationship terrain, but as essential political allies. How this can be done, and why it is so important that it is done, will be the subject of the next chapter when the family-unfriendly workplace comes under the microscope.

Chapter 6

THE FERTILITY CRUNCH III: THE OPPRESSION OF WORKING MUMS (AND DADS)

Women can 'have it all,' if they don't need to do *it all.*

Anonymous

The Personal is Political.

Carol Hanisch

Women don't just *want* to work: they simply *do* work, and can't imagine their lives any other way. Women's jobs are just, as Sylvie put it, the air that they breathe. In fact, the role of paid work in their identity and imagined future is much the same for most women in their twenties, thirties and forties as it is for men. In the same way that nearly all young men in Australia and the United States imagine paid work as part of their future and suffer financially and emotionally when unemployed, few young women these days cast their minds forward to a future in which they feature solely as wives and mothers. In fact, according to researchers Lois Bryson and Penny Warner-Smith, international trends suggest that paid employment has not only become 'normalised' for women; it has become a 'priority, as happened much earlier for men'.[138] When 39,000 Australian women aged between 18 and 22 were asked what they would like to be doing at the age of 35, 91% said they wanted to be employed either full-time or part-time. Only 5% of women said they wanted to be full-time homemakers.

None of this should be surprising given the well-known correlation between female employment and female mental health. Having reviewed over 20 years of women's health data from the United States Institute for Social Research and the National Center for Health Statistics, researchers concluded that compared with a woman's marital and parenting status, 'employment has by far the strongest and most consistent tie to women's good health'.[139] *Backlash* author Susan Faludi says that the importance of paid work to women's self-esteem is both 'basic and longstanding'. Even in the 'feminine mystique' 1950s, when married women were asked what gave them a sense of purpose and self-worth, two-thirds said their jobs and just one-third said homemaking. In the 1980s, 87% of women said it was their work, not their relationships, that gave them personal satisfaction and a sense of accomplishment.

So why do women think paid work is so cool? First, they see it as a source of identity and pride: an important and socially valued way of contributing to the work of society. The economic independence it provides is also, for many women, key. This is particularly so for women who were raised by mothers who lacked qualifications or work experience and felt unfulfilled or even demeaned by the economic dependence involved in being 'just' a housewife: women who wanted something better for their daughters. This is journalist Sushi Das's story, and part of the reason why she has such a great career, but at age 39 is still childless:

> My mother was 20 when she gave birth to me. Many times she has told me that while she loves all three of her children, devoting her life to them robbed her of her youth, and the chance to see the world and enrich her life with more experiences. She tells me she will take her unfulfilled dreams to the grave ... Women in my age group grew up in a world where we did not have to fight to be equal. We always believed we were ... I grew up understanding that I cannot expect a man to provide for me. It is my responsibility to earn a living to pay for a roof over my head and food on the table. The opportunity to have a career was not just a dream to fulfil my personal desires; it was a means to earn a living.

Many of the childless women I spoke with were similarly influenced by their mother's dependence, disappointment and regret. They agree wholeheartedly with Das that they have both a right and a responsibility to pay their own way in life. Museum director Martine, for instance, remembers:

> The only thing my mother ever wanted for me was to be economically independent ... She used to say, 'Have your own money, be independent.' I think the implication was to not only be independent from Dad but be independent from your partner.

Judi remembers disapproving, when she was young, of her mother's economic dependence on her father:

> Had you talked to me in high school, I was like, Mom didn't have a job and I can't believe it and that was terrible and how could she be so dependent?

Darcy, too, has no intention of ever allowing a man to bankroll her life:

> Because I have spent so many years getting educated and working towards doing things, I'm very passionate about work, I couldn't not work ... I've been self-supporting since the age of 16 ... but I also feel very strongly about what I want to do, and I like the particular lifestyle [I have]. I don't expect ... to be supplied with that; I'm very happy to contribute to it.

Brenna saw her mother's reluctance to return to the paid workforce after she and her brother were in school as placing unnecessary strain on her father:

> [My dad] was a policeman. [Mom] stayed home. Even when I was in school my mom didn't work. I don't

agree with that … I think that she could have [gone] out and done something and helped my dad a little bit, so it wasn't so hard on him. I think it's hard to have to work and take care of all the bills … She works now … [and] loves it and is sorry that she didn't do it sooner.

For many women, the importance of work went far beyond its capacity to free them from *financial* dependence on their fathers, boyfriends and husbands. For women like Kylie, paid work is an independent source of economic and emotional power, purpose and pride:

I've just resigned from the position that I've had for the last few years … I had a wonderful time. But [I wanted to push myself out of the] comfort zone … My husband … has been pushing me for the last few years to come and work with him. [But] while I think that it can work to work with your partner … you really need to have that separateness of hats and areas in the business. Like, 'That's your baby, you run it, and this is mine' … But I haven't quite discovered what my area in [his] business would be … Everything that I've done in life I've always loved doing … but it hasn't been mine … I need to find [something that is mine] … [because] I like to be independent.

Jacinta also sees her job — she is an administrative assistant at a carpet company — as offering her much more than a salary. She sees work outside the home as essential to her personal growth:

I'm the office administrator, [but] I'm about to get a promotion. I've been asked if I'd like to step up into an account manager's role, which is something I've never ever done before, but the position's been vacated and the manager's approached me ... It will mean a lot more responsibility and a lot more hours. And I'm really excited about it because it's a really good goal ... [My partner and I] dedicate quite a bit of time to work. Work doesn't always demand of me the hours I put in, but I like to know that things are done properly ... so I tend to do more than what is absolutely necessary, but for me it's necessary.

Does this mean that women never feel pissed off, disappointed or plain unfulfilled by their jobs? That they never wish for a break or to marry or inherit the sort of wealth that could make them the proud owner of their own personal island and getaway jet? No, silly, of course not. As a colleague, a high-powered radio personality, confessed to me on a particularly high-stress day: 'You know, some days I seriously feel the whole career thing is totally overrated.' And it's almost a certainty that the fantasy behind the lottery tickets women in boring, low-paid jobs often purchase includes a scenario where they tell their boss to take his stinking job and stuff it.

But surely high-powered men have days when they'd like to pack it all in, don't they? And men in menial jobs buy heaps of lottery tickets too. The point is that few differences exist any more (if they ever did) in the ways that men and women value paid employment and that on good days, both men and women appreciate the economic security (and therefore independence) and emotional satisfaction paid work can provide. Both men and women need experiences that offer both pleasure and mastery in their lives in order to feel happy and fulfilled. Most of us derive pleasure from our intimate relationships with partners, children and friends, and gain a sense of mastery from meaningful involvement in the work of society. Ironically, paid work can be the linchpin on which both mastery and pleasure hang, for as many women have learned the hard way, without financial independence, their capacity to leave unpleasant — even abusive relationships — is severely restricted.

The work/family conflict

Screwing parents increases circumstantial childlessness
Anyone who hasn't heard of the conflict between work and family has most likely been living under a rock for the better part of the last decade. The issue has been, in the infamous words of the Australian Prime Minister John Howard, a 'barbecue stopper'. Yet despite all the talk, we continue to misunderstand the profound impact the work/life conflict has, not just on parents, but also on those considering becoming them. We continue to believe, in other words, that the sole consequence of failing to support parents so that they can raise their children well and undertake meaningful work simultaneously is making parental lives miserable. We don't recognise that it also contributes to rising rates of circumstantial childlessness.

Big mistake. As the stories of women's lives in this book should make clear, work/family stress profoundly influences not only women's timing of motherhood, but also their decision about whether or not they'll parent at all. Similarly, a growing body of evidence, some of it anecdotal, suggests that men have been similarly put off parenting, and even partnering, by the Herculean struggles of the parents they know to divide childrearing responsibilities fairly between them, and at the same time avoid fatal blows to their career. We've already heard about the anxieties men like Tim Wooster and Andrew Price have about starting families before they achieve some degree of job security.

In the same way a study of European couples showed men delaying the decision to have first and later kids because of anxieties about the impact children will have on their careers, and on their income and housing options.[140]

For decision makers to behave as though their government and workplace policies and practices affect only today's parents, not the potential parents of tomorrow as well, is both naïve and dangerous. Naïve because there is good evidence that some 'pre-mothers' are strongly influenced by the fate of their friends and relatives, and dangerous because policy change is unavoidable if the scourge of circumstantial childlessness is to be overcome.

The conclusion is inescapable: screwing parents increases circumstantial childlessness. Only through improving the lot of today's hardworking mums and dads can we reduce the number of women who are unhappy about missing out on motherhood.

How childless women attempt to 'solve' the work/family conflict
Careers as babies

The simplest way to solve the problem so many women anticipate in balancing work and family is simply not to have kids. This is the course taken by the childless by choice women, and also — though far less voluntarily — by some waiting and watching women, particularly those who are childless by relationship.

Given how often women are accused of choosing their careers over motherhood — read, being selfish cows — it will perhaps not come as a surprise to find that women are sensitive to this charge, and try to avoid getting caught in its net. I heard vehement denials from both childless by choice women and childless by relationship women that their dedication to career was behind their decision not to parent. They seemed aware of the contemporary social equation ('career woman equals selfish cow'), and having only recently seen another label banished ('childless woman equals selfish cow'), they feared being stigmatised as egotistical deviants once again.

Childless by choice women, those who were clear that their childlessness was their own freely made choice, rejected absolutely the idea that career had played a causal role in their decision. It had nothing to do with it, they all were quick to inform me. In fact — and unlike all the other childless women I spoke to — these women went out of their way to emphasise how little value they placed on paid work. The response of Deborah, 38, was typical:

> I don't think I'm a great feminist ... I think a feminist point of view is, 'Oh, you have to have your career and put yourself first and everything' ... I've never been a career sort of person. So I wouldn't have been the type who would have said, 'I've got to pursue my career and do all that, and then have my children when I'm 35' ... I've always treated work as just a means to an end: just a pay packet at the end of the week.

Lorne, a former dancer, also rejects any connection between her choice to remain childless and being career oriented:

> I'm not really sort of ambitious in a career sort of way. It's not like the old glass ceiling and all that sort of crap. I don't know, I just like balance, as I was saying before: work and leisure and all that sort of thing ...

But here's where things really got interesting. In contrast to the childless by choice women, women who were childless by relationship — who saw their childlessness as a consequence of their partner's refusal to become or act as a parent — were forthright about the important role career played in their lives. Kelly is typical:

[Ivan's refusal to have kids] has given me the opportunity to channel my energy and interests into other things, [which is important] ... because I'm not going to have a child. I feel the need to work hard on leaving something else behind ... whether it's people remembering me for something I did for them ... I'd just like to think that there was a point to me being here ... So I started to get involved in the project where I work now. And that's turned into my baby. I have physically created something from nothing ... I advise clients ... Because women have such anxiety about their bodies. 'I'm fat.' Or, 'I'm a size this' ... I just wanted to try and stop people from getting so hung up about that ... I enjoy who I am when I am there. Because people come in and they ask your advice. And listen to what you say.

Why, I wondered, didn't older women who were childless by relationship have the same concern as those who were childless by choice that their decision bit to have children would be described as selfish if it was seen to result from a dedication to career?

The answer seems to lie in the voluntariness of the decision. For women who really choose childlessness, and are therefore vulnerable to the selfish charge, admitting to a passion for career would be to nominate themselves as members of another group of women that society loves to hate. In contrast, those who really didn't choose their childlessness — like women childless by relationship — feel free, once they have made sure others are aware that their childlessness was involuntary, to openly embrace other avenues for meaning and fulfillment in life, like paid work.

Jobs, not careers

I've already discussed the fact that many childless women believe working at home will resolve the clash they anticipate between their desire to work and their desire to be a 'good' mother. Here I want to look at another popular proposal: the downgrading of one's 'career' to a simple 'job'. Many of the women who accept reigning standards for 'good' motherhood, and see the problems caused by the family-unfriendliness of the workplace, conclude that it will have to be their own career ambition that goes. To attract Mr (wants to have children) Right and induce him to have kids, these gals decide they can make do with a 'job' which allows them to retain an independent income but demands they sacrifice the work satisfaction, prospects and conditions that are part and parcel of a 'career'.

When I spoke to 29-year-old Kristina, a travel agent, she rated career highly, and was enjoying the fruits of the considerable effort she had put into developing hers. Having obtained a diploma and done a short course, she got her start at a small family-run agency before moving to a larger one in search of opportunities for advancement. However, Kristina has a strong commitment to having children one day, and when they arrive she wants to take a leaf out of her mother's book and look after them herself. Her solution? To abandon her career for full-time motherhood in the early years, and then re-enter the workforce by taking a 'job':

> My mum … [is] not big on daycare from when they are really little. My mum actually had a business when I was younger, but there's never a day that I can remember that she wasn't there to drop me off at school, or pick me up after. Even if I had to go back to the business with her, she always put me first. Mum and Dad had a [smallgoods] business and they used to work astronomical hours … but Mum was always there for the kids. Even if the kids were actually with her in the shop, she was always there and she'd always make sure we had dinner with her … I think that's

why Mum thinks that back in those days she could do it, so I think she's not a supporter of women going back to work two weeks after you've had a baby … I honestly think if I had a baby, I'd want to stay home with it at least for the first couple of years, and then I think I'd like part-time work. But I always think that if you're going to take the time to have a baby, then for the first couple of years it is important that you are around. But not necessarily all the time, once they get a little older. I mean I think the way that we were brought up was fantastic, because my mum kept active, but I never felt like they were never there for us … If we were sick, she wouldn't go in to work, because it was their business.

Shaney, 37, described her career as 'very important' to her, and speaks passionately about the discrimination she and other women she knows suffer at work because they are female:

I still get angry about [the fact that] women are still — and I see this all the time — not given the credit that they are due just purely because they are female. And I see this in the business world all the time. I managed a company that was in an industry that was very male oriented and it used to make me sick. The number of women in a meeting, including me, that would just be talked over. They wouldn't think of doing it to each other … Often if I or another female started talking you'd be halfway through your first sentence [and the men would act] as though you weren't even speaking, as though they weren't even hearing you speak. That you were just a nothing. And I see that still, even where I'm working today.

Perhaps in part because of these disappointments and frustrations, Shaney is eager to abandon her career when she has children and return to a 'job' when they're at school:

> [If I have kids] I'll probably still work, so it [won't be] entirely wife and mother. Though mind you, I'd love to stay home for a few years and do nothing.

Staying home and 'doing nothing' for years, however, means marrying a man of means. When 32-year-old Lori felt her successful career was impeding attempts to land such a man, she began strenuously insisting that when she became a mother, she'd give paid work up entirely:

> I want … to get married … I'm ready to do that.
>
> *Me:* What kind of person are you are looking for?
>
> He has to be ambitious, similar qualities and traits that I have … successful.
>
> *Me:* Why are ambition and success so important?
>
> I need to live in a comparable place, and lifestyle that I grew up in … I'd stop working when I had kids, because I love kids so much … Like right now, I'm really into my career. I'm really into working, and I'm travelling and all that, but if I had a kid, I'd give it up in a heartbeat. People don't believe that, even my ex-fiancé had trouble, as did his mother. She was like, 'She has a career' and da da da, but I could care less [about a career] at this point, because I've done what I wanted to do. I've become pretty successful in my mind, and have a good name out there. I've established myself and hit goals … I always say to my

friend Lynn (she's working), 'Just get married and [we] won't ever have to work again. [We can] play tennis.'

Some women intend to turn to jobs only temporarily, until the children get a bit older, but anecdotal evidence suggests that things don't always work out that way. In a private discussion with an eminent Australian researcher involved with work/family issues she said many stories were told of professional women who'd found themselves 'stuck' in part-time jobs, and unable to get back into the full-time work they needed if they were to move forward in their career. And anecdotal evidence suggests that whether women want to be there or not, the careers of those working part-time languish in the doldrums. In 1998, freelance journalist and mother Jane Cafarella wrote:

> Those who take advantage of [flexible work arrangements and part-time employment] disadvantage themselves in other ways at work. Their loyalties are seen to be divided and they are taken less seriously. They have fewer opportunities for promotion, they earn less, and those who try to fit in with school hours miss out on important meetings and social gatherings and risk becoming marginalised. And this is unlikely to improve in the short term [given] the current work environment, where even basic entitlements such as sick pay are now considered negotiable and employers are demanding more and more for less and less.[141]

Six years later, little appears to have changed. In an opinion piece in the *Age*, part-time worker Dr Louise Watson argued passionately for the elevation of part-time employees to the status of 'serious worker':

If a woman wants to work part-time and have a career — as opposed to just a job — she has to learn how to disguise [this desire]. Working parents who try to balance their work and family lives face entrenched discrimination. Very few employers provide genuine career paths for part-time workers — either male or female. Part-timers are relegated to the 'mummy-track' or the 'daddy-track', where they are stuck in low-status jobs and denied opportunities for promotion. Corporate culture assumes that part-timers are not interested in building careers because they want to spend time with their families — for some reason, these two goals are seen as mutually exclusive.[142]

I'd love to see some proper research done on this issue so we knew how many part-time workers feel stuck in such work, and that their careers have been negatively affected by working part-time. Then women and men would be better able to judge — before they did it — the effects scaling back their working hours might have on getting back on track later, when they were ready.

Staying home full-time

In 2003, the *New York Times* magazine ran a front-page story about the return of the 'stay-at-home' mum. According to journalist Lisa Belkin, this flight from career represented a refusal of women to submit to the male-oriented demands of work. Having spent their twenties earning postgraduate degrees and forging careers in the law, business and the media, these women were abandoning their careers suddenly and choosing to stay full-time at home when they realised that motherhood was the most important job of all.

Choose? Choose?! Here is just a small sample of the stories Belkin's so-called opt-out generation — women she describes as 'elite', 'successful' and married to men with 'substantial salaries and health insurance'[143] —told her about why they left work.

Columbia law school graduate Katherine Brokaw moved to Atlanta with her husband to ensure a short commute to her law firm. She worked full-time and had a great nanny. But when her daughter was just six months old, Katherine became the lead associate on a major case, which forced her to spend three months working a 'crushing schedule' of up to 15 hours a day, seven days a week while nursing a child who was still not sleeping through the night. When the trial date arrived, the judge postponed the case and then took it off his calendar indefinitely. Later, Katherine found out he'd decided to spend two weeks fishing.

Journalist Sally Sears, a mother of one, took nine years to quit her six-figure job in TV and, according to Belkin, did so with regret. 'I would have hung in there,' she said, 'but the days kept getting longer and longer.' She tried to go part-time but her station refused, saying it was all or nothing. Says Sally, now the homeroom mom at her son's school, 'It was wrenching for me to leave Channel 2. I miss being the lioness of the newsroom — walking through and having the interns say "There she goes." It kills me that I'm not contributing to my [retirement fund] anymore.'

What these stories make crystal clear is that it was not choice, but a palpable lack of it, that drove these women from the workforce. Indeed, one researcher investigating the stay-at-home decision of highly successful women found that a large proportion felt this decision was forced on them by 'long workweeks, unsympathetic employers and inflexible workplaces'. The majority (66%) would have preferred to be back at work.[144] Despite acknowledging the difficulties her interviewees faced in corporate America, Belkin nonetheless implies that these women have bowed out because of a peculiarly feminine desire for 'balance', and a lack of ambition and drive:

As these women look up at the 'top', they are increasingly deciding that they don't want to do what it takes to get there. Women today have the equal right to make the same bargain that men have made for centuries — to take time for their family in pursuit of success. Instead women are redefining success. And in doing so, they are redefining work ... There is nothing wrong with money or power. But they come at a high price. And lately when women talk about success they use words like satisfaction, balance, sanity ... why don't women run the world? Maybe it's because they don't want to.[145]

Belkin's uncharacteristically sloppy analysis here (her work for the *Times* is usually first-rate) falls down in a number of places. First, and most importantly, she assumes that what women do is what they *choose* to do. Not only is such a presumption illogical; it also has little in the way of evidence to back it up. Unfortunately, this has not stopped it corrupting not just the conclusions of journalists, who could be forgiven for not knowing better, but of some sociological researchers, too. I'm speaking here about the work of British sociologist Catherine Hakim, who confidently argued from the facts of female workforce participation that women choose the low-quality work in which they predominate. The reason women choose low-paid, insecure jobs, says Hakim, is that most women (read, the good ones) are like grateful slaves: selflessly dedicated to their children and husbands, and grateful for any work at all as long as it provides the flexibility they need to put their families first.

In a world in which the law, social attitudes and economic realities constrain women's freedom to choose their employment, and practically everything else, it is patently absurd to extrapolate from what women do to what they'd actually *choose* to do were they truly free to decide. To discover the latter it is necessary to ask women, preferably when they are still young enough to either be unaware of or not feel intimidated by the social forces that may later place a ceiling on even their dreams about their future aspirations. On the other hand, those interested in generating data in support of reactionary social agendas will act, as has Hakim, to prop up the 'does equals wants' equation. This is because the 'does equals wants' equation means all is right with current social and economic structures — that women are freely choosing the economic and employment disadvantage they suffer — and business can carry on as usual.

The other irritating thing about Belkin's justification for why she arrived at 'choice' as an explanation of the 'opt-out' phenomenon is her false contention that women today have the same freedom as men to 'take time' out from their family 'in pursuit of success'. The fact that they don't therefore proves that women are fundamentally different from men: less interested in 'money and power' and more focused on 'satisfaction, balance and sanity'.

Whoa there, Nelly! In the world I live in, the consequences for women and children of trading family time for work success are — in the main — totally different from those faced by men. When women trade off family time for paid work, the usual consequence is that their children spend time in paid care, and women face a second shift of epic proportions when they finally do get home. In one Australian workplace, there was a vast difference between the number of senior female managers who did the majority of unpaid work at home (42%) and the number of male managers who did (4%).[146] Indeed, the effects of ambition on maternal well-being are so well known that they partially explain why goal-oriented women decline to have kids in the first place. A recent photo in the *Sydney Morning Herald* said it all. Beside each minister in the Howard Government was the number of children they'd 'produced for the nation'. While male ministers in the most demanding portfolios have between two and five children each, the highest level female ministers, Kay Patterson and Amanda Vanstone, are childless.

As this fertility count suggests, the cost of success for working mums and working dads couldn't be more different. When men bargain away time with their families for work success, their usually full-time wives nearly always pick up the tab. That's why male success is a predictor of more children, not fewer. Internationally, this story is the same. Almost without exception, corporate high-flyers — nearly always blokes — have a full-time wife holding the fort at home. In the rare cases where the CEO is a woman, she has a house-husband.[147]

The point is that as things currently stand, Belkin's assertion that it is different feminine values, rather than harsher female realities, that are driving women to opt out lacks even the most basic evidential support. This is not to say that women and men might not have different definitions of life success, or different levels of willingness to act on them. They might, and they might not: what particular middle-class women are doing in response to extreme levels of work/life stress indicates little either way.

What it does indicate is that in the face of a system that is badly broken, and with little hope of structural adjustment on the horizon, women with fiscal options will exercise whatever options are available to them to fashion the best private solution they can for themselves and their individual families.

The problems with stay-at-home mothers and breadwinning dads

OK, this is the part where people are going to start throwing rocks but I'm going to say it anyway. Women 'choosing' to stay at home as a means of resolving the work/family conflict is a problem. Not, of course, on a personal level. In a society where the demands of work are radically out of kilter with the demands of family life, and in which women bear nearly all the negative consequences of that imbalance, individual women may well be justified in doing what they see as necessary to ensure their family's well-being. Like Allison Pearson's fictional working mum Kate Reddy, many are simply collapsing under the stress of doing it all and have no option but to find a better way — and 'stat'!?

The problem comes when the solutions such well-heeled women arrive at under duress are valorised as answers for everyone, rather than highly personal solutions to political problems. The problem is when such stories are seen as evidence of women's choices, rather than of the fight/flight decisions of cornered animals. When journalists such as Belkin refuse to acknowledge how men's unwillingness to share the domestic burden has severely limited women's work/family choices, they encourage women to direct their anger and frustration in on themselves, rather than at the men and the male-dominated institutions that have failed to provide them with real and deserved opportunities to be both good parents and productive workers. Worse, shoddy journalistic analysis encourages women to blame feminism for telling them they can have it all, rather than the system that, despite concerted feminist efforts, has so far refused to change enough to give working parents and those who want to be them a fair go.

As it happens, Belkin is innocent on this count, but TV news presenter Virginia Haussegger is not, and on the Australian landscape, she is not the only rising feminist-blaming star. The *Australian*'s Miranda Devine and Janet Albrechtsen represent a new generation of female columnists whose ignorance of feminist history is surpassed only by their determination to obscure the real forces that limit women's choices.

Finally, journalists stand condemned for their continuing failure to expose the central fallacy of their endless cant that women 'can't have it all': that it is women's job — and the job of women alone — to make the two-earner household function properly. After all, the underlying 'thinking' runs, it was women who walked out on 'their' job of looking after home and hearth to enter the workplace, and consequently it is their responsibility to clean up the mess that's resulted. Surprisingly, even some well-known feminist activists and bureaucrats are guilty of this sort of woman-stands-alone logic, foremost among them Anne Summers and Australian Sex Discrimination Commissioner Pru Goward. In her recent book *The End of Equality*, Summers repeatedly refers to 'women whose children use formal care' and the fines childcare centres impose on 'mothers' who 'pick up late'.[148] Fathers are never mentioned. Similarly, Goward's recent campaign to increase the family-friendliness of the Australian workplace focused exclusively on maternity — rather than paternity or parental — leave. With this level of analysis from feminist leaders, no wonder so many women feel they have only themselves to blame when they can't make the working mother role fly, and come near to collapse from the stress and guilt of trying.

The classist waffle of choice

Another problem with the 'choice' explanation for working mothers' retreat from the workforce, and many working women's delay of motherhood, is that it studiously avoids the issue of class. You see, the whole idea of motherhood (but not fatherhood) as a temporary career move assumes that maternal careerists are married to men making big enough bikkies to support their 'choice'. Though she declines to let it alter her opt-out thesis, Belkin admits that the mothers at the centre of her story are elite women with rich husbands, which means they can afford the choices they make. At least she's honest. In contrast, Miranda Devine conveniently omits the inconvenience that social class brings to her thesis about contemporary women's bountiful reproductive choices. In 'Yes, sister, choose what you want', Devine lauds something she calls 'new feminism' (which I've never heard of, before, or since), claiming that its bounty is women's reclamation of

> marriage, motherhood, femininity and domesticity as valid feminist choices rather than some sort of betrayal of gender. [The new feminism] can be charted from 2001, when Newsweek ran a cover story with a picture of a pregnant woman and the headline 'The truth about fertility: why more doctors are warning that science can't beat the biological clock.' It was about that time young women started to confront the false belief their fertility would last well into their 40s and they could put off having babies for decades ... new feminists don't have to drool over their babies and their appliances ... They don't have to give birth, or get married. They don't have to be CEOs or run their own successful businesses. The secret of the new feminism is that ... women have the freedom to make the choice that suits them best.[149]

Angela Shanahan is another columnist whose comments on the nature of good motherhood also conveniently omit the financial privilege that enabled her to choose motherhood as a career. Instead, Shanahan pretends that it was her own dedication to the values of maternal self-sacrifice that led her away from work 'done for money' and towards her true maternal 'vocation'. Yet in the same piece, Shanahan admits that it was only hubby Dennis's promotion to a 'well-paid job ... with the *Australian*' that allowed her to do it all for love:

I was offered a full-time job in a selective school —
but I was not prepared to leave a baby in full-time
care. I have an unshakeable conviction that
institutional care is too impersonal for a baby's
emotional wellbeing. The instinctively physical nature
of the mother–baby bond is something too many
women of my generation won't admit and enjoy. For
this reason, I began working less ...[150]

The problem for most mothers is that they lack a loaded
husband. Indeed, some lack any male at all. This means that while
Belkin's opt-out generation, and women like Shanahan, are
undeniably lucky, their decisions — and the unsolicited advice that
comes with them — have little relevance to most women's and men's
lives, and offer few insights into the changes that would have to be
made to government and workplace policies and practices if there
was a genuine desire to ease the burden borne by the majority of
parents who want or need to work. As I argued recently in the
Sydney Morning Herald:

For the rest of us ... the choice is academic, given the
causal pairing of the stay-at-home option with the go-
to-the-poorhouse one. Seen in this light, it's clear that
respect for individual choice offers few answers to
most women and men struggling to solve the
work/life crisis.[151]

This is why when privileged stay-at-home mums claim
exclusive entitlement to the societal 'good mum' seal of approval,
I find it hard to contain my rage. Shanahan, for instance, lauds
her own choice to reject paid care as evidence of her good mother
credentials, but given all she's told us about her husband's earning
power, I'd say we know the truth.

Career motherhood and bitten bums

The class bias of the career mum 'answer' to the life-out-of-balance problem — and the unfair definitions of good motherhood that accompany it — are not the only reasons both should be rejected. Another problem is that opting out, no matter how appealing it may seem at the time, can wind up really biting women on the bum. While career motherhood may seem to offer women, as one of Belkin's interviewees put it, the opportunity for a 'graceful and convenient' exit from high-powered high-stress jobs, women often report high levels of difficulty returning to work — the kind they want to do and at the level they merit — after so many years out of the game. So years from now when some wealthy mother writes an op-ed piece about how no feminist warned her of the risks of staying at home, you can direct her here.

As Belkin notes in her opt-out article, the question of re-entry is the 'hot button' of the work/life debate: a question, she says, on which the future of women and work might hinge. Because if the workplace cannot or will not reabsorb women who left a career for full-time motherhood, the ability of these women to use the opt out strategy to manage work/life stress will be 'no different than their mothers', after all'.[152] According to Sylvia Ann Hewlett, the signs don't look good. Hewlett is the founder of the Center for Work-Life Policy in the United States and the author of several books about the work/family crisis. According to her research, women trying to re-enter professional life after having left it to raise children are finding it 'exceedingly difficult':

> As a society we have become very good at building offramps ... But we are seriously lacking onramps ... These women may think they can get back in, but my data shows that it's harder than they anticipate. Are they going to live to the age of 83 and realise they opted out of a career?[153]

Career mothers may face other problems, too. Recent findings suggest that women who step out of the workforce to raise children never make up the ground lost with their salaries, career trajectory or retirement savings. Research by Bruce Chapman from the Australian National University found that one child reduces a woman's lifetime earnings by $160,000, with each additional child adding $12–15,000 to that figure. These inequalities — and the relative or absolute poverty they result in — tend to impact most cruelly on women whose marriages end up on the rocks. As Summers argues:

> Policies that entice or coerce women from employment are increasing their vulnerability, making them economically dependent and reducing their future options. They may well be on a permanent slippery slope of economic dependency on a husband who, one must fervently hope, will never leave … no amount of legislation can remedy the fundamental financial inequality entailed in a woman's leaving the workforce in order to have children. When she does so, it is usually on the presumption that the marriage will last and that she and the children will receive all necessary financial support.[154]

Of course, as US journalist and author Susan Faludi notes, one of the simplest solutions to the financially devastating impact divorce has on women is to pay women fairly for their work in the first place. Women's pre-marital financial stash, plus their post-divorce work options, in other words, are as much responsible for post-divorce fiscal devastation as are the terms of the settlement. Faludi cites the conclusion of a federal advisory council that if the wage gap between the sexes were eliminated, half of America's female-headed households would be instantly lifted out of poverty.[155] Sadly, for women, this is only one example of how inequality doesn't come cheap.

Traditional families slow down the revolution

When wealthy high-powered mums and dads indulge in 'labour specialisation' — meaning she does all of one thing (unpaid work at home) and he does nothing but the other (paid work at the office) — they disadvantage couples who are struggling to share the benefits and costs of paid work and childcare more equitably. Well-to-do families also critically dilute the size and power of those sections of the workforce — among them actual and prospective parents — that desperately need change.

I've already had my say about the former problem: the main point is that it is simply not possible for a working mother, or a working father who does his fair share at home and whose partner also works, to compete in the workplace with a worker who has a wife at home. But each well-off family also reduces the number of employees in the coffee room grumbling about breakfast meetings and the low value accorded to part-time workers. They ensure, in other words, that there are fewer disgruntled workers plotting to achieve change in ways both large and small. The husband with the wife at home also exerts drag on revolutionary momentum because, as the biggest beneficiary of the unfair advantages his domestic situation confers, he's hardly likely to bite the hand of the family-unfriendly workplace regimen that feeds him.

Another problem with the 'traditional' family is that it ties the breadwinner into long hours and a daily workplace grind that preclude him from participating in a meaningful way in the life of his own family. While some men are obviously more than happy not to 'be there' in any way shape or form, others hate missing out on their children's lives and strongly believe that their absence undermines their children's development and well-being. Writer Steve Biddulph, for example, argues that absent fathers breed weak sons, while researcher Don Edgar contends that children with active, involved fathers have higher self-esteem and increased social competence, and achieve better results at school:

> The father ... has an 'additive' effect. Where the father spent time with his child, showed an interest in what he/she was doing, helped occasionally with homework, was a 'presence' to be communicated with, there were additional and significant improvements in self-esteem, school performance and general social competence. When there was aloofness or conflict, there were damaging consequences for the children. Moreover these positive effects of child–father interaction over-rode the effects of family income, fathers' educational level and family status ... children in two-parent intact families and children in separated one-parent families were doing well if and when the father was playing a continuing role in the child's upbringing.[156]

The point is that active fatherhood requires quantity as well as quality time. Biddulph argues that blokes at the office for more than the standard 40 hours per week simply can't be there as often as their children — particularly their sons — need them:

> The bad news is that even when things are going well in the family, it may not be enough. Even when a father is present, committed and available at weekends and evenings in a healthy marriage and with all the ideal conditions, sons still miss out. It's highly likely that boys have a biological need for several hours of one-to-one

male contact per day. Put another way, to have a demanding job, commute to work in a city and raise sons well is an impossibility. Something has to give.[157]

There is also growing evidence that at least some men find the breadwinner role oppressive, and do not freely choose it. A number of recent Australian studies reveal that fathers are 'now less likely to see their primary role as breadwinners and are more focused on their role in providing emotional support to their children'. One random telephone survey found, for instance, that many fathers see being accessible to their children as 'the most important aspect of their role ... in terms of the impact they have on their children's wellbeing and adjustment'.[158]

Some men say they had little choice about assuming the breadwinner role, claiming that they were pushed into it by their partner's attitudes and behaviour. Says one disgruntled Australian father who works full-time:

> I feel a bit resentful that she'd never worked in the marriage. She made a unilateral decision to stay home with the kids, which is okay, except it involved [the] unilateral decision that I'd work and bring home the bacon, with no flexibility to develop in the way I wanted.[159]

Says another:

> I know [my wife] has changed jobs and careers and that's fine, but she does it with not a lot of consultation. She seems to be able to do that. Whereas if I wanted to change, and up and do something else, it's a family thing — so it's very much still a 'breadwinner' role — although my wife would probably deny that.[160]

Ever sensitive to male oppression and dissatisfaction, Michael Leunig recently depicted the business suit as the Western male's 'burqa', with the stooped and unhappy-looking men wearing the 'fundamentalist garment' described as 'Men trapped and submissive/Men oppressed and hidden/Men as property'.

Growing male dissatisfaction with being 'just a breadwinner' can also be seen in survey results that show a growing number of fathers fed up with having only a few hours each week to spend with their kids. The vast majority cite workplace demands as the source of the problem. In one Australian poll, 68% of fathers said work commitments were the major barrier to their being more involved with their children.[161] Men in The Netherlands state a preference for working fewer hours when their children are young, with many nominating a four-day week as ideal.[162] A 2001 Newspoll of workers that appeared in the conservative broadsheet the *Australian* found one in every four men expressing mild or severe dissatisfaction at the balance between work and family in their own lives.

Gorgeous men

Not all men swan around in Mercs, run big companies, play golf on the weekend and rub shoulders with other oppressors in smoke-filled rooms. Indeed, some are so low down in the various social pecking orders that exist in Western societies that it simply isn't fair to hold them responsible for the oppression of today's working parents, or those of tomorrow.

Another small group of men can also legitimately escape blame for the family-unfriendly politics and practices that are making the lives of parents so hard and ensuring that there are fewer parents in the future. They are men who have the income and educational credentials to be part of the problem, but have chosen instead to be part of the solution. They are single men willing to commit to women they love within reasonable time frames, or when an unplanned pregnancy intrudes on well-laid plans. They are the married men willing to say 'yes' to a partner who wants to get pregnant while she's still young, despite his job anxieties and his knowledge that physiologically, he's still got time. They are the men who refuse to allow jibes about their masculinity or costs to their career deter them from altering their work hours so they can share the domestic work with their partner and be an active father to their kids.

They are the gorgeous men.

One such man is Mick Shuttleworth. While he frankly described himself as someone who got nervous when girlfriends began discussing commitment, because he feared he wasn't 'financially ready to support a family', when his girlfriend became pregnant, Shuttleworth rose to the occasion, taking more than two years off work to look after his daughter, now aged five.[163]

Daniel Donahoo is another man who didn't cut and run when unplanned fatherhood loomed. When his girlfriend became pregnant unexpectedly, he accepted the challenge of children and is happy to report no regrets. 'Everything in society ... [was] saying to me: you shouldn't do this. You're 25, you've got your whole life ahead of you,' Donahoo recalls, '[But children have] given ... meaning to my life. [They] made me actually grow up and take some responsibility.' The problem, says Donahoo, is that men aren't told they can have a fulfilling career *and* a long-term relationship with children. Nor, he adds, is fatherhood 'sold' as the amazing experience that it is.[164]

Our final gorgeous man is 'Ethan White'. Having split with the mother of his child, White refused to become an every-other-weekend dad to his young son Xavier. Instead, he walked into his boss's office and announced that his full-time position as a marketing consultant had just become part-time. It was a bold move, and it worked, though ultimately he found it impossible to keep on top of his workload. At that point he quit, spent a year working for himself, and now that Xavier is at kinder, has a four-day a week job in publishing. While it's been stressful at times, he has no doubt it's been worth it: 'I wanted to play a real role in my son's life, and I do.'

'Oh, all very fine and nice,' I can hear some of you saying. 'But aren't such men — dedicated to becoming fathers, and once there, doing the job well — scarcer than healthy eating habits on Halloween? Aren't such men the cream of a largely crappy crop?' Well yes, and no. Research by eminent American researcher Kathleen Gerson found one-third of men — those she describes as 'autonomous' (and what I'd refer to as a party mix of childless by choice and deadbeat-dad types) — are not interested in becoming a father or in maintaining any contact with their kids after divorce. Another 36%, according to Gerson, were of the 'Father Knows Best' variety, seeing their family responsibilities exclusively in breadwinning terms. However, the final third of men Gerson interviewed were what she termed 'moving towards' active fatherhood and equitable partnerships with their wives.[165] This 'one-third are gorgeous' conclusion gains support from American researcher Arlie Hochschild's observations in *The Time Bind*. Hochschild reports that in one corporate giant company, when male executives with working wives were asked how their lives had changed as a result of becoming a father, one-third replied that they now did more around the house, another third said nothing had changed, while the final third — in a stellar display of passive aggression — claimed they did even less on the domestic front than before.

The truth is that while some men are really trying hard, and often succeeding in their quest for gorgeousness, others carry on as if basic concepts such as equality and shared parenting were as foreign as fractals. Some 40% of British fathers don't even get home from work until after their kids are in bed. One can only hope that recent legal changes entitling working parents to apply for flexible hours will alter this abominable practice somewhat, but who knows? In the late 1980s, one US study found that while many workplaces offered significant periods of unpaid leave to fathers after the birth of their child, few men took more than a few days after their child was born.[166] Fifteen years later, and across the ocean in Australia, things are little different, with only 18% of men using flexible hours to balance work and family (despite their being offered by 93% of companies surveyed), and only 2% working part-time to help care for their own children. Indeed, according to the Australian federal government minister Kay Patterson, 73% of Australian fathers do not use any of the family-friendly provisions available to them. Add this to the fact that of the 30% of employees who regularly work more than 48 hours per week, 80% are men, and we see that the title of a recent article about fatherhood — 'Caring, sharing and hardly ever at home'[167] — seems sadly apt.

But a fair evaluation of gorgeousness shouldn't focus just on what men do; it should also focus on what they claim to *want* to do. As well, it has to take seriously the constraints on men's freedom to choose a more egalitarian partnering style and a more active fathering style.

First, what they say they want. Interestingly, while the public often ponders what the fairer sex 'really want', men are rarely asked about their innermost desires. A 2003 survey of British men found that almost half (!!!) of new dads want to stay at home and look after their newborn babies, 80% wanted to spend more time with their children and 68% said they would happily take the up to two weeks of paid paternity leave now guaranteed by law.[168] A 1999 survey of 1000 Australian fathers saw 68% saying they didn't get to spend enough time with their children.[169] The same desires were expressed when Australian fathers were grilled on similar matters several years later.[170]

So what's the problem? Men are quick to blame corporate America and Australia for halting all attempts at gorgeousness in their tracks. The problem they report, in both quantitative studies and through books like Daniel Petre's and Biddulph's, is workplace inflexibility and the belief that long hours are a sign of commitment to the company and thus necessary to advance their careers. Numerous women, and some men too, however, express cynicism about the validity of the work excuse. They wonder if the truth isn't that men are simply unwilling to make the necessary sacrifices and acquire the requisite skills to do their bit, but know where to lay blame for such shortcomings when social researchers come calling, pen in eager hand. As certifiably gorgeous man Shuttleworth puts it, men are not 'victims'; they are willing participants in a society that asks them to work long hours. Richard Fletcher, from Newcastle University's Family Action Centre, agrees: 'The economic obstacle argument is a myth. When dads are interested and understand what it is they are supposed to be doing, they make the time.'[171]

Such lack of forgiveness should be expected. Men, perhaps even more than women, have invested in the myth that we control our lives. In addition, men who have made sacrifices in order to do the right thing understandably feel bitter about blokes who make excuses for why they don't. Yet there does seem strong, indeed compelling, evidence that men pursuing active fatherhood are being forced to make considerable career sacrifices — the same sacrifices as working mothers, in fact. If we believe this is unjust for women, isn't it similarly unfair to compel it from men?

First the facts: what happens to men who pursue — or intimate that they might pursue in the future — the time and flexibility to do their fair share on the domestic front? There are workplaces where employees on flexible or part-time hours don't suffer career penalties, but they are few and far between. The majority of managers believe, and I'm quoting a stellar Australian example here, that if new fathers show any signs of resistance to the modern 'open all hours for business' workplace culture, then they deserved all the demerit points they get. Another manager in the same survey agreed. He stated unequivocally that men wanting flexible working arrangements were not 'up to the calibre' of worker needed at his enterprise.[172] In fact, one study of Australian male managers found that only 8% believed fathers should be entitled to 52 weeks' unpaid leave after the birth of a child; a mere 32% supported a paternal entitlement of five days' unpaid 'special family leave' per year; and just 22% felt that employers should be more responsive to their employees' problems balancing work and family.[173]

The situation in the United States is little different. There, only 3% of men eligible for paternity leave actually take it,[174] with approximately 90% of companies making no attempt to even *inform* their employees that they are eligible. An alarming 41% of American managers actually see it as unreasonable for fathers to take any family leave at all, regardless of what is said about family-friendliness and entitlements in the company's written policies.[175] Male reluctance to take leave because of a seemingly justified fear of committing career hara-kiri even affects the Swedes. While the recent legislative changes to parental leave provisions there have alleviated the 'he's not serious' stigma through the attachment of a one month 'use it or lose it' clause for fathers and resulted in a rise in the number of men making use of their leave entitlement, low rates of part-time work persist.

What all this suggests is that 'competitive' workplaces are hostile to anyone who removes their nose from the grindstone, not to working mothers *per se*. While social convention and pay inequality ensure that it is largely women who will attempt to modify their work patterns (by working part-time or using flexible hours) to achieve some balance between work and home — and wind up on the mummy-track for their efforts — working fathers who attempt a similar juggling act will suffer similar career misfortune. It is parental practice, not gender, which puts workers at risk of discrimination. This is shown in the harassment one active father suffered at his workplace from a colleague who insisted on scheduling meetings at 8:20 am and then loudly announcing that he'd save this dad a croissant because he was 'never there before morning tea anyway'.[176] It is also borne out by the rise in complaints made by Australian fathers to the Equal Opportunity Commission on grounds of parental status: from 1% of those complaining in 2002 to 16% in 2003.

But while there are men really trying to be active dads, and suffering for it, not all men are fighting the good fight at work. Some, as our 'one-third gorgeous' analysis suggests, are simply traditional blokes, and aren't that way inclined. But another problem comes from a frightening capacity of at least some men to deny the costs to their partners and their children of inequity in their domestic arrangements. Among many examples are those dads who regularly tell researchers that they spend 15–20 minutes with their newborns but are consistently clock in at just 37 *seconds* per day.[177] Another is the continued insistence of most men that they are already 'sharing the parenting equally with their wives'; despite consistent research findings showing that only 1–2% of Australian men have actually significantly increased their involvement in childcare.[178]

The issue is not just denial; it is also definitions. Many men, it seems, feel it's possible to be a good father while being barely present in their children's lives at all. Take corporate lawyer

Rowan Neilson, who proudly tells journalist Kate Nancarrow how he always planned to be a hands-on father. This is why when he comes home to his wife and three children at 7:00 pm every night, he changes nappies, reads books to the kids and, on the weekends, delights in their milestones. Then there's banker Rob MacIsaac, also a father of three, who gets up at 6:30 am to dress and feed the kids before heading out the door an hour later. He then stays at work until 7:00 pm, except for two nights per week when he leaves early and gets to the see the kids for 10 minutes while his wife ferries him from the train station to university where he is studying for his MBA. Every second weekend he does an eight-hour shift with the children while his wife works.[179]

Now, just as a little experiment, let's try substituting the word 'mother' for 'father' in the above stories. How does corporate lawyer Rowena's claim to be a hands-on mother fit with her early starts and arrival home at 7:00 pm each night? How impressed are we with banker Roberta's commitment to 'active mothering' when, without those 10 minutes in the car, there'd be 36-hour stretches when she wouldn't see her children at all?

The point is that while quantity time is built into definitions of good motherhood, 'any time at all' seems to be what contemporary definitions of good fatherhood are all about. This is either because good fathering is still defined as breadwinning (where absence is *de rigueur*) or because men are now kidding themselves that 'quality time' will close the gap between fathering expectations and workplace realities — in the same way that working mothers did in the now-discredited era of the 'supermum'.

In either case, children aren't fooled. New research by Australian researcher Barbara Pocock has found that children yearn to spend more *actual* time with their fathers, and the longer Dad works, the more his kids want to see him. Notably, no amount of time with their mother — whether she was a homemaker or worked part-time — mitigated this longing. The heart-wrenching nature of such findings, rather than their own needs, may be what ultimately compels prospective and actual mothers to insist that their husbands become active fathers. Because much as I hate to blame women for the inadequacies of men, the bald fact is that unless and until women refuse to allow absent men to get away with calling themselves good fathers, and to cover the enormous caring and housework gaps they leave, the status quo will remain. Says researcher Graeme Russell, it is only when women get cranky and insist that their partners 'make the same adjustments [they themselves] are making to their careers' that life-altering changes to employment and domestic life are set in train.[180]

Politics, NOT personal sacrifice

What changes are life-altering? What changes to the way we work and raise children do women, not to mention men, really need if they are to be the sort of parents they want to be — and that their children need — while retaining the power to earn and be successful at work? What sort of changes will be profound enough to encourage waiting and watching women, and their equally anxious male counterparts, to throw caution to the wind and start having the children they'd really like to have? Not, unfortunately, the changes that have been suggested so far by the Australian gurus of the men's movement, Petre and Biddulph.

Petre and Biddulph are clearly — on a personal level — gorgeous men. They are both men who saw problems in their marriages and the relationships they had with their kids, and made big changes in their lives in order to do something about them, and taking significant knocks to their careers in the process. These changes, if I've understood their personal stories correctly, meant reducing the hours they worked enough to care at least part-time for their children. For this, both are to be congratulated.

Unfortunately, it is these men's politics that are sorely inadequate for the gigantic social task I believe they would agree is ahead: reintegrating fathers into the rhythm and responsibilities of family life and integrating mothers fully into the world of paid work. In *Father Time*, Petre argues that men are entitled to full-time jobs that are fast-paced, challenging and meaningful. His basic claim is that men need to balance this with their responsibilities to be at home and participating in their children's lives, and that corporations act counterproductively by promoting long-hour cultures, and the individuals whose success was built upon them.

Yet if Petre's personal work maximum for full-time male executives — 50 hours per week and five weeks per year away from home — were also applied to their wives, there's little doubt that either nanny would be the one doing most of the caring, or both parents would find themselves being charged by the department of social services with neglect. Of course what Petre is really envisioning is a home situation that matches his own: one in which so-called active Dad flies through the door in time to read to the kids, who've already been dragged through the supermarket and fed and bathed by Mum. While he's reading, she will clean the kitchen, do a load of laundry and make the next day's lunches. Despite this, as Susan Maushart sniffs in *Wifework*, Mrs Petre barely rates a mention:

> Does she too manage to work fifty hours a week for pay and still feel sanctimonious about her parenting? Has she also learned the secret of elevating her children to the status of a business meeting? And what about her record on 'getting home for dinner'? Does she, like

Dan, win brownie points just by turning up? And, once she gets there, does a meal materialise for herself and the kids, just as it seems to do for him? Does Mrs Petre get written up in *Family Circle* magazine because she no longer believes her kids' needs must be sacrificed on the altar of her own career goals?[181]

What's at issue here is the unacknowledged, but absolutely essential, role of the mother in not only cushioning the children against the impact of their father's prolonged absences, but also ensuring that the children are sated, sweet-smelling and in their pyjamas when Dad arrives, so he can maximise the few precious minutes of 'father time' he's programmed into his schedule. Such arrangements are so far from any possible conception of equality between the sexes, and from providing women or children with anywhere near the time they need from the man of the house, it's a joke. The only problem is, no-one seems to be laughing. Both Petre and Biddulph are deadly serious.

Or highly realistic. The program for active daddies may seem woefully one-eyed and inadequate to working women spending long hours at the office and listening to their biological clocks ticking, or to exhausted mothers sweating it out by the stove — à la Mary Leunig — while a child gnaws on their shin, but they are not the people Petre and Biddulph are addressing. They are talking to men, and to men who are in another planetary zone altogether. Men who are ringing or responding to the corporate dog whistle that summons executives to informal weekend meetings, and to the office during the week well before 8:00 am, to prove their dedication to the firm. However sad we may find it, for these jokers a 55-hour week *is* a radical concept. More importantly, from Petre and Biddulph's perspective, it is a proposal guaranteed not to send the corporate world into a full-frontal tizz. Why? Because winding back to 50 hours, when 40 remains the official norm, can be seen as workplace reform, rather than as a radical restructure. It's tinkering around the edges, rather than really questioning the very way we organise employment and family life. As most blokes know, anyone who asks questions about the way the globalised economy works to achieve 'efficiencies' and 'growth' — especially if others start listening — stands a fair chance of getting hurt. Perhaps this is why, as a group, men are so unresponsive to radical proposals for change. As Helen Townsend found in her survey of Australian men, they are reluctant to join battles of any sort unless they believe there's a good chance of winning.[182]

The other problem with the active-daddies 'answer' to the work/family bind is that it is just as class-blind as the stay-at-home mum 'solution'. Petre's decision to downsize his workplace commitment to 30 hours in order to study and care for his children was predicated on his successful and lucrative legacy as the managing director of Microsoft Australia. Lucky for him — and for his wife and children, too. But while the over-inflated salaries of the corporate executives Petre seems to be addressing in his book would have the finances to do the same, the rest of us aren't as blessed. Most families these day need two salaries, or at least one and one-half, to stay afloat, which would make any choice to reduce hours (if that reduction meant a cut in pay) unlikely for most men. So while it's nice to see how the other half live, their 'solutions' are of limited value to the rest of us.

But what really angers me about the active-daddies program, indeed the entire manifesto of the men's movement, is its lack of politics: of the joining up, lobbying, petition-signing, placard-carrying kind. Instead of male leaders urging men to band together to defeat oppressive corporate attitudes and practices, they instead advise each man to make an *individual* choice about his work practices. Where they acknowledge the cost of that decision, they advise men to bear those costs alone. If you're a really gorgeous bloke, the implication seems to be, you'll realise that the benefits of being an active dad outweigh whatever work sacrifice — pay cut, daddy-tracking or even sacking — you'll be forced to make.

This is rubbish! In fact, it's exactly the same sort of rubbish that is fed to women about the pleasure really good mothers get in sacrificing career and identity for the love of their kids. Why, might I ask, should *either* parent take it on the chin for doing the socially necessary work of raising the next generation, and actually caring enough to ensure that it's done well? If societies need children and want them raised in particular ways, why should the citizens who step up for the job be made to bear additional and unnecessary burdens, while employers and governments, those institutions that most benefit from increased population, and the mercenary policies that shift the costs away from them and onto individual families, get off scot-free?

Towards full reproductive freedom

The time has come to say enough is enough. That it's become too hard to have children in Western societies today, and that something — other than the present and future backs of working mothers and gorgeous fathers — has to give. No-one has an unfettered right to have a child, but what citizens of Australia and the United States are entitled to is real reproductive choice. By real choice, I mean the freedom to either avoid or embrace parenthood: a freedom that neither women nor men — the parents of the future — have today. Unrealistic and unfair good motherhood standards, and the challenges women face both finding Mr (wants to have children) Right and meshing their workplace responsibilities to the demands of marriage and children, are all serious, and in most instances unnecessary, constraints on women's freedom to have children. For too long, women's misplaced shame has kept them quiet about the obstacles on the path to motherhood, and has led to the problem of circumstantial childlessness remaining unnamed. But until we face the obvious reality that in Western societies today, many women lack the freedom to choose the what, where and when of their reproductive lives, the forces impeding women's free choice will remain in play. Birth-rates will decline, making life for existing parents all the harder as services for children shrivel for lack of an adequate population to support them. As a consequence, the number of women pained by having missed out on motherhood will grow. They will suffer not just because of the lost opportunity to give birth to and nurture young, but because they were denied the freedom to choose.

This is why the growth in circumstantial childlessness matters and should matter to everyone, even if they are convinced (mistakenly, in my view) that declining birth-rates, no matter of what magnitude or how they are globally distributed, are good for the planet. It matters because reproductive rights are a subset of human rights and, as John Stuart Mill has so famously pointed out (see page 52), choice is at the heart of what it means to be human. Choice enables control, and as research repeatedly shows, when human beings lose control over important parts of their lives, their prospects for happiness are diminished. This may be particularly true of reproductive decisions; these can often be at the heart of the way individuals define themselves, and attribute meaning to their lives. This isn't only true of those who want to be mothers, as the stories of childless by circumstance women make clear; it is also true for the childless by choice, who define themselves as 'not mothering'. The point, and I'll return to it in the final chapter where I defend the rationality of a decision to mother, is that while we've thankfully moved past the era where mother was the *only* meaningful role and life path for women, we must take care to avoid — through our social attitudes and work practices — demeaning motherhood's place in women's identity and aspirations, and moving it beyond the reach of all but the well-heeled few. That there is more than one way to live a good life is beyond doubt, but parenting is, and will rightly remain, one way for individuals to pursue what philosophers call 'their own conception of the good'. How could it not be? What sort of people, what kind of society (egotistic? death-worshipping?) places no value on the work necessary to give itself a future?

Removing the constraints on women's freedom to choose motherhood will be hard work. Changing laws and negative social attitudes, like those that long surrounded abortion and childlessness more generally, was hard enough. Forcing the recognition and removal of the social and fiscal limits on women's freedom to have children — a task that must be supported by a more expansive and egalitarian notion of liberty — will be a great deal harder. Many, particularly those who either benefit from such inequities, or whose personal riches enable them to avoid them, may contest the claim that the rest of us are unfairly constrained. They can be expected to invoke the libertarian line that as long as there are no laws preventing pregnancy and parenthood, women are free to choose if and when they parent. That women are choosing to mother less, the argument will run, is an expression of the freedom of contemporary women to choose, not proof of its absence.

Would that this were so. But as researcher Robin Gregg explains, real liberty requires more than being able to decide free from governmental barriers. It also requires having the resources necessary to put one's choice into action. To have the freedom, in other words, 'to make, and the resources to actually exercise, choices'.[183]

What this means is that if we really care about what Australians call the 'fair go', standing back and letting nature or the market take its course will not do. If we want to protect women's reproductive freedom, and raise our birth-rates, we are going to need to act.

What women who want to mother need is a full array of relationship, economic and employment options, and the resources and freedom necessary to select from among them according to their own values. These are the conditions necessary for reproductive freedom to flourish in the developed world at the start of the 21st century. But how do we get there? What changes are needed to contemporary standards of good motherhood? What needs to happen to increase women's odds of meeting Mr (wants to have children) Right before it's too late? What changes to employment attitudes, policies and practices will help women get to motherhood not just once, but as many times as they see fit? Most importantly, in what way — and with whose help — ought women go about pursuing such solutions, once they have been identified?

In the next chapter, I attempt to find out.

Chapter 7

SOLVING CIRCUMSTANTIAL CHILDLESSNESS: ON THE ROAD TO PARENTHOOD TOGETHER

Never doubt that a small group of thoughtful committed citizens can change the world. Indeed, it is the only thing that ever has.

Margaret Mead

First, there was 'the problem that had no name': the malaise that Betty Friedan argued (in *The Feminine Mystique*) had infected non-working mums trapped in 1950s suburbia. Now, there's the problem no-one wants to name — 'And they call this progress?' wonders fictional mother Kate Reddy in *I Don't Know How She Does It*.

Women have long fought for the power to define themselves, the nature of their lives, and the futures they dream of. The power, in other words, to name. Problems without names are ones that can only be known by those who experience them. They can't be sympathised with by the rest of society nor thrown onto the desks of decision makers to be solved. It is all too easy for problems without names to be seen as personal rather than political in nature; problems that women must suffer — in shame and silence — alone.

Circumstantial childlessness is the 21st century's problem without a name. To solve it, the women who suffer from it must step out of the shadows and speak their truths. They must replace their misguided sense of shame with anger and indignation. Because childless women, particularly those for whom the sands of fertility are fast spilling from the hourglass of time, have a right to be angry about their lack of reproductive freedom. They have a right to feel indignant that while they are constantly chided for failing to reproduce, the role that outdated social attitudes and sexist and family-unfriendly institutions — such as marriage and the workplace — play in their decisions goes unmentioned.

It is wrong to blame women for circumstantial childlessness. Sometimes remaining childless is the best, or only, decision they feel they can make. Such decisions are worthy of respect, but they are also worthy of further examination. An examination that reveals the precise nature — and motives — of the forces that constrain women's reproductive options, and their freedom to select from among them. The forces limiting women's freedom to choose include society's unreasonable expectations of mothers and rigid political ideologies about the nature of choice and responsibility, and individual men and male institutions determined to protect their privilege in the face of rapid economic and social change. These forces have resulted not only in a reduction in the numbers of gorgeous men willing and able to pull their relationship weight and father their children actively; they have also undermined women's confidence that if they tie the knot and take the motherhood plunge, they'll be able — in the contemporary family-antagonistic workplace — to be both good mothers and good workers.

The time has come to break the silence. To replace each of the mythical beliefs that shape contemporary discussion of the so-called birth-strike with the truth about women's desires for motherhood and the forces limiting their ability to have the children they want. From this day forward, women must insist on both a moral and political right to what noted US historian Rosalind Petchesky calls the 'social and material conditions' necessary to ensure that they are really free to choose whether they will mother, or live a childfree life.

Circumstantial childlessness: the supporting myths exposed

1   There are only two sorts of childless women: the infertile, and the childless by choice.
2   We must call every woman's childlessness 'chosen', so she can move on.
3   If there ain't a law against it, then you have choice.
4   Non-choosers are losers.

5   Parents choose to have children and so must wear all the costs of raising them.

6   Good mothers don't work, especially when their children are young.

7   Kids ruin a good relationship.

8   Women can't have it all.

Oh, heavy, heavy sigh. Sometimes I think there are more dubious attitudes and scurrilous lies about choice, motherhood, marriage and employment than there are blackheads on a teenager. Most of these ideas lurk where they are hard to see and even more difficult to question: in the unrecognised assumptions that guide the most critical decisions women make about men, motherhood and work and the assertions and slogans of activists, business leaders and political decision makers. The time has come to lay them to rest.

Circumstantial childlessness is real

If we remove the ideological blinkers that have led us to automatically label the childlessness of all fertile women as chosen, we see a very different story, and the evidence for it is plentiful, clear and unequivocal. There is a small number of childless women who chose to be that way, and a larger (and growing) number who want to have children — and will, if the circumstances are right. It's critical that we keep our terms straight when we think, talk or make decisions that affect such women. Choice is choice; circumstance is the result of a lack of it.

Choice requires more than legal freedom (or, we're not as free as we think we are)

Civil rights supporters discovered this after the 14the Amendment to the US Constitution was passed in 1868 but Jim Crow laws in the South effectively prohibited former slaves from exercising their newfound right to vote. The freedom to choose abortion in the first trimester was enshrined in the 1972 US Supreme Court decision in *Roe v Wade* but it wasn't long before Medicaid funding of the procedure was denied to most poor women, abortion rights supporters discovered it, too. The removal of a prohibitive law is the start of freedom, but on its own does not guarantee it. As Petchesky explains, it is the social and material conditions in which people make choices that determine whether they have 'empty' rights, or rights that are real:

> Women make their own reproductive choices, but they do not make them just as they please; they do not make them under conditions they create but under conditions and constraints they, as mere individuals, are powerless to change. That individuals do not determine the social framework in which they act does not nullify their choices, nor their moral capacity to make them. It only suggests that we have to focus less on 'choice' and more on how to transform the social conditions of choosing, working and reproducing.[184]

When the social conditions under which we 'choose, work and reproduce' are oppressive or unequal or exploitative, women's capacity to control their reproductive fate is compromised. This is the story of women who are childless by circumstance. Such women aren't social losers, they are political losers. That is why political action, not personal change by those who can afford it, is the right way to ensure those who want to mother get the chance.

Parenting is not a 'lifestyle' choice
Cars, mansions and yachts are not ends in themselves. At a minimum, buyers hope their cars will get them from A to B, that their house will increase their access to space, privacy and prestige,

and that their yacht will increase their holiday pleasure. Even dogs, though they are sentient creatures and possess their own individual intelligence, can be purchased for the characteristics that most suit the needs of their owner (short-haired, minimal exercise needs, guarding capacities), and can be deposited in kennels or found a new home when their owners go on holiday or take new jobs overseas. Children, on the other hand, are not simply means to their parents' ends; they are ends in themselves. Indeed, the essence of the parenting project is the creation of a new and separate consciousness whose own means and ends may conflict with those of their creators. It is the other-oriented, rather than self-oriented, nature of the parenting decision that profoundly challenges its equation with lifestyle — or consumerist — choices. In addition, while a person can choose childlessness as a basis for developing themselves, or indeed can choose to parent for similar reasons, parenting takes on a social dimension in a way that childlessness does not in the context of a society in which the rapidly declining birth-rates are having catastrophic impacts. Finally, the way the militant childfree falsely describe the decision to parent as a lifestyle choice takes for granted the negative freedom that Western libertarian societies grant to the childless by choice to avoid children, but fails to recognise the absence of the positive freedoms that are necessary to ensure the same reproductive choice for those who wish to parent.

Good mothers can and do work, and can still be great parents

Myths about good mothers are killing us girls, killing us. There is nothing wrong with setting moral standards for parental behaviour. In fact, given the dependence and importance of children, they may be inevitable. The problem is that while unrealistic and gender-biased norms may increase the number of picket-fence mothers, they also reduce the number of women willing to brave motherhood in the future. What a conundrum for 'pro-family' conservatives! While they ponder their way out of it, I suggest that women — those who are mothers, and those who hope to be mothers one day — liberate themselves. Insist on recognition for the moveable feast of good motherhood definitions that exist across cultures! Reject contemporary definitions of middle-class motherhood as classist, and thinly disguised tools of social control! Defend unisex standards of good parenting! Define children as a social good, and demand state support for the work of … Oh well, I can dream, can't I?

Good relationships can — and do — include children

Nothing ventured, nothing gained, as the old saying goes. Relationships need to change and grow, and children can provide the impetus for the deepening of intimacy necessary for a relationship's long-term survival. And don't forget, relationships with children bring meaning and a satisfying intimacy of their own. While the unfair over-burdening of women with the lion's share of the child-raising responsibilities means that mothers must whine about the unnecessary depth of sacrifice men and male-dominated society demand of them, it would be good if mothers could also remember to speak out about the pleasures of relationships with children, and of raising them with someone you love.

Women will have it all when they don't do it all

You know by now what I think of the claim that the work/family crunch is the result of women trying to 'have it all': it's reactionary drivel, dressed up as homespun pragmatism. The only retort to those who insist on describing the problem this way is to ask why, if it is fair that men can have it all when it comes to work and family, that it is so damn unreasonable for women to expect the same? Sure, the way work and domestic life are currently organised, women can't have it all without doing a superwoman with a triple bypass every day, and collapsing every night under the weight of their own guilt, frustration and exhaustion. But the problem with this picture is the way work and domestic life are currently organised. Women aren't the only ones losing out to misplaced social nostalgia about white picket fences. Men are too, not to mention children. The take-home point is this: parents need to share work and family obligations, not only because this is what's fair and because it's the only way to ensure that both have opportunities for mastery and pleasure in their lives, but also because this is the arrangement that's best for children.

Men are the problem, but they've got problems, too

Inside at least one-third of the male population is a gorgeous bloke struggling to get out. Men haven't spent the last four decades under a rock (though I know some of them look that way). They are more than aware of women's expectations on the intimacy front, and that they are failing to meet them. Many also know, or suspect, the pleasures of fatherhood, and worry about the impact — on themselves and their children — of not being around when their kids are young. Yet like women, they hesitate to wear the exorbitant career costs society impels them to accept for doing the right thing by their partners and kids. Who can blame them? So the next time you feel like throttling some male commitaphobe, or catch sight of a harried-looking father trying to slip out the office door at 5:00 pm, remember that they have problems much like ours, and in the political fight to reorganise work so that families can form and thrive, they are the circumstantially childless women's and the working mums' most important allies. Defeating circumstantial childlessness requires recognising the basic fact that men are not our enemies; they may even be our salvation.

Changing the way we think about childlessness, choice, motherhood, children, the workplace and the power and potential of different sorts of men is essential to challenging the myth of a birth-strike, and recognising how circumstantial childlessness is undermining women's reproductive freedom, and contributing to fertility decline in the West. But we must go further. We must not only name the problems, but also name the solutions — and the tactics needed to achieve them — before it's too late. Because the truth is that an entire generation of women has been, or stands on the cusp of being, lost to circumstantial childlessness. Without immediate remedial action, we stand poised to lose another.

Most fish prefer a bicycle

Judging by the women I spoke with (and by the upsurge in popularity of titles like *If Men Are Like Buses Then How Do I Catch One?* and *So You'd Like to Increase Your Attractiveness to Men*), women still want to 'get with' men as much as they ever did. Not just for love, companionship, or even (as one sassy single put it) 'entertainment' — though these things are important — but also to have children. As researchers Bob Birrell and Virginia Rapson note, even for an educated woman with a solid career and cash to burn, when the biological clock starts ticking, a stable partnership 'bestow[s] considerable benefits': namely, an on-site sperm donor to create, and a father to help raise, her child.

Most women know this. And if it is the case that some tail-end baby-boomer women and older Gen Xers were confused about their own physiology, recent media blitzes and much publicised hand-wringing from fertility experts will have left the remainder of the female population in little doubt. Teaching physical facts is one thing, but using those facts to push mothers back behind the picket fence or maintain the child-antagonistic status quo is quite another.

There have been a number of examples of this recently, including Australian experts urging young women interested in mothering to avoid disappointment by abandoning their career plans in favour of early marriage and motherhood. Another less salutary suggestion has been that 30+ women seeking children should abandon all their standards as they hunt for a man, and grab anyone that can successfully inseminate them; disposing of them later if necessary. According to Dr John McBain, whose avuncular counsel on this matter appeared on the front page of the *Australian* in 2003, women were justified in 'manipulating circumstances' to ensure that they had a man on hand when time began running short. Indeed, McBain advises women in relationships with reluctant dads to do whatever it takes to get pregnant because 'sometimes men need to be helped to see themselves as fathers.'[185]

If such advice were any further off, it would curdle. I'm sorry, but it's simply not on to tell women to purposely procreate with a guy they know they won't be able to stomach long term. It's virtually making divorce their child's birthright, and a bitter divorce at that, should Dad work out, or even suspect (as he surely will), that as far as Mum was concerned, he was never more than a glorified sperm donor. Talk about feeling used! And can't you just see the accusatory headlines that no amount of 'but McBain told me to do it' will counter: 'Husband Sues for Deception and Sperm-Napping: Claims Ex-Wife Married Just to Have Children'. Trust me, girls, if ever there was a maternity fall-back plan with 'Danger! Wrong Way! Go Back!' written all over it, this is it. Ugh. The whole idea gives me the creeps.

Another proposed salve for the pain of circumstantial childlessness comes from ethicist Julian Savulescu. Savulescu advises women to freeze part of their ovaries and store them at a local tissue bank. With their fertility on ice, they can then adopt the same leisurely pace men now enjoy in preparing for parenthood, and wait until they are financially and emotionally ready and well ensconced in a relationship with Mr Right before taking the maternal plunge. Savulescu argues:

> Social progress has outstripped our biology. Women are having children later because today they are educated and have careers. Freezing eggs ... gives women the same choice as men have: to be educated, work and have children at the time of their choosing.[186]

Savulescu's idea is a classic in the annals of 'personal solutions for political problems'. It requires no social change, or even social coordination, to implement. Any well-heeled career woman who is willing to undertake the necessary surgery and pay the yearly storage rate can 'choose' to store her ovarian tissue until the right time in her career and relationship trajectory arrives for her to become a mother. Personal fertility crisis solved!

Or is it? So far no pregnancies have been achieved using reimplanted ovarian tissue, and at this stage too little is known about the freezing, unthawing and re-stimulation procedure to say when, if ever, it will become reliable enough to (sorry, I have to say it) bank on. In addition, the motherhood-at-any-age solution wilfully ignores evidence that suggests that older mothers have a harder time coping with motherhood than do younger ones because their previous autonomy makes it harder to adapt their own needs to the demands of the baby.[187] In addition, anecdotal evidence suggests older mums may find baby-care far more physically exhausting than younger ones. Freelance journalist and cartoonist Jane Cafarella writes:

> Life with small children is demanding and relentless. No matter how invincible a woman feels at work, and no matter how much she prepares for her new job of motherhood, nothing can prepare her for the physical and emotional challenges. Everyone seems to forget, or ignore, the fact that it is not just the reproductive system that ages. You may be wiser, but you may also be exhausted. As someone who has had two children eight years apart, I can tell you that it was much easier the first time. I had more energy and patience and fewer conflicts between the desire to work and the desire to parent.[188]

I must also admit to wondering exactly what, in the absence of female biological imperatives, would provoke men to get off their delaying duffs and become 'ready' for parenthood.

More important, though, is the fact that the pursuit by better-off women of personal solutions to work/family imbalance leaves the rest of the sisterhood hanging out to dry. There is nothing *inherently* wrong with women's time-limited fertility. The problem is that the social conditions and work practices governing our lives have turned female physiology into a 'problem' that needs 'fixing'. But hey, here's an idea. What about 'fixing' the attitudes, institutions and policies that constrain women's (and men's) freedom to partner and have children before time naturally runs out? This is a solution that would remove the pressure on women to undertake invasive and unnecessary surgery, and would benefit women and men across society, not just the better-resourced few.

But what happens once the ovarian tissue-freezing solution is out there? The prospects for universal change diminish. This is because the women able to choose it are a large enough group to sap the political muscle of those fighting for change. The work/family boat will sink, with everyone unable to afford his or her own personal lifeboat going down with the ship. In fact, once again, women who jump ship are likely to worsen employment conditions for those left behind. If thirty-something Darleen with her eggs in storage makes it clear to her boss that she can do everything her childless colleagues and those with wives at home can do, and more, no woman *un*willing to make a similar pledge of low-maintenance fecundity on demand will stand a chance of either beating her to the job, or up the ladder. Given that average weekly hours for many in the workforce are skyrocketing, it's simply terrifying to think what might happen when the minimally braking impact of women's biological imperatives and their consequences — namely children — are removed from the equation. Further, who's to say, what with demanding clients and heaps of money at stake, that managers will *ever* grant their employees permission to take time off to get pregnant? 'Can't you wait until next year?' they'll bleat, and because technically they can, women will be obliged to either say 'yes' or suffer the consequences.

I realise this makes me sound like a reproductive technophobe, but I'm not. I have no problem with technological advances that actually increase all women's reproductive freedom and control. In fact, there's a new test available in Australia that can measure a woman's ovarian reserves, and therefore the degree of risk she is taking by delaying pregnancy. Once the bugs are ironed out, and if it's affordably priced, I'll welcome it as a useful tool for contemporary working women wanting to book a seat on the motherhood train. But technologies are just tools. They are not sexy toys whose mere existence compels their acceptance and use. If such tools fail to facilitate the sort of global social changes that improve the quality of all women's lives, they should be rejected.

Why should women panic-bolt or manipulate their way into unhappy relationships, or feel compelled to use invasive and unproven technology, to solve the problem of circumstantial childlessness when it's the organisation of work in Western societies that is at the heart of the problem? Why should we not search for equitable and sustainable social solutions that benefit both women and men?

Two problems, one solution

The solution to the work/family problem, in a nutshell, is to generate more gorgeous men. Current shortages are due to the unnecessarily high costs both women and men pay, or fear they'll pay, if they share both the economic and the domestic responsibilities. Make it possible for parents to raise kids without being forced to sacrifice their commitment to equality, their relationship with one another, their careers or their financial security, and you create the conditions for more men and women to put up their hands for the job of parenting. You create the conditions, in other words, in which the problem of circumstantial childlessness is either eliminated or significantly reduced.

Part-time work
Some might think the solution here is to establish a right for working parents to work part-time. But I'm not convinced. Sure, part-time work is currently the best of a none-too-stellar array of options available to working women forced to do it all. But as I've already discussed, part-time work, along with parental leave and flexible work arrangements, creates exploitative cul-de-sacs that prevent career development and advancement because of the illogical belief that anyone working part-time or flexibly can't be 'serious'. It also pays poorly, in part because it tends to be done

overwhelmingly by women, and 'women's work' — primary school teaching, nursing, social work — is consistently less valued, and therefore less well paid, than that traditionally done by men (who dominate in the sciences and the business executive field).[189] One American study found that over a fifteen-year period, the average woman worker earned $449,101 less than her male counterpart; this meant she earned 38 cents for every dollar a male earned. This massive discrepancy was due in part to the wage gap but was also a result of the working patterns characteristic of mothers, in which part-time work features, and breaks in employment abound.[190] What all this means is that the only way part-time work can form even a partial solution to the work/family conflict is if women start getting paid the same as men for the same day's work and (relatedly) if traditional 'women's work' starts to pay as much as jobs in which male workers dominate.

This could happen. Employers could have a change of heart: they could decide that their part-time workers are as loyal and 'serious' as their full-time ones, and even do their bit to ensure women achieve their long-standing goal of pay equity. But there is some way to go. According to the Gender Issues Research Center, in only 8.5% of major fields do US women earn 100% or more of men's salaries. This represents just 2% of women's employment. In about half the employment fields (which account for 48% of female employment), women earn just 87% of men's salaries.[191]

But even if such changes did occur, they wouldn't solve the problem of full-time workers resenting the break parental part-timers get from the oppression caused by the intensification of work and the open-all-hours culture of the corporate world. Despite the losses part-timers accept — in salary and career advancement — for the 'privilege' of working part-time, there is increasing evidence to suggest that full-time workers resent their part-time parental colleagues and feel they are being cheated: of the same opportunity to reduce their full-time hours, and by being forced to wear the consequences to their own workload of the part-time worker's absence. This is why I have to be frank and say that, human nature being what it is, I have grave doubts that any 'special privileges' type of solution to the work/family crunch will ever fly.

Whatever change is going to be put in place to enable parents, and those who want to be parents, to be egalitarian partners, active parents and responsible workers, it's going to have to be available — and of benefit — to all workers equally. At the heart of such a change is a fundamental shift in our perception of workers. At the moment, we pretend that all workers are the same, and that none has significant responsibilities outside the workplace. What we need to start realising is that nearly all of them do have such responsibilities — or will, or would like to.

Real solutions are radical

'Radical' is a word we've all come to fear, but what does it actually mean? The Oxford Dictionary defines it as 'affecting the foundation, going to the root'. Radical change isn't about tinkering around the edges (as ovarian tissue-freezing and part-time work solutions do) but leaving the foundational assumptions, structures and beneficiaries of the situation untouched. It's about finding the root of a problem and having a go at fixing things there.

According to high-profile Australian historian Marilyn Lake, at the heart of the problem is the question of time. In particular, the lack of time in contemporary societies to meet existing relationship and caring responsibilities, and to generate new ones. In a seminal article on the work/family crunch, Lake argues that for women to achieve at work, they need equity in the home (while men, I would add, need less oppressive employment conditions if they are to have equity in the home). While childcare is an important part of the women's liberation equation, says Lake, it isn't the whole story, or even the most important part. What is imperative is the reconstruction of society in general, and the workplace in particular, men and women enabled to share the work of raising children equally. 'In an ideal society,' writes Lake, 'we would all share the satisfactions of productive and creative work with the responsibilities and rewards of caring for people.' Such a vision cannot, she notes, be achieved without a 'direct challenge to the … organisation of work'.[192]

For Lake, if we are to have the time necessary to properly manage such crucial areas of life, a reduction of the standard working week to around 30 hours, or a few hours short of four 8-hour days is required. Such a reduction wouldn't just be for parents; it would be for everyone. Such a change is long overdue in the 21st century, in the same way as the introduction of the 40-hour week was long overdue at the start of the 20the century. It would allow parents of older children to pick their kids up after school and cover school holidays, and it would allow those with young children to pool their hours to cover half the working week, and share the remainder with grandparents (who, if they still work, would have more time, too), other parenting couples, a childcare centre, or another child-minder. For the childless, time to develop a life outside the office could be put to use engaging in meaningful activities, like forming and nurturing romantic relationships, while empty-nesters would have time to look after their ageing parents, their grandchildren and, eventually, one another. Finally, a 30-hour week would allow those without pressing relationship demands to really live: to engage in further study, learn an instrument, read, travel or volunteer in the community, for example. In addition, a reduction of working hours offers the potential for workloads to be redistributed, from the overworked to both the under-employed and the unemployed, with a consequent reduction in the individual and societal costs associated with joblessness and overwork.

I know a 30-hour week seems, given the current insanity of corporate culture, like so much Boston crème pie in the sky, but by world standards, it's far from outlandish. In 2000, the French brought in a 35-hour week. This was designed to increase employment and productivity, and make the lives of individuals and families less conflicted and more — get this — enjoyable. Despite the usual Henny-Penny predictions from the business community about unsustainable costs, uncompetitiveness, the certain collapse of the French economy (insert more predictable corporate yada-yada here), several years on, the sky not only remains in its usual firmament locale, but French citizens enthusiastically support the changes because they've delivered such vast improvements in the quality of life. In addition to improving the quality of jobs (an issue likely to be of real concern to 'fully employed' US workers who are compelled to hold down two minimum wage 'McJobs' to make ends meet), the 35-hour week has lowered unemployment. The Jospin Government attributes at least one-fifth of the new jobs created in France from 1997 to 2001 to the 35-hour work week.[193]

What would happen if governments in other Western countries actually sought to represent workers and small business owners, who are often forced to work long hours to remain competitive with the corporates, and demanded an end to the employment status quo, in which corporations keep the number of available jobs artificially low in order to max-out the hourly contributions of those they do employ, with little concern for the detrimental impact such work conditions have on workers and their families' well-being? What if, instead, governments committed themselves to ensuring that all workers had access to the sort of humane employment conditions that would allow them to claim back their lives? What if, in the absence of such a concerted government push, workers started asking those claiming to represent them why at a time in history when Western citizens are enjoying unprecedented levels of health and wealth, our quality of life — as measured by the time we have to live, to love and to contribute to a better future — is declining?

I'm not being naïve about this. I know it would take a lot of fraternising and hard work from a coalition of grassroots organisations and trade unions around the world to achieve such radical workplace change. But using the same technologies that have so ably assisted the implementation of the open-for-business-all-hours philosophy — the internet, faxes, mobile phones and email — anti-globalisation activists proved in Seattle that it could be done. Indeed, the chances of being able to gather forces and link hands to fight for increased time are good, given the enormous pool of stakeholders who stand to gain from such fundamental workplace change. If the French example is any guide, opponents would be restricted to employees who've internalised the corporate agenda, CEOs, and some small business people. Against them would stand, literally, the might of the people: those of all ages, and of both genders, who care for young and old, and those who would like to do some relationship-building and caring in the future. In particular, against them would stand thwarted mothers like Kylie, for whom a reduced working week would be a huge plus: it would enable her to discover and maintain the career that is key to her identity without requiring her to sacrifice too much time with her kids. We would also find women like waiting and watching Jacinta in our midst: for her, the capacity to better merge career and maternal responsibilities without ruining her relationship is central to her decision to have kids. Waiting and watching women like Bethany would also be likely to come on board, in the knowledge that reduced hours for her husband Jack would make it easier for him to say 'yes' to sharing the work and her consequent capacity to conceive while she's still young.

While the 30-hour week is the major plank of my proposal to reduce circumstantial childlessness, other economic changes will also be required if we are to create more gorgeous men and facilitate their partnering and procreating with child-desiring women. Job security is a big one: it is essential if we are to get waiting and watching women (and men) who are nervous about the impact parenthood could have on their economic security to stop dithering and make a move. It seems clear that governments did not foresee the impact on birth-rates of allowing businesses the 'flexibility' to contract and dispose of labour as needed, and it is high time, as Fagin once said, to 'think this one out again'. Emergency leave and flexible working hours are also important, and while ideally they would be available to all, they are definitely essential to any parent-facilitating employment package. The same holds true for parental leave arrangements (with built-in financial incentives for parents to share leave between them), low-cost high-quality childcare, quality government schools and tax and child endowment benefits. All are necessary parts of defraying the cost of parenthood, and thus reducing parents' need to work overtime to make ends meet.

But hang on a minute. Didn't I just get through arguing that workplace policy should not favour parents over the childless, or those whose kids have grown? I did, but largely — as you'll recall — on practical grounds. It is parents who lose out when they are the only ones accorded the 'special privilege' of part-time or flexible hours. They lose not just in their struggle to be seen as 'serious', but because of the resentment they endure from their non-parenting colleagues. Guaranteeing the basic conditions required for people to be both good workers and good parents is the only way I can see — in a buyer's labour market — to ensure that parents aren't punished for caring for their kids. But I do see children as a public good, a direct, substantial and meaningful contribution to the future. In the same way that it is fair for governments to provide tax relief for those who contribute to charity, it is legitimate for them to give particular benefits to those who do the work of raising children — children whose taxes and labour will in the future benefit everyone. In doing this, governments both reward parents, and encourage others to become parents in the future. Specific support for parents, such as tax benefits, or public investment in schools, should only cease — and we are light years from this point at the moment — when it becomes so generous that it actually induces people who actually don't want children to have them anyway. While it may infuriate militant childfree activist Tom Nankivell to be told that his decision to remain childless in and of itself benefits no-one but himself and significantly advantages him in the workforce, the facts speak for themselves. Indeed, such facts make clear why there is no other word for his bid for additional benefits in the form of tax rebates for services he doesn't use other than 'selfish'. Should he choose to use the time his choice affords him to do something to benefit the wider community, I would be the first to put my hand up to suggest he should be rewarded, and further encouraged through the use of taxpayer funds, rather than unfairly accused of having his snout in the trough. The irony of Nankivell's self-righteous anger and exaggerated sense of having been put upon by hardworking others is that while he denies the social contribution parents make, it is the children of the parents he accuses of selfishness who will pay the taxes that support the hospitals and nursing homes he'll need when he grows old and sick. And, in the absence of children of his own, they will almost certainly be the staff who nurse and comfort him when his time is at an end.

Know the old joke about the Irish traffic cop? A bunch of visitors in a car stop to ask him the way to a well-known tourist haunt. 'Oh, that's easy,' he says. 'It's … you just … well if you go …' He pauses. 'That's funny,' he says, scratching his head. 'I don't think you can get there from here.'

The powers that be put a lot of energy into making us feel like that police officer. That the most logical solutions are too outlandish to even be spoken out loud, let alone achieved. That the status quo is not just the way it is, but the only way it can be — for the sake of the economy, of course. That we simply cannot get to a world in which women are truly free to have the children they want from the society we live in now.

Well I say phooey. Western societies have long gone past sense when it comes to talking about the economy; they have lost sight of the fact that economies are meant to serve people, not the other way around. The question is, which people is the economy currently set up to serve, and if we were to change things, who would be served worse, and who better? If there isn't time for the average person to have children, to raise them well and to enjoy them, then as a nation our priorities are out of order, and any economic system that produces or tolerates that disorder needs to be castigated.

Besides, most big business claims about the unchangeable fundamentals of economic management are just propaganda. Take the constant assertion of Australian and American businesses that their top priority when making decisions about how the company operates is to increase shareholder value. If this means, as it so often does, that staff have to take a cut in pay or conditions, or even lose their jobs, chief executives consistently suggest that that's just the way it has to be because the first responsibility of a corporation must be to its shareholders. Well, this is just rubbish. In Japan, Germany and France, business is accountable to multiple stakeholders including employees and customers. These arrangements, an outgrowth of both corporate law and corporate practice, ensure that the impact of corporate policy on these groups is considered before decisions are made. My point is that there is nothing necessary or inevitable about the way business conducts itself: with all the power in the world, big business has a choice. If the chief executives of the Fortune 500 companies decided tomorrow that they wanted to reduce the hours of the standard working week, in a few months' time, the wheels would be in motion. Anything can change, and does, if those with power want to change it. The question is are parents, and those who want to become them, powerful enough, and united enough, to convince the powers that be that the time has come for such a change?

A parents' movement (or why circumstantial childlessness isn't a feminist issue)

Women owe the feminist movement a lot. In addition to speaking out about sexual harassment in the workplace, glass ceilings, ongoing pay inequity or the tragic consequences for women of work/life imbalance, it's been the women's movement — and only the women's movement — that has fought for women's access to employment, and cared about our fate once we got into the big, wide world of work. So perhaps it seems unfair to argue, as I'm about to do, that feminists should step back from the work/family issue, and hand it over to an (as yet nonexistent) organisation that is better equipped to continue the fight: a parents' movement. My reasons for this are simple. First, in theory, the question of workplace and domestic equity are not women's issues alone. Second, and more importantly, if women are to achieve such equity in practice, they have to see men as fellow sufferers of domestic inequity and join hands with men and political allies in the fight to achieve change. A unisex fight for unisex parental freedoms is not, by definition, a fight for the feminist movement, and historical feminist antagonism to men and male interests makes the need for a new movement to mount the crusade for workplace equity even more imperative.

Bringing men in at the ground level of a newly formed parent's movement not only instantly doubles the potential support base but it also greatly increases the odds of success. Let's face it, in our world, issues of importance to men are seen as more universal, and get far more attention, than those that matter 'only' to women. In the same way that if men could get pregnant abortion would be a sacrament, expect that when men cry foul about family-unfriendly work practices, union bosses, CEOs and political leaders will be more inclined to listen. Remember, it is only because childless workers and men with stay-at-home wives can — and do — succumb to whatever unreasonable demands the 'open all hours' workplace makes of them that employers get away with imposing such unreasonable demands on the workforce. Once a critical mass of wannabe and actual mothers and gorgeous men refuse to dance to the corporate tune, things will start changing, and fast.

This is set to happen in the not-too-distant future anyway. In the wake of the demographic bulge of baby-boomers' kids (currently in the career starting blocks), succeeding generations will be relatively, and increasingly, small. This will tilt the power balance between worker and employer back towards the worker. The scarcer workers are, the more power they'll have to name their price, and while a handful may opt for ever more dollars to compensate them for endless hours away from home, I'm betting that most will use their bargaining power to obtain greater job security, and to reduce and increase the flexibility of their hours. Not only will such changes lead to more happy families; they will lead to more families full stop, as circumstantial childlessness is reduced by men and women having more time to meet, marry and mate — and to have the number of children they want.

The problem for the circumstantially childless women of today and tomorrow (the women of Generation X and the leading-edge kids of the baby-boomers) is that such changes won't come soon enough. These women will be past, or almost past, their fertile years by the time the cavalry of family-friendly work practices brought on by a seller's market in employment pulls into town. This means that if we are to avoid losing such women to the scourge of circumstantial childlessness, political action to bring such changes forward in time must be taken now. A parents' movement will enable the considerable energies of such women, who have the most to lose in the short term and who don't (yet) have the children (and the consequent time demands) that make activism so much more difficult, to be harnessed for change.

This is not to say that the women's movement should butt out of the fight for work/family balance. In the 21st century coalition building is the name of the social change game. A parents' movement would have to build links with the women's movement, the men's movement, the union movement and those 'grey power' organisations that represent the interests of grandparents who are pressed into long hours of childcare by their harassed and overworked adult children. The post-40 set also need time out to care for their aged parents and eventually each other (studies show that older men take as much time off work to care for ageing parents and partners as do older women). All of these groups, in other words, have an interest in a 30-hour working week, as well as in other workplace arrangements that are designed to increase job security, and improve the quality of life of those who have obligations to care for others.

Reproductive freedom and rationality

There are two issues that are fundamental to most choices, but certainly to reproductive choices. The first question we must address is whether or not individuals are entitled to make their own decisions about parenthood. If the answer is yes, the second issue rises to the fore: if we are free to make such decisions, are all of them good ones to make?

I have already argued, as emphatically and passionately as I can on paper that yes, women are entitled to full reproductive choice. For me this freedom goes well beyond an absence of laws forbidding adults to have kids. At the heart of such freedom is the social and material resources necessary to actually make and implement both a decision to avoid parenthood and a decision to embrace it. The denial of such freedom is a denial of the basic human entitlement all people have to live — in fundamental ways — what they see as the good life.

But are all reproductive choices equally good — or moral — ones for women to make? As a society, our preoccupation with this question outweighs that of any civilisation that has come before us. This should not be surprising, for it is due in large part to our unprecedented capacity to control if we will have children and how many children we will have. Women's historical inability to exercise significant control over their fertility (as well as the sexist belief that women were driven to mother and care for their young by instinct, not rational decision) explains why the philosophical shelves are almost totally bare when it comes to discussions of motives for or justifications of decisions to parent. After all, choice to do something doesn't exist unless one has the power to *not* do it.

But it's been roughly 40 years since the introduction of The Pill, and 23 years since French historian Elisabeth Badinter, in her seminal *The Myth of Motherhood*, put the belief that women mother their young instinctively to bed. Excuses for the complete absence of philosophical attention to the parenting decision are starting to wear thin. The time has come for philosophers, feminists and other social activists to step up and articulate a defence of motherhood as a rational and a moral choice for comtemporary women to make.

This case will be difficult to mount: landmines abound in all directions. Motherhood must be defended without re-inscribing the age-old oppressive equation of woman = mother, and in such a way that we do not return to the bad old days where childless women were scorned or pitied. Such a defence must laud as worthy the altruism at the heart of many women's decision to have kids, but at the same time launch a full-frontal assault on the self-sacrificial component of longstanding definitions of good motherhood. It must call on values often poorly articulated in the public domain — ones like faith, trust, other-centredness, care, responsibility, commitment, generosity — and contrast them (at times unfavourably) with old-time liberal democratic favourites such as knowledge, independence, freedom, autonomy and self-reliance.

It will be hard, but not impossible. In the next and final chapter I'm going to do as I've argued others must: search for the concepts and struggle for the words to say what many of us believe in our hearts and now needs to be spoken aloud.

CODA: WHY MOTHERHOOD IS A RATIONAL CHOICE TO MAKE

Many persons have a wrong idea of what constitutes true happiness. It is not attained through self-gratification but through fidelity to a worthy purpose.

Helen Keller

For me, the most heart-rending observation of the many circumstantially childless women I interviewed was that they'd be fools to have children. How, they asked me, wide-eyed, could it make sense to have children when the choice (and its outcome) would consciously and deliberately undermine every value they held dear? The values they'd painstakingly organised their lives to reflect — robust bank accounts, full-steam-ahead careers, unpressured and romantic intimate relationships and those values connected to their own needs and desires for security, mastery and control: lives that children would surely mess up. 'I hear you never have sex again,' one woman confided in a horrified whisper. And they'd heard more. Parenthood would rob them of comfort and luxury options for spending their time (like sleeping in, or going away to a resort to play golf on weekends) and worse, it would strip contingency from their lives. They'd be trapped, as Barbara, the woman anxious about making any commitments that would stop her being able to drop everything and go waitressing in Santorini, said; denied the freedom to change their lives at any time. 'Why would you have a baby?' this 43-year-old woman asked me plaintively several times. 'Why would you?'

The sad thing is that there are no ready-made answers for those wondering if a decision to parent makes sense. We know why freedom matters, why choice is important, why money is good, but in Western cultures like Australia and the United States, there is an absence of words and concepts that can explain why creating new relationships and maintaining them makes sense, and more, why doing this might be a good — or even the right — thing to do. When it comes to the childbearing decision, and parenting more generally, the values-illiteracy we suffer is severe.

What we need is a world in which, to quote feminist philosopher Joan Tronto, 'the daily caring of people for each other is a valued premise of human existence'.[194] This is not to say that we don't value the moral qualities demanded of parents (generosity, commitment, responsibility), and the qualities of good relationships between parent and child (loyalty, trust, intimacy). The trouble, it seems to me, is rather that we don't value them in the same way we value other things. We tend to see such values as 'nice', but somehow distinctly different from, say, 'liberty and justice for all'. We don't see them as fundamentally reflecting who we are and what we ought to be doing, and at the heart of a description of what makes for a meaningful life. Should there be a conflict, we see it as justified that such other-oriented values get 'trumped' or overridden by the self-oriented ones. When this happens, the message is clear: caring is a dispensable part of what it means to be human and to live a meaningful life.

Another consequence of the low-on-the-totem-pole status of other-centred values is that the particular moral values expressed by a decision to parent are left unexamined. While philosophers have discussed every nuance of concepts like autonomy and justice, they simply aren't interested enough in parenting to wonder exactly what moral qualities are expressed by a choice to parent. In part, this is because of the longstanding belief that women's desire to mother and mothering behaviour is instinctual rather than moral. But it may also be because on some level, many philosophers agree with the growing view in society that a decision to parent simply doesn't make sense on rational grounds.

Part of our confusion about the worth of other-centred motivations and behaviour can be traced to the insidious creep of the equation of human nature and rationality with self-interest (and other-centred behaviour as inhumanly strange and irrational). This view of human nature was rejected during the 1500 years that Christian values dominated Western thought, but gained prominence during the 17th and 18th centuries through the theories of Thomas Hobbes and the economist Adam Smith. Today, entire schools of political and economic thought — the academic disciplines to which the general public has greatest exposure — are premised on the claim that humans inevitably act in their own self-interest, and that leaving them free to do this brings about the morally best outcomes. This philosophy was expressed perhaps most succinctly by the film *Wall Street*'s protagonist, Gordon Gekko, in his assertion that 'greed is good'. Such assertions have had enormous sway, despite ample and growing evidence, some of it from 'prisoner's dilemma' research (in which research participant 'prisoners' who are unable to communicate with one another must decide what to tell the 'police'), that the search for meaning, and the good of others, are also profound motivators of human behaviour, and that cooperation and trust are sometimes necessary to bring about optimal outcomes. Indeed, what some of this research shows is that knowing that another has benefited or that one has acted morally can be a sufficient inducement or 'pay-off' for co-operation.[195] What this suggests is that by nature, we humans aren't just motivated by what's in it for us. We are also motivated by love and duty.

Another problem with our culture's disrespect for and lack of interest in other-centred values is that a lot of the time, we are pretty confused about when we should act — and indeed even when we are acting — from a motive that is self-oriented, and when we are acting from one that is centred in our concern for others. Laney's worry that her desire to have a child in order to give to it makes her 'selfish' is a classic example:

> For many years I had this fantasy that I would have
> kids, and hadn't really worked out why, why I had this

desire to have kids, and I think that a lot of it was around me rather than the kids. So it was for my needs rather than a child's needs.

Me: What where those needs?

… filling the hole that I felt was in my life. And, this will sound corny, like I have so much to give. And I thought that was what I wanted … to have this thing in my life that belonged to me, that would fill this hole, whatever. I don't think they're the right reasons … Because I [would be] trying to right something that was wrong and I think that that is not a good reason to experiment on a child … It's like trying to sort myself out by doing something with a child: my needs, rather than the child's needs.

With all due respect to Laney, who was one of the most open and endearing women I met while researching this book, it is just plain psycho-babble to describe one's need to give to others as selfish. In the first place, despite all the Hobbesian hype, the fact that Laney's decisions regarding children are motivated by other-centred rather than self-centred impulses is normal, rational and — dare I say it — commendable. The desire to give is not a pathology. Second, it's simply impossible to be directly motivated to care for others (such as future children) if the others concerned don't yet exist. This means that the needs — good, bad or indifferent — of women and couples to have children, and perhaps an abstract love of children, will always be the prime motivations for deciding to have a child. The fact that they are good motives, not based in the direct requirements of a particular child, is what makes them defensible and highly ethical. Third, insofar as Laney seems afraid that by deciding to mother she can fairly be accused of having a child as a means to an end, she should put this worry to bed — for good. Neither Laney nor any other mother-choosing women can be fairly accused of using their child as a means to an end (an ethical no-no) by deciding to have them. This is because, as philosopher Susanne Gibson explains, parents are perfectly entitled to treat their child (future or present) as a means to their own ends as long as they don't treat the child *solely* as a means, but also — at the same time — as an end in itself. So as long as Laney intends to, and in fact does, treat her child as an end in itself once it is born, she can rest assured that she has done nothing wrong.

This is not to say that all motives for childbearing are good. Women and men can decide to have children for all sorts of morally neutral or unworthy reasons: to fit in with what their friends are doing, please their parents, or because they are afraid of or morally opposed to abortion, to name a few. In the same way, the childless can have reasons for their choice that are highly moral: to dedicate themselves to a disabled sibling, for example, or to serve the public through their work or artistic endeavours, or by finding a cure for disease. As noted feminist philosopher Virginia Held argues, it's not the decision you make about having children, but the motives you have for the decision you make, that matter: 'Men (and women) can die out of loyalty, out of duty, out of commitment, and they can die for a better future. Women can give birth or refuse to give birth from all these motives and others.'[196]

But while childlessness may set the stage for a woman to pursue a morally meaningful life, parenting is itself a stage on which morally meaningful activity can take place. This is why it makes sense for a woman to choose mothering as her means to pursue a morally meaningful life. At the core of parenting is the act of caring, and to care requires particular emotional and intellectual qualities and competences. According to moral psychologist Carol Gilligan, it is just as rational to see society as held together by a web of relationships that guarantee care as it is to see it as held together by a system of rules that guarantee justice. Indeed, in a world in which others are not viewed primarily as restrictions, but as what make one's own existence possible and meaningful, parenting not only makes sense, it is an expression of one's moral values and a means of achieving them.

Those who seek to maintain the web of relationships that give their lives meaning must accept responsibility for others, and develop the sympathy necessary to meet their needs for care. Parents must act from care, and perform acts of care. It is clear that not all of the things required of parents of either sex come naturally, and acquiring them demands emotional capacities, intellectual qualities and competences that characterise moral behaviour. In particular, argues feminist philosopher Sara Ruddick, reflection, knowledge, and the capacity for reason are necessary for parents to perform what she sees as their three tasks: they must make a commitment to protect and attend to their child; they must recognise and respond to their growing child's emotional and intellectual development, as well as to their increasing need for independence; and they must ensure that their child develops in socially acceptable ways, without over-emphasising conformity or unquestioning obedience to authority.[197]

Feminist philosopher Tronto takes Ruddick's description of the moral requirements of parenting further by expanding the definition of 'care' to include, among other things: noticing that care needs to be given in the first place; assuming responsibility for care; and considering the reaction of the other to the care being given. Most importantly, Tronto specifies precisely what is being asked of carers in moral terms: that they be attentive, responsible, competent and responsive. Importantly, she notes that parents are unable to care properly for their children if they are unaware of their own needs, or have failed to satisfy them.

This addendum is critical. It means that while choosing to care is rational for both men and women, and that deciding to parent and parenting are moral things to do, parenting isn't about self-abnegation, or even self-sacrifice. It's about care.

This is no minor matter. If to give is human, but also rational and right, then we can dismiss as sexist bunkum the claim that women's desire to mother is either programmed directly into their genes, or an outgrowth of their naturally giving (even masochistic) nature. Further, if caring is human, rational and right, then the decision to create new relationships characterised by care isn't the irrational decision of a pure-relationship saboteur, but the rational choice of a person with complex and expansive understandings of meaningful intimacy. This will be a great relief to a number of the childless women I spoke to, who desperately wanted their heartfelt desire to displace their own needs from the centre of their lives and dedicate themselves to a vulnerable, dependent other to be seen as an expression of their rationality, normality and humanity.

More importantly, emphasising the rationality and morality of motives and behaviour that spring from the human impulse to care, particularly when care involves self-awareness and self-regard, may help women to avoid the martyrdom trap. It will enable us to speak highly of the impulse to care, while simultaneously allowing them to defend ourselves as sensible beings who draw a line under other-centred behaviour at the point at which we feel we're becoming suckers. It will also provide the basis for us to reject conservative claims to valorise self-abnegating women as moral saints. Indeed, if there's one thing the phenomenon of circumstantial childlessness proves, it is how the absence of opportunities for present-day mothers to meet both their own needs and the ideological and practical demands of good mothering is undermining their confidence in their ability to care, and thus their willingness to mother.

Reproductive freedom accords us our privacy, our dignity, and the freedom to choose what we define as a meaningful life. This is why we believe it so wrong for a society — through act or omission — to deprive its citizens of such freedom. However, the concept of reproductive freedom cannot help us understand why some values and some choices might be better than others. It cannot explain why motherhood is a rational, and moral, thing to do.

I do not believe that everyone should choose to parent, that choosing childlessness is selfish or wrong, or that parenting is the only way to live a moral life. I do, however, believe that for a range of reasons, including our understandable desire to put an end to the stigma and discrimination suffered by the childless, we have forgotten the importance of explaining why the decision to parent is a morally laudable decision, and lost the words to explain why raising children is one way to lead a meaningful life.

The reason why a decision to parent makes sense and is moral lies in our humanity, which leads us to find satisfaction and meaning in balanced lives: lives dedicated to the pursuit of both pleasure and mastery; to our own good, and that of others. Parenting is one way to enjoy the pleasure of human relationships, and to respond to the rational human impulse to dedicate some of our lives to the good of others. It is wrong to question the rationality of those who want to care. It is wrong to make the practical demands of motherhood unnecessarily onerous and to ignore the unwillingness of fathers to do their fair share, while at the same time making women's willingness to deny their own needs the test of good motherhood. It is as wrong to deny women the freedom to mother as it is to make motherhood seem an irrational choice for a woman to make.

Women don't want to be suckers, or moral saints. Many just want to be mothers, and they deserve that chance.

Notes

1   Petchesky 1985, 11
2   Wicks and Mishra 1998
3   Hewlett 2002
4   McDonald 1998
5   Franklin and Chee Tueno 2003
6   Kelly 2002
7   Madrick 2004
8   Summers and Hogan 1994
9   Cook 2000
10   Baruch, Barnett et al. 1983, 41
11   Siedlecky and Wyndham 1990, 17, 18
12   Chesnais 1996, 731
13   McDonald 1997, 7
14   Goward 1998, 15–16
15   Summers 2003, 57, 59
16   Singer 2004
17   McDonald 2001
18   Chesnais 1996, 733
19   De Vaus 2002, 26
20   Veevers 1980, 29
21   Veevers 1980, 26
22   Campbell 1985, 71
23   Veevers 1980, 49
24   Faux 1984, 4–5
25   Campbell 1985, 60
26   Ireland 1993, 83
27   Faux 1984, 3–4
28   Mill 1859
29   Alexander, Rubinstein et al. 1992, 619
30   Leland 2004
31   Gregg 1995
32   Gregg 1995, 144
33   Das 2004
34   Murrell 2004
35   Dornan, in McIntosh 1998
36   Leidig 2003
37   Maushart 2001
38   McDonald 2002, 426
39   McDonald 2002, 426
40   Faux 1984

41   Moore and Moore 2000, 83, emphasis in original
42   McIntosh 1999
43   As quoted in Belkin 2000, 34, 35
44   Nankivell 2001
45   Watkins 2000
46   Cannold 1999
47   For extracts of her piece, see Cannold 2000
48   Cannold 2000
49   Giddens 1992
50   Smart 1997
51   Cooper 2004, 15
52   De Vaus 2002
53   Alexander, Rubinstein et al. 1992, 620
54   Summers 2003, 25
55   Ehrenreich 1979, 281
56   Morton and Morton 2000
57   O'Reilly 2004, 764
58   Daniels and Weingarten 1988
59   Mackay 1997, 165
60   Biddulph 1994 and 1995
61   Edgar 1997, 251
62   Edgar 1997, 255
63   Whitehead 2001
64   Summers 2003, 22–23
65   Summers 2003, 25
66   Fogler 2000
67   SA Working Woman's Centre 1991; Department of Productivity and Labour
     Relations 1996–1999
68   Stewart 2001
69   News Office 1999
70   Halliday 2004
71   Edgar 1997, 254
72   Nancarrow 2004; The Staff of Catalyst 1988
73   Edgar 1997, 180
74   Summers 2003, 188
75   See, for example, Ochiltree 1994
76   Overington 2003
77   Watson et al. 2003, 13–14
78   Watson et al. 2003, 14
79   Cunningham 2004
80   Birrell, Rapson et al. 2004, 14–15
81   Netherlands Family Council 2000, 17–18, emphasis in original
82   Netherlands Family Council 2000, 19, emphasis in original
83   Latten en Cuyvers 1994, as cited in Netherlands Family Council 2000
84   Newman 2004
85   Das 2004, 13
86   Maushart 2001, 35
87   Maushart 2001, 36

88   Gilder 1986, 39
89   Ehrenreich 1983, 12
90   Ehrenreich 1983, 46
91   Faludi 1999, 30
92   Birrell, Rapson et al. 2004, vii
93   Birrell, Rapson et al. 2004, vii
94   Birrell, Rapson et al. 2004, 15
95   Birrell, Rapson et al. 2004, 15
96   Watson et al. 2003
97   Birrell, Rapson et al. 2004, 30
98   Bone 1998, 13
98   Wicks and Mishra 1998, 92
100 Summers 2003, 26
101 Summers 2003, 55
102 Birrell, Rapson et al. 2004, 44
103 Hrdy 1999, 233–234
104 Hrdy 1999, 217
105 Watson, 86, 97–98
106 Birrell, Rapson et al. 2004, 17
107 Cannold 2002
108 Reaney 2004
109 Cunneen and Stubbs 2003, 79, 80, 82
110 Poynting, Noble et al. 2003, 134
111 Angry Harry 2004
112 Morton 1997, 32–33
113 Morton 1997, 33
114 Birmingham 2000
115 Dennis 1992, 61
116 Quoted in Cannold 2002, 21
117 Birrell, Rapson et al. 2004, 56
118 Birrell and Rapson 1998, 49
119 Birrell, Rapson et al. 2004, 26
120 Button 2000
121 Fisher and Charnock 2003, 9
122 Birrell and Rapson 1998, 52
123 Morton 1997, 281
124 Briscoe 2004, 19
125 Sherry 1999
126 Briscoe 2004, 21
127 Reddan 2002
128 Das 2004, 5
129 Das 2004, 5
130 Birmingham 2000, 46–47
131 Das 2004, 5
132 Dowsett 2003, 27
133 Wallerstein, Lewis et al. 2000, 56
134 Netherlands Family Council 2000
135 Dennis 1992, xxvi

136   Dennis 1992, 234
137   Das 2004
138   Bryson and Warner-Smith 1998, 3
139   Faludi 1991, 36
140   Netherlands Family Council 2000
141   Cafarella 1998
142   Watson 2003
143   Belkin 2003, 'The opt-out revolution', 44
144   Hewlett 2002, 95
145   Belkin 2003, 'Abandoning the Climb and Heading Home'
146   CCH Australia 1994, 303
147   Beard 2000, quoted in Summers 2003, 188
148   Summers 2003, 57
149   Devine 2004, 11
150   Shanahan 2001
151   Cannold 2004
152   Belkin 2003, 'The opt-out revolution'
153   Hewlett, quoted in Belkin 2003, 'The opt-out revolution'
154   Summers 2003, 156–157
155   Faludi 1991, 25
156   Edgar 1997, 267
157   Biddulph 1994, 1995, 113
158   Hand and Lewis 2001, 26
159   Townsend 1994, 195
160   Hand and Lewis 2001, 26
161   As quoted in Hand and Lewis 2001, 26
162   Netherlands Family Council 2000, 3
163   Story told in Das 2004, 5
164   Story told in Das 2004, 5
165   Gerson 1993, 11–12
166   The Staff of Catalyst 1988
167   Bachelard 2001, 22
168   *Manchester News* 2003
169   Russell and Bowman 2000
170   Hand and Lewis 2001
171   Burgess 2003, 11
172   Nancarrow 2004, 6
173   As quoted in Petre 1998, 128
174   The Staff of Catalyst 1988
175   The Staff of Catalyst 1988
176   Nancarrow 2004, 6–7
177   Petre 1998, 24
178   Burgess 2003, 10; Nancarrow 2004, 6
179   Nancarrow 2004
180   Nancarrow 2004, 4, 6
181   Maushart 2001, 112
182   Townsend 1994
183   Gregg 1995, 12

184 Petchesky 1985, 11
185 Jackman 2003
186 Savulescu 1998
187 Walter 1986
188 Cafarella 1998
189 Madrick 2004
190 Hewlett 2000; Madrick 2004
191 Gender Issues Research Centre 2004
192 Lake 1986, 135, 136
193 Trumbull 2001
194 Tronto 1993, x
195 Mansbridge 1990
196 Held 1993
197 My understanding of Gilligan's, Ruddick's and Tronto's work draws on the insights of Maihofer. See Maihofer 2000.

Select bibliography

60 Minutes (2002). Poll: are couples who remain childless selfish?, *60 Minutes*. http://sixtyminutes.ninemsn.com.au/sixtyminutes/stories/2002_04_14/story_554.asp.

Alexander, B and Rubinstein, R et al. (1992). 'A path not taken: a cultural analysis of regrets and childlessness in the lives of older women'. *The Gerontologist* 32(5): 618–626.

Angry Harry (2004). 'Angry Harry, Angry Harry', 21 April 2004. http://www.angryharry.com/.

Australian Social Science Data Archive (2002). Negotiating the life course 2000: Wave 2. Australian Social Science Data Archive. http://assda.anu.edu.au/codebooks/NLC00_web/15vars.html.

Bachelard, M (2001) 'Caring, sharing and hardly ever home'. *Weekend Australian*, Inquirer (1–2 September): 22.

Baruch, G, Barnett, R et al. (1983). *Lifeprints: New Patterns of Love and Work for Today's Women.* US, McGraw-Hill.

Beard, A (2000). 'Traditional roles with a twist'. *Financial Times* (UK, 5 October).

Belkin, L (2003). 'Abandoning the climb and heading home'. *New York Times Magazine* (26 October): 42–47, 58, 85.

——, (2000). 'The backlash against children'. *New York Times Magazine*: 30–35, 42, 56, 60–63.

——, (2003). 'The opt-out revolution'. *New York Times*: 42–47, 58, 85.

Biddulph, S (1994, 1995). *Manhood: An Action Plan for Changing Men's Lives.* Sydney, Finch Publishing.

Birmingham, J. (2000). 'Who's afraid of her?' *Good Weekend* (26 August): 46–47.

Birrell, B and Rapson, V (1998). *A Not So Perfect Match: The Growing Male/Female Divide 1986–1996.* Melbourne, Centre for Population and Urban Research: Monash University.

Birrell, B, Rapson, V et al. (2004). *Men + Women Apart: Partnering in Australia.* Melbourne, The Australian Family Association, Centre for Population and Urban Research: Monash University.

Briscoe, J (2004). 'The baby gamble'. *Good Weekend* (17 April): 18–23.

Bryson, L and Warner-Smith, P (1998). 'Employment and women's health', *Just Policy* 14 (November): 3–14.

Burgess, R (2003). 'When dads do time'. *Age,* Good Living (20 November): 10.

Button, V (2000). 'A woman, a dream and a prime minister'. *Age* (2 August): 2.

Cafarella, J (1998). 'The real cost of delaying motherhood'. *Age* (4 June): 18.

Campbell, E (1985). *The Childless Marriage: An Exploratory Study of Couples Who Do Not Want Children.* London and New York, Tavistock.

Cannold, L (2004). 'A pregnant pause for waiters and watchers'. *Sydney Morning Herald*: 15.

——, (2004). '"Choice" a hurdle for new feminism'. *Sydney Morning Herald* (27 July): 11.

——, (2002). 'Redefining fatherhood: lowering the temperature of debates about the use of donor sperm by single women and lesbians', *Australian Journal of Professional and Applied Ethics* 4(2): 19–33.

——, (1999). 'Vexed in the city: why motherhood beats the driest martini'. *Age* (13 November): 9.

——, (2000). 'Women's desire for babies comes from the heart, not the patriarchy'. *Age* (9 December): 7.

CCH Australia (1994). *Work and Family Responsibilities: Adjusting the balance*. Sydney, CCH Australia with the assistance of the Work and Family Unit of the Commonwealth Department of Industrial Relations.

Chesnais, J-C (1996). Fertility, family and social policy in contemporary Europe. *Population and Development Review* 22(4): 729–739.

Colbatch, T (2000). 'Childless future for more women'. *Age* (22 March): 1–2.

Cook, A (2000). 'Childlessness neither selfish nor a choice'. *Age* (28 March): 14.

Cooper, A (2004). 'High infidelity'. *Sunday Life* (29 August): 12–15.

Cullen, D (2001). 'Unequal opportunities'. *Age* (7 May): 8–9.

Cunneen, C and Stubbs, J (2003). 'Fantasy islands: desire, "race" and violence', in Tomsen, S and Donaldson, M, *Male Trouble: Looking at Australian masculinities*. Melbourne, Pluto Press: 69–90.

Cunningham, S (2004). *Geography*. Melbourne, Text.

Daniels, P and Weingarten, K (1988). 'The fatherhood click: the timing of parenthood in men's lives', in Bronstein, P and Cowan, CP, *Fatherhood Today: Men's Changing Role in the Family*. New York, John Wiley & Sons: 36–51.

Das, S (2004). 'It's all too hard'. *Age* (2 March): 4–5.

——, (2004). 'More babies: men have a role to play, too'. *Age* (2 March): 13.

De Vaus, D (2002). 'Fertility decline in Australia: a demographic context'. *Family Matters* 63 (Spring/Summer): 14–21.

Dennis, W (1992). *Hot and Bothered: Women, Men, Sex and Love in the 1990s*. Melbourne, Penguin.

Department of Productivity and Labour Relations (1996–1999). Home based work: an information paper. The Government of Western Australia. 1 May 2000.

Devine, M (2004). 'Yes, sister, choose what you want'. *Sydney Morning Herald* (1 July): 11.

Dowsett, G (2003). 'Masculinity, (homo)sexuality and contemporary sexual politics', in Tomsen, S and Donaldson, M, *Male Trouble: Looking at Australian Masculinities*. Melbourne, Pluto Press: 22–39.

Edgar, D (1997). *Men, Mateship and Marriage: Exploring macho myths and the way forward*. Sydney, HarperCollins.

Ehrenreich, B and English, D (1979). *For Her Own Good: 150 Years of Experts' Advice to Women*. New York, Anchor Press/Doubleday.

——, (1983). *The Hearts of Men*. New York, Anchor Press/Random House.

Faludi, S (1991). *Backlash: The Undeclared War Against American Women*. New York, Crown.

——, (1999). *Stiffed: The Betrayal of the Modern Man*. London, Chatto & Windus.

Faux, Marian (1984). *Childless By Choice: Choosing Childlessness in the Eighties*. New York, Anchor Press/Doubleday.

Fisher, K and Charnock, D (2003). *Partnering and Fertility Patterns: Analysis of the HILDA Survey, Wave 1*. HILDA Conference, Melbourne University.

Fogler, L (2000). 'Work@Home: want to make lots of money, look to the stars'. Idea Cafe Inc. www.ideacafe.com/workathome.

Frankl, VE (1959). *Man's Search for Meaning: An Introduction to Logotherapy*. Boston, Beacon Press.

Franklin, J and Chee Tueno, S (2003). 'Graduate and childless'. *Quadrant* (July–August): 52–55.

Gender Issues Research Centre (2004). *Women and Employment*. Gender Issues Research Centre. http://www.gendercenter.org/genderwork.htm.

Gerson, K (1993). *No Man's Land: Men's Changing Commitments to Family and Work*. New York, Basic Books.

Giddens, A (1992) *The Transformation of Intimacy: Sexuality, Love and Eroticism in Modern Societies*. London, Polity Press.

Gilder, G (1986). *Men and Marriage*. Gretna, Pelican.

Goward, P (1998). *Women in the Post-Industrial Society*. Speech by Pru Goward, First Assistant Secretary, Office of the Status of Women, to the Sydney Institute.

Gregg, R (1995). *Pregnancy in a High-Tech Age*. New York and London, New York University Press.

Halliday, C (2004). 'At home with dad'. *Sunday Life*, 11 July: 23–25.

Hand, K and Lewis, V (2001). 'Fathers' views on family life and paid work'. *Family Matters* 61 (Autumn): 26–29.

Haussegger, V (2003). 'The sins of our feminist mothers'. *Age*, 23 July: 11.

Held, V (1993). *Feminist Morality: Transforming Culture, Society and Politics*. Chicago and London, University of Chicago Press.

Hewlett, SA (2000). 'Have a child and experience the wage gap'. *New York Times*, 16 May.

Hewlett, SA (2002). *Babyhunger: The New Battle for Motherhood*. London, Atlantic Books.

Hrdy, S Blaffer (1999). *Mother Nature: Natural Selection and the Female of the Species*. London, Chatto & Windus: 233–234.

Ireland, MS (1993). *Reconceiving Women: Separating Motherhood from Female Identity*. New York and London, The Guilford Press.

Jackman, C (2003). 'Start seeking Mr-Not-Quite-Right'. *Weekend Australian*, 10–11 May: 1.

Kelly, P (2002). 'It's Breeding Obvious'. *Australian*, 4 September, 13.

Lake, M (1986). 'A question of time', in McKnight, D, *Moving Left: The Future of Socialism in Australia*. Sydney, Allen & Unwin: 135–148.

Leidig, M (2003). 'Panic as sperm donor revealed as baby killer'. *Age*, 5 November: 10.

Leland, J (2004). Why America sees the silver lining. *The New York Times*: 1.

Lisle, L (1996). *Without Child: Challenging the Stigma of Childlessness*. New York, Ballantine Books.

Mackay, H (1997). *Generations: Baby Boomers, Their Parents & Their Children*. Sydney, Pan Macmillan.

Madrick, J (2004). 'Economic scene: the earning power of women has really increased, right? Take a closer look'. *New York Times*, 10 June: 2.

Maihofer, A (2000). 'Care', in Jaggar, A and Young, IM, *A Companion to Feminist Philosophy*. Massachusetts, Blackwell.

Manchester News (2003). New dads want to stay at home. Manchester Online. 17 March 2003. http://www.manchesteronline.co.uk/news/s/53/53896_new_dads_want_to_stay_at_home.html.

Mansbridge, JJ (1990). 'On the relation of altruism and self-interest', in Mansbridge, JJ. *Beyond Self-Interest*. Chicago and London, University of Chicago Press: 134–143.

Marshall, H (1993). *Not Having Children*. Oxford, Auckland and New York, Oxford University Press Australia.

Maushart, S (1997). *The Mask of Motherhood: How Motherhood Changes Everything and Why we Pretend it Doesn't*. Sydney, Vintage.

——, (2001). *Wifework: What Marriage Really Means for Women*. Melbourne, Text Publishing.

May, ET (1995). *Barren in the Promised Land: Childless Americans and the Pursuit of Happiness*. US, Basic Books.

McDonald, P (1998). 'Contemporary fertility patterns in Australia: first data from the 1996 census'. *People and Places* 66 (11): 1–12.

——, (2001). 'Fertility and the 3 types of women: it's not that simple'. *Age*, 18 September: 13.

——, (1997). *Gender Equity, Social Institutions and the Future of Fertility*. Canberra, The Australian National University.

——, (2002). *Population-E* 57(3): 426.

McIntosh, D (1999). Child-free zone. *Sunday Life*: 6–10.

——, (1998). Going it alone. *Sunday Life*: 10–12.

Meyers, DTJ (2001). The rush to motherhood — pronatalist discourse and women's autonomy. *Signs* 26(3): 735–774.

Mill, JS (1859).Chapter 1, online version: http://www.utilitarianism.com/ol/one.html.

Moore, D and Moore, S (2000). *Child-Free Zone: Why More People Are Choosing Not To Be Parents*. Sydney, David Moore and Susan Moore.

Morell, CM (1994). *Unwomanly Conduct: The Challenges of Intentional Childlessness*. New York, Routledge.

Morton, T (1997). *Altered Mates: The Man Question*. Sydney, Allen & Unwin.

Morton, T and Morton, A (2000). 'Where is the father?' *Age*, 4 May: 17.

Murrell, C (2004). 'One picket fence does not suit all'. *Age*, 4 March: 14.

Nancarrow, K (2004). 'Father tim'e. *Agenda*: 4–7.

Nankivell, T (2001). 'Snouts in the trough'. *Australian*, 3 September: 11.

Netherlands Family Council (2000). *Partner Interaction: Partner Interaction, Demography and Equal Opportunities as Future Labour Supply Factors*. Brussels, Netherlands Family Council.

Newman, L (2004). Geographical differences in fertility rates in Adelaide: a reflection of the social conditions of parenting? Paper delivered at Institute of Australian Geographers Conference, Glenelg, South Australia.

News Office (1999). Marriage wanes as American families enter new century, University of Chicago research shows. Chicago, The University of Chicago.

Ochiltree, G (1994). 'Effects of child care on young children: forty years of research'. *Australian Institute of Family Studies: Early Childhood Study Paper No. 5*.

O'Reilly, A (2004). *From Motherhood to Mothering: The Possibility of Empowered Maternity*. York University, Toronto.

Overington, C (2003). 'Rebirth of the stay-at-home mum'. *Age*, 12 July: 7.

Pearson, Allison (2002) *I Don't Know How She Does It*. New York, Knopf.

Petchesky, RP (1985). *Abortion and Woman's Choice: The State, Sexuality and Reproductive Freedom*. Boston, Northeastern University Press.

Petre, D (1998). *Father Time*. Sydney, Pan Macmillan.

Poynting, S, Noble, G et al. (2003). 'Protest masculinity and Lebanese youth in Western Sydney: an ethnographic study', in Tomsen, S and Donaldson, M, *Male Trouble: Looking at Australian Masculinities*. Melbourne, Pluto Press: 132–155.

Reaney, P (2004). 'Here's proof: there is a need for men after all'. *Daily Telegraph*, 14 May: 16.

Reddan, E (2002). 'No Virginia, feminism is not to blame for your solitary pain'. *Age*, 30 July.

Russell, G and Bowman, L (2000). *Work and Family: Current Thinking, Research and Practice*. Canberra, Department of Family and Community Services.

SA Working Woman's Centre (1991). *Home Is Where the Work Is*. Adelaide.

Safer, J (1996). *Beyond Motherhood: Choosing a Life Without Children*. New York, Pocket Books (Simon & Schuster).

Savulescu, J (1998). 'Pursuing a Great Advance for Women'. *Age* Letters: 3 September, 14.

Schwartz, J (1993). *The Mother Puzzle: A New Generation Reckons with Motherhood*. New York, Simon & Schuster.

Shanahan, A (2001). 'Joys of motherhood brook no competition'. *Australian*, 5 September: 15.

Sherry, C (1999). 'Motherhood: the feminist blind spot'. *Age*, 13 May: 15.

Shoebridge, N (1998). 'Look and learn: how not to sell to women'. *Business Review Weekly*, 14 September: 87.

Siedlecky, S and Wyndham, D (1990). *Populate and Perish: Australian Women's Fight for Birth Control*. Sydney, Allen & Unwin.

Singer, J (2004). 'Kids a luxury item'. *Herald Sun*, 26 February: 19.

Smart, C (1997). 'Wishful thinking and harmful tinkering? sociological reflections on family policy'. *Journal of Social Policy* 26(3): 301–321.

Stewart, M (2001). More and more men decide to be stay at home fathers. Slowlane.com. 24 April. http://www.slowlane.com/articles/media /more_men_decide. html.

Summers, A (2003). *The End of Equality: Work, Babies and Women's Choices in 21st Century Australia*. Sydney, Random House.

Summers, A and Hogan, C (1994). 'Maybe baby'. *Good Weekend* (12 March): 14–19.

The Staff of Catalyst (1988). 'Workplace policies: new options for fathers', in Bronstein, P and Cowan, CP, *Fatherhood Today: Men's Changing Role in the Family*. New York, John Wiley & Sons: 323–240.

Townsend, H (1994). *Real Men*. Sydney, HarperCollins.

Tronto, J (1993). *Moral Boundaries: A Political Argument for an Ethic of Care*. New York, Routledge.

Trumbull, G (2001). France's 35 hour work week: flexibility through regulation. The Brookings Institute. http://www.brookings.edu/dybdocroot/fp/cusf/analysis/ workweek.htm.

Vandenheuvel, A (1991). The most important person in the world. *Family Matters* (29): 8–13.

Veevers, JE (1980). *Childless by choice*. Canada, Butterworth.

Wallerstein, J, Lewis, Julia et al. (2000). *The Unexpected Legacy of Divorce: A 25 Year Landmark Study*. New York, Hyperion.

Walter, CA (1986). *The Timing of Motherhood*. Lexington MA and Toronto, Lexington Books.

Watkins, S (2000). 'To breed or not? It's your choice'. *Age*, 20 April: 15.

Watson, I, Buchanan J, Campbell, I and Briggs, C (2003). *Fragmented Futures: New Challenges in Working Life*. Sydney, Federation Press.

Watson, L (2003). 'Corporate culture still insists that work and family don't mix'. *Age* (12 July): 15.

Weston, R and Parker, R (2002). Why is the fertility rate falling?: A discussion of the literature. *Family Matters* 63(Spring/Summer): 6–13.

Whitehead, MM (2001). The poetics of Michael Leunig. English Honours thesis, University of Sydney. http://www.users.bigpond.com/schelle/essay/thesis.html.

Wicks, D and Mishra, G (1998). 'Young Australian women and their aspirations for work, education and relationships', in Carson, E, Jamrozik, E and Winefield, T, *Unemployment, Economic Promise and Political Will*. Brisbane, Australian Academic Press.

Will, GF (1999). A radical proposition. *Washington Post* (4 February).

Williams, Z (2004). You'll understand when you have kids. *Good Weekend* (14 February): 42–44.

Ziman Tobin, P and Aria, B (1998). *Motherhood Optional: A Psychological Journey*. New Jersey and London, Jason Aronson.

Index